Illustrations

page

ART AND DESIGN  EDUCATION SERIES

d

Longman Group UK Limited
*Longman House, Burnt Mill, Harlow, Essex, CM20 2JE, England
and Associated Companies throughout the world.*

First published 1990
ISBN 0 582 040299

British Library Cataloguing in Publication Data
Issues in design education.
   1. Education. Curriculum subjects. Design
   I. Thistlewood, David
   745.407

Library of Congress Cataloging-in-Publication Data
Issues in design education / edited by David Thistlewood.
     p. cm. – (Art and design education series)
   In association with the National Society for Education in Art and
Design
   Includes bibliographical references.
   ISBN 0-582-04029-9: £8.95
   1. Design – Study and teaching – Great Britain. I. Thistlewood,
David. II. National Society for Education in Art and Design (Great
Britain).
NK1170.I87   1990
745.4′07′041 – dc20   90-5899
                                                   CIP

Set in Linotron 202 10pt Plantin
Printed in Singapore
Produced by Longman Singapore Publishers (Pte) Ltd

Contents

Contents

Acknowledgements

We are grateful to the following for permission to reproduce photographs:
Architects' Journal, 41a, 41b; Baynes, K, Figs 8, 9, 10, 11, 12, 13, 14, 15; Devon County Council/Clement, R, Figs 18, 19, 20, 21, 22, 23, 24; Diderot *Encyclopédie*, Fig 50; Hedrich Blessing, Chicago, Fig 40; Hudson, T, Cover Illustration and Figs 26, 27, 28, 29, 30; Liverpool University/Thistlewood, D, Figs 1, 2, 3, 4, 5, 6, 7; *RIBA Journal*, Figs 38, 39; Roberts, P, Fig 8; Schools Council/Adams, E, Figs 31, 32, 33, 34, 35, 36, 37; Sheffield City Polytechnic, Figs 52, 53, 54, 55, 56; Trustees of the National Gallery, London, Fig 16; Yale University Press, Fig 17; Yeomans, D, Figs 42, 43, 44, 45, 46, 47, 48, 49.

Cover: Creative Technology; course director Tom Hudson (Chapter Ten).

Introduction

The new thinking in Britain, as exemplified by the National Curriculum Design and Technology Working Party, is that Design must be universally taught throughout compulsory education. It must not be modelled on the old Craft, Design and Technology (CDT) for, although there are pockets of creative excellence in this subject field, it has become generally characterised by the impartation of methods, routines and formulae. The new approach (to judge by the very brief policy statements that have so far been published) will stress innovation and origination, lateral besides linear thinking, beneficial opportunism, and the kinds of mental and material exploration that educate cognition, feelings and motor skills in unison. And, analogously, the school curriculum will provide for this new subject, not by building a monolithic discipline around it, but by requiring school managers to organise systems of beneficial opportunism on its account, by recognising design-sustaining activities in all other subject areas and coordinating them in such a way that the sparks of creative design may bridge them. We have had the well-intentioned rhetoric: now must begin a distribution of appropriate experience across the whole of the teaching force, for all teachers will be required to contribute parts to the whole.

This volume, then, has several related purposes. The first is to indicate the sorts of design issues that are already being explored across all spheres of education in Britain, from primary to tertiary and from general to specialist. Current 'official' thinking has not come out of the blue: it has been sustained by the debate that is reported in the chapters that follow. The Working Party's proposals make sense to those teachers who are already teaching Design only because of their familiarity with this wider context. This suggests the second purpose of this volume, which is to propagate the *debate* for the benefit of those other teachers whose services will be called upon (teachers of mathematics and the sciences, English and modern foreign languages, history and geography, music, physical education and drama) who so far have had little opportunity to consider this new dimension of their future work.

The third purpose is to summarise current and recent issues in design education for the benefit of teachers of Art and Design, representatives of whom have been the principal contributors to the debate. All along they have maintained the relevance of their subject to the national need to establish a 'design culture'. Throughout the past decade, while government resources have supported 'problem-solving' and 'linear thinking' curricula, the National Society for Education in Art and Design has provided a focus for Art and Design's claims to recognition. The vast majority of the country's qualified designers took Art and Design throughout their secondary education, and then studied in Colleges or Faculties of Art and Design. Long-standing exceptions to this are architects [1] and the kinds of inventor-fitter that our engineering industries consistently produced until these industries collapsed in the 1980s. Government resourcing of other initiatives has made negligible difference to this general pattern, and teachers of Art and Design have continued to bear most responsibility for identifying and nurturing potential designers. This is why, for the sake of complete reporting, this volume includes tertiary education as part of the logical continuum. Now that official favour has turned towards their disciplinary values, teachers of Art and Design demand full opportunities to exercise them in comprehensive curricular development. This requires explicit statement because there is a danger that the Design and Technology Working Party's findings may be interpreted differently – suggesting, for example, that Art and Design may add colour and originality to a coordinated mixture dignified chiefly by science and technology.

That this would clearly be a misconception is established by John Steers in Chapter One. This charts well the recent history of the Working Party's deliberations, and records several shifts in their thinking as a result of the representations of outside bodies such as the NSEAD. Some of these changes have been subtle – for example, their slight reorientations to take account of issues of gender and disability. Others have been fundamental – particularly the downgrading of entrepreneurial 'exploitation' and the promotion of 'value-adding' concepts such as aesthetic appreciation and synthetic creativity. This is the language of Art and Design; and if it is used consistently throughout primary and secondary education in the teaching of Design as a 'cross-curricular' subject (with Art and Design as a parallel 'foundation' subject providing reinforcement, enhancement and, where appropriate, leadership) the future for a design culture in Britain will never have been more promising.

That this integration of 'Design' and 'Art and Design' is both educationally and culturally essential is argued here by Philip Roberts and Norman Potter. Philip Roberts explores distinctions between 'the routine exercise or task' (that has been the staple concern of Manual Training, Woodwork, Metalwork and, most recently, CDT) and 'existential problems of meaning, identity and value explored, expressed and celebrated through practical learning' (an apposite summary of the habitual concerns of Art and Design). He defines these respective sets of concerns as 'conventional' and 'not conventional' educational practices, and offers a curricular model in which they are taught discretely but also overlap. This view (first published by the NSEAD in 1982 [2]) is precisely what is now encapsulated in official policy.

Norman Potter's arguments are even older, but, considered heresies in their day, they are now to be seen as remarkably prophetic. Over twenty years ago he was castigating as socially immoral the idea of design as wholesale exploitation, and he was substituting a humbler and yet more crucial role for designers, embracing the conservation of finite terrestrial resources and the provision of expertise to self-help communities. His criteria of 'good design' exclude all aspects that are geared exclusively to 'selling', and include all that are identified with satisfying genuine needs while *accounting* for the renewable and non-renewable energy, materials and efforts these require. Teachers, therefore, who wish for elaboration beyond the Working Party's mere deference to such concerns ought to consult Chapter Four and the standard text from which it is reproduced [3].

They ought also to consult the review, provided by Ken Baynes in Chapter Five, of a decade's investment in defining a Design dimension for the curriculum. His contribution is more profound than the Working Party's Report, and it is imbued with the experience of implementation in countless primary schools, secondary schools and colleges throughout the country – an experience far greater than the Working Party's collective achievement. What probably guaranteed an initial rejection of his ideas is the fact that they are based on extending the contribution that Art and Design makes to general education. Now that authorised attitudes are aligning with his, his arguments provide non-specialist teachers and school managers with the best possible means of familiarising themselves with educational concepts they will soon be required to cope with. This model, too, was published by the NSEAD two years before the Working Party first met [4]. Even so, we are reminded by Christopher Crouch in Chapter Six that a 'design culture' is not an invention of the 1980s, but is a phenomenon with a past – or rather a variety of pasts – the study of which is essential as a discipline in its own right, as a means of avoiding repetitive mistakes, and therefore as a means of contributing to the careful husbandry that Norman Potter advocates.

The belief that a Design curriculum should be substantially founded in Art and Design, and in particular should feature a development of intelligence towards the expressiveness of materials that traditionally has been associated with *Craft*, is tendered by Peter Dormer in Chapter Seven. He represents a shade of opinion that regards Design as 'applied art'. For him the fundamental essence of Design is the expressive interaction with basic materials and processes that distinguishes the craftsperson, and he presents a very convincing view that this is the necessary source for replenishing applicable creativity. In the following chapter, John Fulton underlines this message, pointing out that it has been a central concern of Art and Design since the implementation of the 1944 Education Act, and that 'play' with material possibilities is one of the instinctual activities that come naturally at the very threshold of learning. As such it cannot be encouraged enough in primary education. Neither can it be overdone in education as a whole for, according to Peter Dormer's arresting observation, Design must not be regarded as a cultural inessential because when it fails it occasionally results in loss of life.

That it *is* a matter of encouraging a natural inclination in the young child – to explore and express with materials and images – and not one of inculcating alien disciplines, is argued by Robert Clement in Chapter Nine. He also suggests ways of providing for this normal attribute and for consolidating upon it as a foundation for what must follow in secondary education. The two most telling concepts of this part of the book are Robert Clement's conclusion that technology serves Design in a creative, rather than manipulative, capacity [5]; and Tom Hudson's assertion, in Chapter Ten, that every individual is capable of inventing technologies appropriate to their needs. This ability comes first from a sound education through art and in visual literacy, which encourages the kind of total creative immersion in experiments with design *potential* that has characterised all the great quantum leaps in originality – as manifested by history's foremost artists and inventors. Inside the Design and Technology Working Party's Report this concept is trying desperately to find articulation. It has been expressed by Tom Hudson consistently in NSEAD conferences and those of its predecessor (the National Society for Art Education) and its affiliate (the International Society for Education through Art) since 1970 [6].

The burden of their work's potential to harm or curtail life is one that architects, and many designers of industrial products, must always carry. Schools of architecture in Britain were originally departments within art colleges, but since 1968 they have increasingly modelled themselves on the free-standing University or Polytechnic department. Many have dropped the requirement for their matriculating entrants to have studied Art and Design, and all have severed the formerly-close association between their offered qualifications and those gained by artists and other kinds of designer. This has been effected in the name of 'professionalism'. The fundamental error in this has been identified by Eileen Adams, Ken Baynes and others, and, in Chapter Eleven, Eileen Adams charts the attempts they have made to remedy it, and the substantial successes they have enjoyed, since 1976. It is by the worst possible oversight that *Art and the Built Environment* – the generic name that describes their various national and regional projects throughout this time – has had no place in the Working Party's terms of reference. However, detailed knowledge of it is already in the teachers' realm, through the originators' own disseminating efforts, Schools Council publications, and, since 1982, the conference proceedings and the journal of the NSEAD [7].

In Chapters Twelve and Thirteen, David Willey and David Yeomans address the discipline that architecture has courted most over the past twenty years – technology; but what they describe is something that does not at all seem beyond the experience of artists. David Willey posits a 'making' tradition that is at odds with a 'conceiving' tradition; but the ideas he attaches to each belong equally to Art and Design: particularly the principle that an intimate understanding of relevant technology should inform the way a created artefact is constructed. In Art and Design there is no essential dichotomy between this and the belief that artefacts are informed by conceiving them imaginatively; for it is normal for these two 'traditions' to interact at each minute stage of artistic activity. By a similar token, the *technical* knowledge of structural performance in buildings and feats of engineering that David Yeomans describes (a close identification, through projected feeling, with the distribution of loads and the forces of resistance) requires an ability to sense empathetically that is one of the principal attributes engendered by *aesthetic* analysis.

Technologies have intrinsic aesthetics. What Christopher Frayling deplores in Chapter Fourteen is the false application of a 'hand-crafted' aesthetic onto the products of technologies that require no manual intervention in their shaping. This is done either by formal imitation or, more usually, by association through advertising; and increasingly it is done to exploit nostalgic familiarity with a golden past. An education in Design that had no place for Art and Design would not automatically challenge such falsity; however, there are few things to which Art and Design is more hostile than the hollow concept, the fake experience, and Christopher Frayling's concerns endorse the need for a strong Art and Design representation in our design culture. To the inevitable objection that modern technological provisions are far too expensive for Art and Design in education, Michael Yeomans has an answer. In Chapter Fifteen he suggests a far-reaching partnership with industry that would combine the best of today's academic expertise with the most realistic experience of designing in the real world. Again this particular concept has a twenty-year pedigree, while that of art colleges participating in (rather than slavishly serving) industry goes back to the Education Act of 1918. The Design and Technology Working Party's neglect of this principle – which begs to be introduced into late secondary education – is inexplicable, but of course it is an obvious option for school managers in terms of local schemes of implementation.

My own contribution to this volume is to maintain that a concept of *drawing* that is the basis of Art and Design education – exercising both the imagination and a form of cognitive modelling that has recently been labelled 'imaging' – is also *the* essential discipline of designing. I also suggest a scheme for the categorisation of Design for educational analysis. In one aspect the designer deals with an archetypal form, the characteristics of which have materialised through generations of development. A second orientation requires the invention of new forms that invalidate all their predecessors. And a third obliges the designer to be conscious of working within an historical continuum, and to respect the 'given' while positing solutions that were impossible before today. It is fair to say that the Design and Technology Working Party has only really considered the second of these categories. That this is an unnecessarily restricted view will become clear to teachers and school managers as they read this volume, and especially as they begin to enhance their standard obligations under the terms of the National Curriculum by means of their own experimental practices.

DAVID THISTLEWOOD

References

1 In 1968 at an RIBA seminar, now universally referred to as the 'Oxford Conference', it was decided to phase out Architecture's dependence on Colleges of Art, and to model Schools of Architecture on the University or Polytechnic department possessing greater access to the fruits of technological research. Only a few Schools now require evidence of artistic ability in potential students.

2 ROBERTS, P. 1982. What is Design? *Journal of Art and Design Education*, 1, 2, 1982, pp. 269–78.

3 POTTER, N. 1969. *What is a Designer?* London, Studio Vista; revised eds (1980, 1989) London, Hyphen Press.

4 BAYNES K. 1985. Defining a Design Dimension of the Curriculum *Journal of Art and Design Education*, 4, 3, 1985, pp. 237–43.

5 First published in CLEMENT, R. 1984. Developing Craft Activities in Schools *Journal of Art and Design Education*, 3, 3, 1984, pp. 291–302.

6 Particularly the XXth INSEA World Conference *Art in a Rapidly Changing World* (host organisation NSAE), Coventry, 1970.

7 BAYNES, K. 1982. Beyond Design Education *Journal of Art and Design Education*, 1, 1, 1982, pp. 105–14.

Chapter One

JOHN STEERS Design and Technology in the National Curriculum – First Steps

Introduction

The Education Reform Act 1988 requires every state-maintained school in England and Wales to provide a basic curriculum for all registered pupils of compulsory school age. This national curriculum comprises the core and other foundation subjects, specifying in relation to each of them attainment targets, programmes of study and appropriate assessment arrangements. The core subjects are identified in the Act as mathematics, English and science. Welsh is identified as a core subject for schools in Wales which are Welsh-speaking. The foundation subjects are history, geography, technology, music, art and physical education and in secondary schools, a modern foreign language specified in an order of the Secretary of State. Welsh is included as a foundation subject for schools in Wales which are not Welsh-speaking.

Design and Technology Working Group

The Education Reform Act requires the Secretary of State to establish a working group to advise him on attainment targets, programmes of study and assessment arrangements for each of the core and foundation subjects. In April 1988, Kenneth Baker, then Secretary of State for Education and Science, announced the setting up of the National Curriculum Working Group for Design and Technology. The group, chaired by Lady Margaret Parkes, was required to produce an interim report by 31st October 1988 and to give final advice by 30th April 1989 – although in the event the report was not published until 20th June.

The objectives of this Chapter are to record (from an admittedly partial point of view) the principal recommendations of the reports, to note some of the immediate discussion and to summarise the responses of certain informed bodies – in particular the National Society for Education in Art and Design.

The design and technology brief demanded that the interim report should include an outline of:

a) the contribution which design and technology should make to the overall school curriculum and how that will inform the Group's thinking about attainment targets and programmes of study;

b) its provisional thinking about the knowledge, skills and understanding which pupils of different abilities and maturities should be expected to have attained and be able to demonstrate at key stages;

c) its thinking about the programmes of study which would be consistent with the attainment targets provisionally identified [1]. The working group was required to submit a final report in which it set out and justified its final recommendations on attainment targets and the programmes of study for design and technology. In addition, it was required to recommend attainment targets and programmes of study for design and for information technology in the first two key stages, for primary pupils, to supplement the recommendations of the Science Working Group.

The Terms of Reference for the working group define the approach to be followed thus:

> In approaching its task the working group is to view technology as that area of the curriculum in which pupils design and make useful objects or systems, thus developing their ability to solve practical problems. The working group should assume that pupils will draw on knowledge and skills from a range of subject areas, but always involving science or mathematics. They should be taught the principles and practice of good design, the application of theoretical knowledge, and within that context the practical craft skills needed for realising their designs in wood, metal, plastics, textiles and other materials. They should also learn about the variety of modern materials and technologies in use in the industrial and commercial world. Pupils should prepare for the world of work by learning how to work in teams as well as by themselves; by understanding the importance of functional efficiency, quality, appearance and marketability; and about the importance of working within financial and technical constraints. Modern business practice increasingly involves the use of IT. Technological education should equip pupils with basic IT skills and develop an awareness of the potential use of IT and computer technology whether in the business office, or manufacturing or commerce [2].

The Contribution of Art and Design to Design and Technology

A number of organisations, notably the Design Council, the Crafts Council, the Association of Advisers for Art and Design, the National Society for Education in Art and Design and the art and design specialists within Her Majesty's Inspectorate, sought from the outset to impress upon the working group the significance of the contribution which art and design should be expected to make to the area of the curriculum under consideration. While each of these organisations submitted separate evidence to the working group, regular meetings ensured that common arguments were advanced.

At an early stage, the NSEAD submitted a paper to the Design and Technology Working Group entitled *Technology as an Essential Component of the Art Design Curriculum* [3]. The introduction sought to establish the fundamental relationship between the subject areas:

2

The practice of Art and Design is based upon an understanding of techniques. These range from the *practical processes* necessary for the production of objects and artefacts through to *methodologies and strategies* employed to realise particular design objectives. Technology is built upon an understanding of the properties and characteristics of materials and systems and the related processes of making, forming and manufacturing. In common with other 'practical' subjects, but perhaps more directly than most, *at all levels* the teaching and learning of Art and Design demands an understanding of appropriate technology and its application to the pursuit of particular, desired ends.

The Interim Report of the Design and Technology Working Group

The *Interim Report* of the Design and Technology Working Group [4] was published in November 1988 and it received a cautious welcome from most of the professional associations. A meeting of Design Education Forum convened by the Design Council on 14th December 1988 provided evidence that there was considerable common ground between representatives invited by the Forum members: the Council for Environmental Education (CEE), Council of Design and Technology Associations (CODATA), Standing Conference on Schools Science and Technology (SCSST), National Association of Teachers of Home Economics (NATHE) and the National Society for Education in Art and Design (NSEAD). Lady Parkes and members of the working group who were present were urged to give further thought in their final proposals to primary education, to the importance of creativity, intuition and drawing in the design process, and to gender issues.

In its response to the *Interim Report* the NSEAD made the following general observations (the majority of these points were reiterated by other organisations). The opening remarks refer to the difficulty the working group obviously experienced as a result of *technology* being defined as a foundation *subject* in the Education Reform Act and the way in which this tended to conflict with the cross-curricular approach to design and technology advocated in the *Interim Report*.

> The Society is very sympathetic to the Working Group's broad view of the range of design and technology activities in primary and secondary schools. The Society recognises that the Education Reform Act 1988 (ERA) has designated 'technology' as a foundation subject. We believe that technology is the purposeful use of man's knowledge of materials, sources of energy and natural phenomena and may not be a subject in the usual sense. Furthermore, while we believe that design can be usefully seen as an over-arching curriculum activity we are far from convinced that this applies equally to technology. We do not believe therefore that it is helpful to regard design and technology as a compound noun: the study of design may lead to designing, the study of technology does not lead to a comparable activity. It is

3

our view that some of the important cross-curricular implications of the report are confounded by the failure to make this distinction [4].

The key reference to this matter is contained in Paragraphs 1.23 to 1.26 of the *Interim Report*. The Society wholeheartedly endorsed the view, and the consequent implications for the curriculum, that

the body of knowledge in support of design is unbounded; designers have the right and duty to draw upon knowledge from whatever sources seem likely to assist them in their quest for a solution.

There was considerable strength of opinion that this statement should not be compromised because it is precisely for this reason that design, if not technology, can be considered a genuinely cross-curricular activity.

The NSEAD expressed the belief that in terms of overall balance the *Interim Report* placed insufficient emphasis on aspects of two-dimensional design and in particular on visual communication through drawing. The response stressed that greater emphasis should be placed on the importance of imagination and curiosity in the design process. Also, because questions of aesthetic judgement necessarily permeate all phases of design activity there should be recognition that such issues are always fundamental to considerations of function and form.

The Society recognised that responsibility for design and technology in the primary phase was only included at a late stage in the remit of the working group but trusted that greater consideration would be given in the final report to this phase of education. In particular, the Society reminded the working group of the excellent Design Council report *Design in Primary Education* [5] and emphasised that this document had recently set out a coherent and practical philosophy for the worthwhile introduction of design and technology related activities into the integrated primary curriculum. The further point was made that there is much in this report that could be of use in framing proposals for the secondary phase.

A number of omissions were pointed out and in their final report the Society hoped that the working group would give further thought to multi-cultural and gender issues in order to ensure that the proposals provide genuinely equal opportunities for all pupils. It was suggested that the aesthetic and environmental elements of design might be given greater emphasis, perhaps by including community and environment as two of the contexts for design – thus also dealing with the significant omission of a strong environmental education element in the proposals.

The Society welcomed the recognition by the working group and the Secretary of State that an enhanced

in-service training programme will be needed to help teachers to come to terms with the new requirements, and additional

specialist accommodation and equipment will be required.

However, it was emphasised that it would be crucial for successful implementation that responsibility for coordination of the design and technology area of the curriculum be accepted in each school by a senior member of the management team who should not be closely identified with any existing subject or faculty. As a consequence of this proposal it followed that part of the INSET programme should be directed towards headteachers and deputy headteachers who will have the responsibility of managing the curriculum and establishing resource priorities. It is vital that senior staff should understand that established subjects in secondary schools should not be dismembered as a result of insensitive administrative decisions aimed at creating a 'tidy' administrative structure. Subjects such as the sciences and art and design, for example, will contribute to the design and technology area but by no means will this be the only contribution these subjects make to the whole curriculum. Finally, and still by way of introduction, the Society called upon the working group to provide an *explicit* statement of the aims of an education in design and technology.

In a paragraph-by-paragraph detailed consideration of the proposals the Society suggested that the working group state unequivocally that design and technology are essentially *cross-curricular* activities rather than a subject. It was emphasised that pressing practical reasons existed why this area of study should not be too closely identified with any one existing subject for fear that this would distort the necessary overall balance. The NSEAD expressed concern about the philosophical problems of providing substance and structure for a foundation 'subject' which has no intrinsic discipline of its own but rather is dependent on skills and aptitudes developed in other disciplines – art and design, mathematics, English language, materials science and technologies, for example.

The Society felt that the *Interim Report* allowed for a somewhat limited interpretation of what constitutes design and technological activity. Although, to be fair, this could be traced to the initial brief, including such statements as

> The working group should assume that pupils will draw on
> knowledge and skills from a range of subject areas, *but always
> involving science or mathematics* [my emphasis].

The Society concluded by reiterating support for the *Interim Report* as a basis for the further development of this vital area of the curriculum and summarised its response by suggesting that the following points were worthy of further consideration in the final report:

> a) There should be a greater emphasis on creativity, curiosity,
> imagination and the aesthetic dimension.
> b) Recognition is needed that the way of thinking which governs
> the route leading from ideas to tangible designs often involves a
> considerable element of intuition. Many of the most innovative
> ideas are initially intuitive and subsequently are rationalised to
> meet a variety of constraints.
> c) The stated attainment targets tend to have an overly product or
> engineering design emphasis.
> d) Schools should be warned not to interpret the report so that
> certain 'contexts' are equated with specific subjects.
> e) As written, there is a danger that if read consecutively as a
> design process, the attainment targets will establish too narrow a
> framework for innovation.

5

Information Technology

A chapter of the *Design and Technology Interim Report* is devoted to Information Technology. Paragraph 9 of the Terms of Reference states:

> The use of computer and information technology and other advance technologies in control, simulation and data storage and retrieval is becoming increasingly important in our society. This fact should be reflected in the use of computer and information technology across the school curriculum. Each subject group as it is set up is being asked to consider the scope for using computer and information technology in its subject and to frame appropriate attainment targets. However, the design and technology group is asked to provide within the national curriculum a focus for the development of computer and IT awareness, and skills such as keyboard skills and basic programming, by recommending appropriate attainment targets at the four key stages together with a supporting programme of study related to IT and basic computer skills and to awareness of the uses of advanced technology [6].

There seems to be general agreement that the development of information technology capability is an essential part of the education of every pupil. The NSEAD recognises that both design and technology and art and design can have a particularly significant role in helping children develop this ability. However the Society believes that education in this area should be developed through active learning rather than didactic theoretical approaches and that, as a general principle, it is more important to develop an understanding of the design and technology potential of IT than to focus on narrowly conceived IT projects. It also has to be recognised that the introduction of a basic IT education for all pupils has profound implications for school-based resources and for initial and in-service training programmes.

The working group was required '. . . to consider the scope for using computer and information technology in its subject and to frame appropriate attainment targets'. However, off the record, a member of the working group has pointed out that, despite this, none of the recommendations is likely to constitute a mandatory entitlement because of the all-too-obvious resource consequences. Ralph Tabberer, Schools Director NCET, says in *Educational Computing:* 'What is becoming clear is that virtually every area of the curriculum, if not every teacher, will be expected to teach with and about IT.' However, he also says that the current INSET scheme for IT '. . . is labour-intensive and its expense, if it were to be spread over, say, a three year period to cover all schools under the National Curriculum, would be enormous' [7].

There is little in the *Interim Report* that sheds light on this crucial issue, although the resource implications are not included in the remit of the working group. The report also makes little reference to the use of IT in relation to the visual, aesthetic or creative aspects of computer education, in art, or elsewhere in the curriculum.

6

In response to particular points in the *Interim Report* the Society made the following comments:

> We note the reference (paragraph 3.2.2.) to graphics and art systems as aids to trying out and developing design ideas. This cannot be divorced from wider visual, creative and aesthetic considerations and we believe that the effective handling of a broad range of IT applications will require a strong emphasis on visual literacy [8].
>
> We note the reference (paragraph 3.7.) to effective use of IT to develop ideas so as to present information in the appropriate forms, such as text, sound, pictures, tables, or a combination of these. However, we are aware that most of the computers that are currently available in schools are designed for word processing, data bases and spreadsheets. Few computer and software combinations at present offer the ability to combine sound and vision effectively and this should be noted [9].

A more thorough consideration of the cross-curricular significance of IT can be found in the recent HMI publication *Information Technology from 5 to 16* in the Curriculum Matters series [10]. In relation to the aesthetic aspect of the primary curriculum, HMI comment that children need opportunities to explore such creative activities as drawing, painting and modelling through the use of Information Technology alongside the more familiar and established media. HMI continue:

> By exploiting IT in order to develop creative and aesthetic aspects of the curriculum, children should by the end of the primary years:
> a) be able to create and store pieces of visual imagery and/or sound compositions;
> b) be able to access and re-work existing sounds or images to produce controlled results which express their ideas;
> c) be able to use IT sensitively in relation to different viewers or audiences.

Further objectives are established in relation to 'Designing, making, measuring and controlling the physical environment' and particular mention is made of the roles of science, mathematics, art and design, technology and environmental studies. The objectives identified by HMI are further developed in the section on the aesthetic aspects of the secondary curriculum. It is stressed that a school needs to formulate a plan for the development of skills and attitudes related to IT through activities across the curriculum. Information Technology concepts are listed subject by subject and it is noted that many of the skills and attitudes overlap. HMI stress that 'this is intentional and emphasises the major messages of IT for the learner within different contexts'.

The particular contribution of Art to the development of pupils' understanding of IT is identified by HMI as being able to help children make appropriate use of IT in the following contexts:

> a) Use computer-aided design to develop, organise, evaluate and refine ideas in visual form.
> b) Use IT to support existing art and design media, as well as to generate imagery.

c) Be able to select with discrimination from a range of input devices, such as a mouse, keyboard and digitiser, and to comprehend the basic capacity of a system to perform a particular task.

d) Use IT databases of materials, media, technical data, records and resources.

Given the necessary resources and training, it seems unlikely that the majority of art and design teachers would quarrel with the objectives identified by HMI. The Design and Technology Working Group's *Interim Report* emphasises (page 65) that they consider that IT is

an important tool for supporting design and technological activity . . . . Examples of this appropriate use include graphics and art systems as aids to trying out and developing design ideas . . . for creating artefacts, or desk top publishing systems for presentation and reporting [11].

While such statements are welcome they cannot resolve the obvious problems which inevitably will inhibit rapid implementation of the proposals.

The *Final Report* of the Design and Technology Working Group

The *Final Report* of the Design and Technology Working Group was released on 20th June 1989 [12]. In a covering letter to the Secretaries of State, Lady Parkes wrote:

Our approach to design and technology is intended to be challenging and new. The aim of our proposals for design and technology is to prepare pupils to meet the needs of the 21st Century; to stimulate originality, enterprise, practical capability in designing and making and the adaptability needed to cope with a rapidly changing society.

Paragraph 1.2 of the *Final Report* develops this statement, declaring that the approach builds upon existing good practice in primary and secondary schools and involves:

the development of design and technological capability 'to operate effectively and creatively in the made world' as the overall objective for the subject;

contexts for design and technological activity which are broad balanced and relevant;

within the attainment target framework, the coordination of design and technological activities currently undertaken in art and design, business studies, CDT, home economics and IT;

the use of knowledge, skills and understanding drawn from the core subjects of mathematics, science and English;

attainment targets which reflect the holistic nature of design and technology;

the description in programmes of study of a core of knowledge, skills and values as resources to be used in design and technological activity.

8

Paragraph 1.5 states:

> In our work on attainment targets and programmes of study we
> have aimed to ensure that they provide the means by which
> pupils develop the ability:
> to intervene purposefully to bring about and control change;
> to speculate on possibilities for modified or new artefacts, systems
> or environments;
> to model what is required in the mind, symbolically, graphically
> and in 3-dimensional forms;
> to plan effective ways of proceeding and to organise appropriate
> resources;
> to achieve outcomes of good quality which have been well
> appraised at each stage of their development;
> to appraise artefacts, systems and environments created by
> others;
> to understand the significance of design and technology to the
> economy and to the quality of life.

The attainment targets for design and technology are summarised thus:

PROFILE COMPONENT 1 – DESIGN AND TECHNOLOGY

AT1 – **Identifying needs and opportunities**

Through exploration and investigation of a range of contexts
(home; school; recreation; community; business and industry)
pupils should be able to identify and state clearly needs and
opportunities for design and technological activities.

AT2 – **Generating a design proposal**

Pupils should be able to produce a realistic, appropriate and
achievable design by generating, exploring and developing design
and technological ideas and by refining and detailing the design
proposal they have chosen.

AT3 – **Planning and making**

Working to a plan derived from their previously developed
design, pupils should be able to identify, manage and use
appropriate resources, including both knowledge and processes, in
order to make an artefact, system or environment.

AT4 – **Appraising**

Pupils should be able to develop, communicate and act
constructively upon an appraisal of the processes, outcomes and
effects of their own design and technological activity, as well as of
the technological activity of others, including those from other
times and cultures.

PROFILE COMPONENT 2 – INFORMATION TECHNOLOGY

AT – IT

Pupils should be able to use IT appropriately and effectively to
communicate and handle information in a variety of forms and
for a variety of purposes, and to design, develop and evaluate
appropriate models of real or imaginary situations.

The *Final Report* recognises that design and technology on occasions
need to call upon the specialist knowledge and skills of other foundation
subjects '. . . particularly history, geography and art'. The working

group notes (paragraph 1.13) that it will be necessary to cross-reference attainment targets and programmes of study when they become available.

The working group acknowledges that their report does not necessarily encompass all aspects of design. Examples are given in relation to environmental design and aesthetics. Paragraph 1.22 notes that in design and technology

> ... the fluency of pupils in the design 'language' of form, pattern, colour, texture, shape and spatial relationships is of crucial importance. Their command of this 'language' and judgement of how to apply such considerations could clearly be developed further in art.

Chapter 1 continues with a discussion of the contribution of design and technology to cross-curricular issues and themes before considering equal opportunities. The working group's basic premise is that design and technology includes activities of equal relevance to boys and girls and it is essential that they have the opportunity to work in a balanced range of contexts. In a welcome and unequivocal statement on gender the *Final Report* emphasises:

> It will not be possible for pupils to satisfy the requirements of our attainment targets and programmes of study by working in a narrow vein of activities, e.g. boys working on mechanical and constructional tasks while girls concentrate on catering and textile-related activities. (Paragraph 1.42)

Chapter 1 concludes with a section on ethnic minorities which declares that teachers should take a positive attitude to the opportunities presented by the cultural diversity in British life. The working group acknowledges that

> The variety of cultural backgrounds of pupils can broaden the insight they all have into the range of appropriate, alternative solutions to perceived problems. There are rich opportunities here to demonstrate that no one culture has a monopoly of achievements in design and technology. Appreciations of this kind could both contribute to better international understanding and yield direct economic benefits later in life.

Chapter 2 details the profile components, attainment targets and programmes of study for design and technology. At the time of writing (June 1989) it is not possible to enter into a considered analysis of this complex chapter beyond perhaps observing that, despite the overall emphasis on a cross-curricular approach, a disproportionate number of the examples given appear to be drawn from the CDT area.

Chapter 3 is concerned with Information Technology. The working group identifies five aspects of IT capability: Developing Ideas and Communicating Information; Information Handling; Modelling; Measurement and Control; and Applications and Effects. However, the report makes it clear that some of these elements should be regarded as an integral part of design and technology and therefore do not merit separate attainment targets – hence the more limited attainment target for IT which is summarised above.

Chapter 4 discusses the assessment of design and technology and IT.

It is clear that a number of crucial issues have yet to be resolved by Government such as the relationship between GCSE and assessment at level 4 (age 16). The School Examination and Assessment Council (SEAC) is expected to advise on 'the development, implementation and operation of the assessment system'. With regard to Standard Assessment Tasks (SATs) the working group make it clear that their preferred solution is one in which the assessment is based on a task undertaken as part of the normal progression of the pupil's work in the pupil's design and technology curriculum: the idea of a 'bank' of externally established standard tasks is rejected.

Provisional Conclusions

It is only possible to come to a few tentative conclusions about the place of design and technology in the national curriculum and, in particular, about the likely relationship between this curriculum area and art and design. The proposals may be further amended as a result of another round of consultation before Orders to give statutory force to the attainment targets and programmes of study are made under section 4 of the Education Reform Act. If all proceeds according to plan the attainment targets and programmes of study for all pupils in England and Wales in the first year of each of key stages 1, 2 and 3 should be introduced in Autumn 1990. Those for key stage 4 should be introduced in 1993, once pupils entering that key stage have completed the programmes of study for key stage 3. It should be remembered that while Orders will prescribe attainment targets and programmes of study for each of the core and other foundation subjects:

a) The Orders will determine *the minimum requirements* for each foundation subject. What is taught may go much wider;

b) there will be scope for the teaching of other subjects, and of *cross-curricular issues*;

c) Section 4(3) makes clear that the Orders may not prescribe any amount of *time* which should be spent on all or any part of a programme of study;

d) Section 4(3) also makes clear that the Orders may not require particular *ways* of providing a subject in the school timetable; and

e) The Orders will not prescribe *teaching methods* or approaches, *text books* or other *teaching materials* [13].

The Times Educational Supplement greeted the final report by declaring, 'A gigantic new faculty for design and technology is about to be born in every secondary school which will rival – if not dwarf – the largest English, science and humanities departments' [14]. While this may be one possible interpretation of the report, the working group has recognised that there may be many ways in which the necessary collaboration between subjects might be realised. However, they acknowledge that, '. . . unless the teacher expertise is brought together, pupils are unlikely to achieve the goals we outline in paragraph 1.5'. In paragraph 1.9 the working group emphasises, 'Those responsible in schools for the organisation and deployment of resources will also need to be aware of the requirements of the subject.' Thus oblique recognition is given to the advice of a number of respondents to the interim report who, like the NSEAD, called for the responsibility for coordination of this area of the curriculum to be given to a member of the senior management team rather than, for example, to an existing head of department.

If indeed, as many members of the working group privately claim, the proposals are a radical departure from CDT orthodoxy, it is equally clear that they are not necessarily seen as such by all concerned. Peter Davidson, Technology Adviser for Cleveland, praises the Working Group for choosing 'Attainment Targets based on a CDT process model which has become so well established' [15]. (A model, it should be noted, which has been condemned by Ken Baynes as 'first generation design education thinking'.) The rigid design process model is not one endorsed by the majority of art and design teachers. Surely such views are profoundly retrograde if they seek to impose a 'logical', process model of design and technology and to ignore more intuitive/affective modes of learning? There is growing recognition of the interdependence of the cognitive and affective in design – and art – education. As the NSEAD stated in its response to the interim report:

> . . . we do not feel at all happy with the polarities suggested in
> . . . (paragraph 1.10). To design any object or system it will be
> necessary to 'know that' as well as 'know how'; the implication
> that it is possible to make something without some level of
> understanding is unhelpful. For example, most educators now
> unflinchingly regard art and design activity as cognitive. That is,
> whatever else they may be, these activities are seen as occasions
> for mental activities, some shared with other pursuits, others of
> special importance to the arts; it is essential to be able to 'read'
> and to 'write' the symbol systems pertinent to art and design [16].

The establishment of the Design and Technology Working Group before that for art inevitably gives rise to concern that the high ground, so far as design and IT are concerned, will have been captured before the content of art is even discussed. On the other hand this situation provided an opportunity to prepare draft documents before the Art Working Group was convened in June 1990. It was crucial to use this time to good advantage and, in particular, to give careful consideration to the relationship between the two subject areas. While the Government does seem to recognise that art makes a major contribution to the curriculum as well as to design and technology education, art and design teachers cannot be complacent.

Most head teachers are unlikely to recognise the importance of art, both as a foundation subject with its own attainment targets and programmes of study and as a key contributor to design and technology in the curriculum, unless art and design teachers continue to emphasise the point. If art is to be adequately resourced to maintain the present wide range of activities and experiences it will be necessary to reiterate the arguments *and* provide the evidence of good design education practice in art departments.

Whatever the eventual outcome there is no doubt that the Design and

Technology *Final Report* is of crucial concern to every art and design teacher [17]. It is also beyond doubt that art and design teachers are being called upon to make a substantial contribution, equal to any existing subject, to this new curriculum area. This is over and above the statutory obligation to provide art as part of the national curriculum. There is no expectation on the part of the working group or the Government that art should be wholly subsumed into design and technology – or for that matter into a creative/expressive arts grouping: every school is required to make appropriate provision for art as a foundation subject in its own right. Once this point is firmly established the next step will be for each and every school to consider how best to deliver all the core and foundation subjects that are the basic entitlement of their pupils, taking into account resources and the expertise of available staff. There are no short cuts. It will be some years before all the building blocks of the national curriculum are in place, and much longer before the current innovations can be properly evaluated.

References

1   DES/WO. 1988. *National Curriculum Design and Technology Working Group – Interim Report*. London, HMSO.
2   *Ibid.*
3   NSEAD. 1988. 'Technology as an Essential Component of the Art and Design Curriculum', *NSEAD Newsletter*, May 1988.
4   NSEAD. 1989. *NSEAD Responses to the Interim Report of the National Curriculum Design and Technology Working Group*. Occasional Paper, Corsham, Jan. 1989.
5   DESIGN COUNCIL 1987. *Design in Primary Education*. London, Design Council.
6   DES/WO. 1988. *Op. cit.*
7   DAVIDSON, P., B. KELSEY, P. MCGEE and R. TABBERER. 1989. 'The National Curriculum: Making IT Par for the Course', *Educational Computing*, April 1988.
8   NSEAD. 1989. *Op. cit.*
9   *Ibid.*
10 DES/WO. 1989. *Curriculum Matters 5–16: Information Technology*. London, HMSO.
11 DES/WO. 1988. *Op. cit.*
12 DES/WO. 1989. *Design and Technology for Ages 5 to 16*. London, HMSO.
13 DES/WO. 1989. *From Policy to Practice*. London, HMSO.
14 NASH, I. 1989. 'Design Team Unfurls a High-Tech Umbrella', *Times Educational Supplement*, 23 June 1989.
15 DAVIDSON *et al.* 1989. *Op. cit.*
16 NSEAD. 1989. *Op. cit.*
17 For an account of the NSEAD's response to the *Final Report* see the *Journal of Art and Design Education*, Vol. 9, No. 1, 1990.

Chapter Two

DAVID THISTLEWOOD The Essential Disciplines of Design Education

Designing is an activity that engages all human faculties. It is the means by which environmental conditions are ameliorated and managed, a historic process that began with the adaptation of furs as clothing and continues today with the deployment of weather-tracking satellites or the creation of buildings that have their own intrinsic climates. Designing provides the means by which we are enabled to perform activities beyond the unaided capabilities of the human frame. This development is no less historic, having begun when flints were used to skin carcasses cleanly instead of tearing with teeth and fingers; it is equally evident today in millions of routine applications from opening cans to accessing the cores of nuclear reactors. It has enabled remote communication, intercontinental travel, space exploration, ocean-floor exploitation. It has provided the means of beneficial intervention in ageing and sickness. There is no human activity that is not facilitated or enhanced by its applications. This is immediately apparent when disaster strikes – flood, earthquake, war. These circumstances need only result in very small reductions in the availability of designed artefacts for life to become unsupportable. In a very real sense, designing is not 'just' an indispensable human faculty: it is the coordination and efficient marshalling of all branches of knowledge.

The fact that the naked ape has survived and thrived in unpromising surroundings may suggest that designing has been an *inevitable* aspect of human evolution. However, we know that certain societies throughout the world, having achieved a complement of designs consistent with supporting life adequately, have ceased to design new artefacts for indefinitely long periods. There may be material and ecological merits in this phenomenon, but it is significant for another reason: it suggests that designing is *not* an inevitable human attribute, but one that must be sustained by motivating needs. It must also be sustained by education – each generation must pass on the ability to design. This encompasses the origination of new artefacts and applications, the refining of existing ones, and the knowledge not to interfere drastically with ones that have been perfected over centuries of use. Sensibility towards one of these criteria does not necessarily extend to the rest. The years of the first lunar landings were also the heyday of the platform shoe.

This latter observation is not entirely flippant. There are distinctions to be made between three principal kinds of design orientation. In one the designer deals with an *archetypal* form – a shoe, a saucepan, a saddle – the characteristics of which have materialised through generations of development. Significant departure from these characteristics leads at best to less-fit artefacts and at worst – witness the platform shoe – to retrograde mutations. 'Archetypes' in daily use today include bowls, jars, musical instruments, tables, chairs, traditional water-craft and age-old implements like spades, hammers and cutting blades. The history of these artefacts has been coeval with human history. They seem to have evolved with Darwinian efficiency in tandem with the human form itself, and at their simplest and most effective they provide the closest possible correspondence between user and use. Such things as these do not commemorate acts of individual, original designing but they clearly embody extensive processes of trial, error, reshaping, adaptation and constant critical use. They represent a phase of human design enterprise before authorship was celebrated. The contemporary designer's contribution to their re-presentation consists in attending to secondary features such as materials, colours and decorative treatments: *essential* forms have ceased, or virtually ceased, evolving and are correspondingly non-negotiable.

A second orientation obliges the designer to invent new forms that *invalidate* all their predecessors. Electronic typesetting has invalidated hot metal. Every improvement of fuel-efficiency in motorcars invalidates the profligacy of earlier developments. Who today would design a sewing machine with a cast-iron treadle, or a hand-powered dental drill? This design orientation is dedicated to the principle of improvement. Each stage of development fosters the belief that perfection has, for the moment, been attained. The Boeing 377 Stratocruiser represented the *ultimate* facilitation of intercontinental travel in 1949 just as the BAC/Aerospatiale Concorde did in 1976.

In a third orientation the designer is conscious of working within an historical continuum. Buildings are the most obvious manifestations of this tendency, and it is clear that new buildings – whether domestic or institutional in scale – have pedigrees that determine their critical reception. They are compared with antecedents that are still evident in the world around them, which in effect constitute a museum of architecture and building. Although houses have a familiar symbolism and of course an archetypal function – shelter – they have no 'essential' forms in the sense in which a shoe has essential form: all kinds of shells, from windmills to barns and chapels, may become serviceable dwellings. Estates of shed-like structures are built speculatively for subsequent use as factories, workshops, warehouses, offices or superstores. Their forms are not specific to any one of this multitude of purposes. It is because buildings do not have such fundamentally necessary forms, but rather histories of more or less valid *alternatives*, that the study of history is vitally important to designers of these particular artefacts. The truth of this carries, for the same reason, to the designing of graphics, interiors, fashion and textiles.

Discussion of the three design orientations offers insights into some of the essential disciplines of designing today. It should be said at once that there are many kinds of designed artefact that relate across these categoric divisions. The Edison lightbulb, for example, is a rare instance of an 'archetype' that originated seemingly from nowhere, that is, without a history of prior evolution, and has not departed significantly

15

from the form in which it was originally conceived. The cat's eye carriageway indicators in our roads conform to this same principle. The modern bicycle was the result of a quantum 'evolutionary' development from the velocipede, and has remained an 'archetype' ever since. In the realm of 'historicist' artefacts a nuclear power station, considered as a group of buildings, clearly is an exception to the rule that architecture has no essential forms, for it obviously belongs to a category of structures that must be perfectible. There may be justification for considering power stations as 'engineering' rather than 'architectural' problems for this reason. However, the three orientations – 'archetypal', 'evolutionary' and 'historicist' – are sufficiently exclusive for them to be useful in theoretical discussion.

It may be seen that working with 'archetypal' forms, and working with those 'evolutionary' forms that invalidate their predecessors, have a certain similarity that distinguishes them from the third, 'historicist' category. 'Evolutionary' designing is a process that aspires to the ultimate creation of non-negotiable, perfected types that are in principle similar to traditional 'archetypes'. They become valid by superseding earlier manifestations of themselves, which are thus relegated to obscurity. For example, the sequence of product development that has resulted in the latest kinds of self-setting cameras has long ago negated the functional, economic and even aesthetic values that once were associated with fixed focus box cameras. In the line of evolution of this artefact, the Canon Sure Shot is nearer to perfection than the Brownie 127. 'Historicist' designing, on the other hand, aspires to the ultimate creation of the greatest possible variety of valid alternatives. Britain's most notable twentiety-century cathedrals – Liverpool Anglican, Liverpool Metropolitan, and the rebuilt Coventry – have in no sense invalidated York, Durham or Salisbury: they have extended and enriched the range of this particular family of artefacts.

'Evolutionary' designing compresses (and in this sense emulates) the centuries-long processes of development that have produced 'archetypal' artefacts. Much of this emulation is effected by means of 'accelerated use' – by subjecting artefacts to harsh regimes of durability-testing and programmes of mechanical wear-and-tear. This is pragmatic research and development. Much else, however, is achieved by imagining desirable but currently impossible outcomes – the opposite of pragmatism. Horse-drawn vehicles changed remarkably little over centuries, but once steam and then internal combustion locomotion were invented the design of horse*less* carriages began to change with bewildering frequency. Human imagination took hold, and designers began to chase 'impossible' dreams of speed, fuel efficiency, safety, seductive shapes, and their mass production.

However, the energetic evolution of the motorcar has resulted in drastic reduction of formal variety: today's cars of comparable performance possess remarkable family resemblances despite their various origins of manufacture, suggesting that this artefact is nearing 'archetypal' perfection. Yet it should be borne in mind that other products (for example, the standard 35 mm single lens reflex camera as typified by the Nikon

16

F or Asahi Pentax) once seemed to have attained similar perfection before radical product developments (in this case miniaturisation, compactness, and infra-red self-focusing) superseded them. The concept 'evolution' is not entirely appropriate here unless it incorporates the kind of quantum leap (evident in the development of the bicycle) that in nature produces new species types. Conventional concepts of 'evolution' are similarly inadequate for coping with the accelerated development of, say, aeroplanes or medical technology. They have been motivated by conceptions that would have seemed romantically foolish only two generations ago.

Imagining, then – a mixture of romantic dream-fulfilment and pragmatic pursuit of remote possibilities – is one of the essential *initiating* activities of designing. As such, it applies less to 'archetypal' designing (though material, chromatic and decorative re-presentation depend upon the imagination in different ways). In 'evolutionary' designing, imagining becomes the means of effecting vital developmental shifts. And in 'historicist' designing this activity consists in quarrying the past for forms that may be endlessly re-permutated, as well as in giving shape to the new. However, imagination is not the sole required attribute of a designer. This individual needs to be able to externalise his or her imaginings and make them real. From the earliest times this has been effected through drawing, a kind of drawing that is immediately responsive to the promptings of the imagination, and that apprehends and clarifies ideas in process of refinement. The term 'to image' describes this vividly, and imaging – a type of cognitive modelling that apprehends sensations, intuitions and perceptions and gives them concrete, *developable* form – may be seen as the essential *enabling* activity in designing. 'Imagining' and 'imaging', in mutually responsive accord, constitute the means by which new concepts are apprehended, refined and realised. It may be said with certainty that they are among the most essential disciplines of design education.

Coordinated, they constitute a process in which imaginative speculation gradually assumes tangible form through spontaneous drawing. The closest equivalent of this is the kind of immediate, expressive drawing that is one of the essential disciplines of art education. But there are differences of purpose. In art it is both discipline and goal – spontaneous imaginative drawings are aesthetically beautiful in themselves. In design this drawing consists in channelling the imagination towards ends which, even before they are entirely apprehended, are *real* and external to the imaging. This relationship has certain ramifications that are too obvious to require elaboration. In the realm of education it means that art is an indispensable foundation subject for design. And the vital part that aesthetic shaping plays in designing tends to result in products that fulfil aesthetic, besides many other, criteria of value.

Now, as I have suggested, this activity of speculating towards tangible forms is not only vital to human survival but also involves the coordination and efficient marshalling of all branches of knowledge. The need for its inclusion in our general educational provision is therefore beyond question. Britain has tended to educate its *vocational* designers particularly well, and in this respect it has been copied, and has had its best

17

designers recruited, by the rest of the world. But provisions for designing in general education have been patchy and poor. There must be very many reasons for this great omission, but the following are likely to be among the most significant.

Cross-curricular activities of the kind that would encourage the marshalling of several branches of knowledge – aesthetic sensibility, literacy, numeracy, logical argument, scientific and technological understanding, a historical perspective, a knowledge of contemporary events – have been discouraged in our highly compartmentalised system of organising the curriculum. Designers have tended not to enter teaching, preferring instead to exercise their chief vocation. Designing is not easily taught: it is far more practicable to teach a form of pseudo-designing in which pupils draw and make pastiches of existing consumer products. This often generates visually attractive studies that are convincing to those parents and educationalists (and the majority of the population) who have not themselves benefited from a design education.

But the most compelling reason for omission is probably this: the 'evolutionary' orientation in designing – the one that produces society's engineering structures, its consumer durables, its modes of transport, and its life-supporting and life-enhancing inventions of all conceivable kinds – is the one for which there is probably greatest need in general education. However, its inclusion establishes a precedent for this sphere of education, in the sense that successful outcomes of 'evolutionary' design teaching may only be measured by the degree to which the teaching in question is transcended by pupils. Of course this happens occasionally in other subject areas, where the most successful pupils gain insights that enable them to surpass in achievement the sum total of what has been taught them. But for *designing* to be taught successfully this must feature in strategies for teaching whole classes. *Any* pupil who does not surpass in achievement all that has been invested through teaching will be engaging in an activity that is not designing.

This observation gives rise to important questions. What might constitute a normal investment of teaching? Will the teacher of design be provider, or be coordinator of teaching that originates elsewhere? And how might teachers expect the relevant investment, from whatever quarter, to be exceeded by their pupils? All the various branches of knowledge that are considered to be contributory – from aesthetic sensibility to knowledge of contemporary events – have long educational perspectives. Serious teaching of these subjects will continue to occur in other areas of the curriculum, and *some* of the principal responsibilities of the teacher of design will be to marshal these disciplines, encourage their interrelationship, and provide stimuli for their enhancement in the context of designing. But if designing is to be regarded as a subject of central importance in our strategic educational provision, we must address its *own* essential disciplines. It is a strange conception of a 'core' subject that would rely upon a range of other subjects for its main investments of teaching, and merely provide a context for their reassociation. Its own essential disciplines lie outside its coordination role and *within* the nature of the way designers engage and process their ex-

18

ternally derived information. *Here* is where we may discern an educational essence, and also begin to see how it may reciprocally enhance learning in other critical areas of the curriculum.

Before I elaborate on this observation, however, there is another component of design teaching to be acknowledged – technology, or rather technologies. This is of course fundamentally necessary learning. It *directly* embraces methods of manufacture and fabrication, from handicraft to mechanical and industrial processes; and it also *indirectly* deals with technologies that are 'packaged' in product design. For example, audio-visual home entertainment systems, within a given range of performance, consist in similar technology, packaged as variations on familiar themes. The same is true of all manner of domestic appliances. Because there is often a surprisingly loose fit between contents and container, the latter may be designed independently in education as it often is in professional life. But educational opportunities are lost if pupils are encouraged to be impressionistic about, say, the internal workings of a washing machine.

Designing with technologies, in order that they may be put to appropriate uses, is an important responsibility of the designer. There is also a concomitant responsibility to respond to new technological developments, and be informed – even led – by them. And there is a corresponding requirement to conceive of designs that test the present limits of technological feasibility, and thus demand their further advancement. But do these vital *responsibilities* constitute essential *disciplines* of designing? The answer is 'no': they remain vital responsibilities beside the host of other social, material, economic and cultural obligations with which designers are charged.

It is possible to ignore all such obligations entirely and still engage in this activity we call 'designing'. History is full of anti-social or uneconomic artefacts – from the V2 rocket to the De Lorean car and Sydney Opera House – that have nevertheless been celebrated as designs. It is true that they have often had an aesthetic significance that has outweighed their social or economic failings. It is true also that the world is replete with artefacts that fulfil functional purposes with matter-of-fact honesty, but which lack aesthetic value, and we tend to say of these that they have not been 'designed' at all, or, derogatorily, that they have been 'designed by committee' or 'by market research'. By this we mean that their forms have not been graced with aesthetic sensibility. We may recognise when they *have* been so graced, even when the aesthetic in question has ceased to be significant, as when for example we regard a Victorian Gothic teapot or a jazz-modern, streamlined toast-rack with amused respect. There is therefore a sense – more than a sense, a fundamental certainty – that designing is *intrinsically* concerned with aesthetic formation, and that the purpose of this pairing of action and criterion serves to engage a host of *extrinsic* social, material, economic and cultural associations, including the technological.

How then does this fundamental interaction of designing and the aesthetic imperative manifest itself? It clearly is manifested in appreciation. We know what we like, and if we take instruction in aesthetics we may learn why we exercise our affections, we may extend our range of appreciation, and we may change our preferences. On this basis it is not unreasonable to suggest that every citizen is entitled to be educated in twentieth-century design aesthetics so that his or her responses to the world of designed artefacts may be informed rather than arbitrary. There is a precedent for such a mass educational provision, though it is not one that is particularly helpful today.

One hundred years ago there existed in Britain a system of general education embracing definitions of quality in design and decoration, and in the styling and fitting-out of domestic and institutional buildings. There was a universally applied rationale for teaching, based on imitative drawing of what were considered authentic works of design and architecture. The most respected concepts were of Greek or Roman origin, or at least of classical descent. Recommended models either replicated the Greek or Roman, or else introduced their abstract proportions into specifically modern artefacts, structures, and materials such as iron and plate glass. This system of ideas permeated the whole of society, from the most cultivated to the least educated, for its combined logic of aesthetic values in art, design and architecture was taught to every young person in maintained education. It was a system based upon copying authorised examples of good design circulated by the South Kensington (now the Victoria and Albert) Museum. The underlying purpose of such a vast and expensive national effort was eventually to achieve a workforce capable of neat and competent craftwork, naturally respectful of the kinds of decorative details with which designers, and industrial and building workers in general, would be expected to be familiar throughout their productive lives.

The necessary skills of the common workman, as perceived at the time, included the marking out, scaling up or down, and transferring of patterns (applicable to all manufacturing and decorative trades), and the recognition of true, standard types of ornamentation so that degenerate forms would be unlikely to slip into usage. The responsibility of the designer was perceived narrowly as to apply the authorised aesthetic to an ever-increasing array of products and inventions. Decorative artist and artisan were thus linked by an unbroken circle of concepts: a recognised authority derived a curriculum from an appreciation (however debased) of classical form, and instilled in ordinary people an automatic respect for this aesthetic in buildings of all kinds and (as ornamental derivatives) in industrial production.

In this way there existed an 'environment' of mutually dependent aesthetic principles incorporating art, design, architecture and education. The point is not whether it was *valid* but that it *existed*. Its greatest benefit was its *coherence* relating, within a single framework of ideas, design in education, design in recommended professional practice, and a notional set of applied aesthetic values representing the highest desirable standards of the day. Its chief disadvantage – the one which now inclines us to diminish its relevance – was the fact that it could not accommodate *change* in any one of its principal parts: education, design, or aesthetics. When any of these became transformed in some way, however slightly, the consistency was broken, the mutual harmony destroyed, and instead of an *integrated* set of principles there was disintegration.

By contrast, throughout the twentieth century there has been constant, unbridled change of aesthetic identification in design. The Arts and Crafts Movement, Art Nouveau, Futurism, Art Deco, Purism, International Modernism, Constructivism, Elementarism, the Festival of Britain Style, Brutalism, Post-Modernism and a host of other movements have been more than stylistic fashions. They have been radically different states of design consciousness, equal alternatives to the few cultivated states – Italianate, Greek, perhaps Egyptianate and Gothic – that prevailed earlier. Within less than a century design has changed utterly in conception and purpose, the ramifications of which are most obvious in 'historicist' contexts.

For example, by overstating space and understating form today's architects have succeeded in eliminating the frontier between inside and outside, and the visual barriers between the lower and upper parts of buildings. Environmental design has become characterised by openness, the intersections of horizontals, verticals and diagonals, the interplay of hard and soft textures, reflections in metals, plastics, glass and water, and the movements of people and vehicles. There is no cultivated procedure for 'reading' its forms and spaces (in the ways in which Italianate, Greek, Egyptianate and Gothic styles were 'read', and their deployment appreciated, by an informed élite).

When designing was concerned with using style as a means of connecting elements (architecture, landscape, decoration, works of art, furniture), the art of appreciation was largely intellectual – a question of understanding whether style had been correctly applied. Now that designers are concerned with the juxtapositioning of elements – setting each beside others without contrived, stylistic connections, to achieve mutual contrast and mutual enhancement – appreciation is more likely to be intuitive and comprehensive. In other words, designed environments might today be appreciated as if they had *not* been designed – as natural landscapes or ancient urban spaces are appreciated – for their 'accidental' juxtapositions and their 'unforeseen' changing relationships. A premium is placed on variety and vitality, gained by bombarding the senses with lines, rhythms, forms, spaces, colours, textures, and movements, performing feats unusual in stylistic design but common in everyday life. This has given rise to a historically unprecedented eclecticism of taste. It is true that partisan arguments have arisen during this expansion of aesthetic consciousness, but there is a widespread acceptance of diverse architectural styles in our streetscapes – providing that buildings exhibit 'good manners' in relation to their surroundings.

In creative education this expansion of taste ought now to mean that pupils may be encouraged to develop uniqueness of *individual* expression, while at the same time reviewing the possibilities inherent in *all* modern aesthetics. A hundred years ago there was an identity of belief and action. Today's eclecticism camouflages both the absence of, and the need for, an educational consensus. One major difference between then and now – perhaps the most important – is that then our major museums were the repositories of standards in art, design, architecture and creative education, whereas today they are not. The South Kensington Museum coordinated and led the whole of British design education. In recent times the Council for Industrial Design, which became the Design Council, was earmarked for this responsibility, but no one any longer pretends that a single, centralised institution can fulfil it.

An appropriate museums policy is the first thing that is needed in a national effort to educate all citizens in designing. A network of regional Design Museums should be established (having the admirable National Museum of Photography, the Museum of the Moving Image and the London Design Museum as their role models) to conserve, present and educate in standards of excellence. It is not hard to imagine such an institution typically housing its holdings in three distinct categories – 'archetypal', 'evolutionary' and 'historicist'. The first would celebrate the consistent validity of traditional utensils and implements that have served humanity so well that they are to be regarded as efficient extensions of the human frame. This category would shade into the 'evolutionary' in the presentation of specifically modern 'archetypes' such as cameras and microscopes – efficient perceptual extenders of human capabilities – that are still in constant process of development themselves. This second category would serve to remind us of ranges of artefacts that have been superseded in the progressive refinement of evolving types. The obvious surrealism inherent in communities of objects in which, say, a Schlicht's Momentograph camera suggests prescience of the Hasselblad 500C, or an Imperial Leicester typewriter sits with equal validity beside a modern word-processor, would contrast sharply with the third, 'historicist' category, where the same principle evokes no comparable sense of dislocation.

We are used to streetscapes containing architectural artefacts ranging from Roman to medieval and to modern: our civilisation supports this range because visual variety is desirable and, more importantly, because it embodies the history of our culture. Society *can* support this historical range because the necessary sustaining technologies are essentially similar for the vast majority of building types. However, the sustaining technologies for horse-drawn vehicles, Model T Fords and Ford Escorts are fundamentally dissimilar, and this is a principal reason why these temporarily familiar aspects of our streetscape are eventually superseded. They slip out of sustentation as technology evolves. Their cultural significance may *only* be retained if they are *maintained* in special environments.

We therefore need museums to conserve transportation vehicles and all other 'evolutionary' artefacts. We need museums to husband 'archetypes' – examples of implements and utensils that represent touchstones of excellence and fitness. We need museums to care for original 'historicist' artefacts from the past, such as examples of clothing design or the design of reading matter, that are ever-present in eclectic imitation and inspiration today, but too ephemeral to survive as original artefacts in the external world. We do not need to conserve architecture *as artefacts* in special environments, though: the world at large is our museum of these phenomena. We do, however, require museums to conserve associated ephemera such as architectural drawings and other documentary records, as we do in relation to the histories of 'evolutionary' artefacts.

If or when such a museums policy were implemented, the question would be: how would pupils interact with holdings that embody a culture, and that also objectify the means by which it has been created and sustained – that is, designing? A general answer – obvious and consequently in danger of being overlooked – is to emphasise the importance of drawing in design education. This means cultivating *in appreciation* attitudes to drawing that have been, and are, cultivated by designers *in creation* – when they are 'imagining' and 'imaging'.

An appropriate encapsulating term for this is 'developmental drawing' (Figs. 1–7). It materialises as a sort of fluctuating diagram – an often unprepossessing image hacked about, over-scored, erased, redrawn, pushed out of shape, retightened, bearing the marks of struggle and the imprint of the designer's creative personality. Its images may be recalled and further elaborated, refined, reduced, reshaped, distorted and reformed, explored and regrouped, indefinitely. It blurs distinctions between analysis and synthesis: it is the heightening of intelligence towards

1 Sketchbook detail: design speculation assuming tangible form through spontaneous drawing.
UMA MAHAVEDA, third year student, Liverpool University School of Architecture.

2   Sketchbook detail
astylistic juxtapositioning
of objects in space.
SHERI PYRON, graduate
student, Washington State
University School of
Architecture, Liverpool
University School of
Architecture Exchange
Programme.

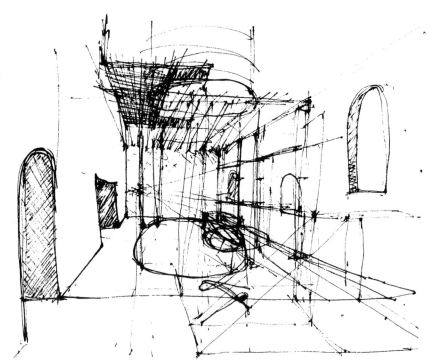

3, 4, 5   Sketchbook
details: a series of
'fluctuating diagrams' of
designs exploring
originative, structural and
historicist concepts at
various developmental
stages.
DAVID COTTAM, fifth year
student, Liverpool
University School of
Architecture.

6, 7 Sketchbook details: spontaneous drawings of designs for a hotel complex, incorporating knowledge of precedents (Japanese architecture and the 'Prairie' houses of Frank Lloyd Wright).
UMA MAHAVEDA, third year student, Liverpool University School of Architecture.

discovery as it follows the shaping of individual products, and the product-to-product development of types. It thus inculcates a sense of evolutionary design sensibility for application to particular instances of problem-engagement.

How would this be supported by the categorisation of design orientations that I have advocated? An education in developmental drawing would begin by reference to 'archetypes', and at this stage would consist in objective visual analysis of forms representing the ultimate perfection of types. This would feature accurately sighted observation, measured representation, and conventional analysis as evidenced in plans, sections, elevations and orthographic projections. In spirit it would synthesise the 'visual' and 'manual' aspects of drawing education that have previously been compartmentalised in 'art' and 'design' curricula.

Skills developed in this arena would be transferable to the study of 'evolutionary' forms. Conceptual complexity would be substantially increased here, because the objects of study – society's engineering structures, consumer durables, modes of transport, life-supporting and life-enhancing inventions – have records of *individual* product development as well as histories of contributing to the evolution of product types. To make analytical drawings of the Morris Mark I Mini, for example, would be to draw *upon* this historic artefact as a means of drawing *out* a stage in the development of this gradually perfecting type we call the 'motorcar'.

A third stage in this approach to design education would engage the 'historicist' category, further complicated by the fact of its featuring non-chronological sequences of influence. Time witnesses the origination of new forms for houses as it does for cars, but in the case of architecture, and other 'historicist' realms of designing, earlier forms are not superseded by later. They co-exist; earlier may exhibit prescience of later manifestations; and later may embody conscious formal references to earlier forms in ways that would be inconceivable, for example, in camera design (though it must be admitted that modern radios are sometimes disguised as wireless sets, exploiting a nostalgia for the early manifestations of this artefact). In other words, the study of 'historicist' artefacts, through drawing, involves complicated lateral paths of influence as well as connections back and forth through history, in place of the simpler, one-directional paths that are to be detected in the 'evolutionary' category.

In tandem with a progressive approach to analytical drawing, a design education should present sympathetically ordered experiences in synthetic creativity, or imagining and imaging. Thus analysis of 'archetypes' should be accompanied by studies in designed decoration, in the use of alternative materials, and in 'styling', a cultural phenomenon that actually applies across all three categories. Designers do not reinvent cups, bowls and plates: they may use new materials, originate novel decoration and devise minor stylistic variations upon these 'archetypal' forms. It therefore seems realistic to invite pupils to do the same. This is by no means simplistic. A chair, for example, is an 'archetype' (a provision of seating elevated a comfortable distance from the floor, offering lumbar

27

support and, optionally, support for the forearms and the head). However, the range of materials from which it may be fabricated is almost endless; and it has been subject to every conceivable stylistic reinterpretation. A Jacobean chair, an Art Deco chair, a de Stijl chair, a Post-Modern chair: these are worlds apart and yet they have 'archetypal' form in common. There is also a sense in which this artefact is 'historicist', for all of its possible stylistic manifestations are mutually inclusive in interior design.

When it comes to 'evolutionary' designing, another level of complexity becomes apparent, comparable to that affecting analytical study of this category. It seems legitimate to ask pupils to design 'evolutionary' strings of artefacts – for example, devices for measuring time which use shadow, waterpower, clockwork, electric, electronic and solar technologies. It also seems legitimate to offer them realistic assessments of the depletion of strategic materials and energy sources, so that they may begin to predict the future directions of 'evolutionary' trends. 'Historicist' designing raises complexity yet another gear. A typical set of problems may feature, say, dwellings responding to post-and-beam, loadbearing brickwork, structural frame, pneumatic, and tensile membrane technologies, but these problems would be strung laterally as well as linearly – for example, requiring pupils to design *communities* of such radically different, but desirably compatible, forms.

I return to the premise that designing is of inestimable value in general education, and I reiterate that it is wrong to posit a core subject that merely coordinates the derivatives of other areas of the curriculum. Its purpose must be to develop modes of thinking, understanding and intervening in the world of constructive events – modes that are peculiar to itself and which complement the mathematical, scientific and literal modes that it adopts from elsewhere. Designing in education – in common with other, traditional core subjects – requires the interrelation of conventions and unique percipience. Like mathematics, science and English, it is committed to the shoring-up of conventions, honing and rationalising our collective memory of useful forms and techniques. Unlike these other disciplines, it places a premium on pupils' transcending received wisdom. This is its 'creative' aspect, and whereas creativity has been considered a useful adjunct to other core subjects, it is indispensable to designing.

Nothing can be said to be creative that does not transcend received wisdom in some slight way. A pupil may begin by perceiving matters in conventional design analysis, and in the course of working with them attain all that may be attained by means of mathematical, scientific and literal modes of rational thought. If there then occurs, through imagining and imaging, an act of *visual* understanding that radically changes the significance of analysed forms and releases them from their conventional origins, the whole of the pupil's study will be graced with creativity: understanding will emerge, unfold, develop. If, on the other hand, a study begins with some intensely revealing insight or conception, which its originator, in order to make it work, then drops into a conventional mould – a hackneyed form or an approximate technology – the result

28

will be to negate the initial creativity. Nothing will emerge, unfold or develop; and moreover an initial *potential* for creativity will be restrained by convention. Designing enhances the rest of education when it brings these principles to all other subjects in the wider curriculum and demands their assimilation. A 'design culture' will manifest creative writing, intuitive mathematics, inventive science and constructive views of world events besides a full complement of ingeniously conceived artefacts and environments. In a real sense the latter will be the achievements of an informed and supportive society, channelling through the creative imaginations of its designers.

Chapter Three

PHILIP ROBERTS 'What is Design?'

That the question 'What is design?' can be posed, apparently seriously, is a source of vexation to many teachers. For the answer is, after all, self-evident: it is what we practise! The question is deceptively simple, however, and on closer examination not so innocent either. Part of its interest is that it leads to the consideration of 'process' and 'product' views of education, especially in terms of epistemology. We may consider two different kinds of response.

One response might consist in specifying certain public knowledge, contained and examined within particular disciplines. That is to say, a particular view of what constitutes knowledge is contained in the possible answer to a supplementary question, '*What* is to be taught?' In this view, knowledge may be seen in 'thing' metaphors – as product; and the answer to the question is contained in the teacher's implied acceptance of the received state of knowledge in his field of competence. Now, contrast this with the notion of art and design activity as process: exploring, discovering, creating a personal route to (presently unknown) personal or (presently unknown to the pupil) public knowledge. In this view, the appropriate supplementary questions that might throw some light on 'What is design?' might begin with 'Why . . .?' or 'How . . .?'

The first response (illustrated in a statement such as, 'The planning and the making, in these ways, of these artefacts constitutes "design"') rests on already-established knowledge. The route to such knowledge is a route to be followed, and there is a necessary conjunction with physical artefacts. The second looks forward into the 'unknown' (illustrated in a question such as, 'If I do this, might I find that . . .?'). The route to knowledge is to be created or found by the knower-to-be: the creator of the to-be-created knowledge. From an epistemological and a language viewpoint, the first sees knowledge in 'thing' metaphors, with process secondary. The other puts processes of knowing and learning superior to (their) product: that is, knowledge as an objectified achievement is, at this stage, secondary. The two views, of process and product, begin to merge when process begins to shape product. Our knowledge is then seen as a consequence of our activities of finding, of finding that (such is the case), or of creating. This is to begin to relate educational experience, through curricular activities called art and design activity, to a theory of knowledge. The complications begin in earnest when 'product' is used to speak, without discrimination, of the artefact as well. By then we have possibly illustrated our failure to recognise and pursue the possible distinctions between 'knowing that' and 'knowing how'.

Practice is the heart of the matter. The function of the question, 'What is design?' is to help us perceive more clearly our present practices, problems and opportunities, and understand better the complexities of change in people, and, more specifically, the educational activity. It is a question posed by practitioners who are concerned with theory derived from and based on practice, rather than with trying to fit pupils and practice to *a priori* theories of what is supposed neatly to happen.

Imagine that in two schools pupils may be observed making coffee tables. In one of the schools this is recognised (by an observer) as a design educational experience; in the other, our observer describes the activity as a 'routine exercise'. Why might one school's activity apparently be recognised as a design educational experience, and the other's not? Why and how and when is one set of activities (that is, the achieving of the coffee table) recognised as a routine exercise and the other set of activities as embodying responses to existential issues of meaning, identity, and value that have been recognised by the pupil in company with the teacher?

To add to the difficulty, let us suppose that both sets of activities have been called designing, or 'design problems', by their respective participants. The issue can be presented in another way: both the 'similar' situations may be called problems, but surely there is a distinction between a routine exercise or task (labelled as a problem) and existential problems of meaning, identity and value which are being explored and expressed and celebrated through 'practical learning activity'? This question begins, perhaps, to point to a problematic area. For it is clear that much of the work done in the 'practical subjects' is concerned with physical artefacts: with such tangible products as pictures, chairs, engineering tools, dresses. In suggesting, albeit minimally, the possibility of discriminating between, on the one hand, artefacts of this kind and, on the other, sets of activities, we are suggesting some consideration of the weight of possible emphases on (isolated) artefacts and (continuous) process, and, ultimately, on the issue of the separation of the knower and the known. This will lead towards some consideration of the nature of knowledge – especially the distinction between 'knowing that' and 'knowing how', revealing contrasting epistemological views perhaps implicitly held by practising teachers.

It might be useful to consider a further comparison in an attempt to illustrate the possible objectifying of activity, with its attendant consequence of process being understood primarily in terms of product in conjunction with artefacts, or in 'thing' metaphors of knowing and understanding. Take first the case of a pupil who plans and makes a box. Consider him (with his activity) against the pupil who graphically records movements around a kitchen, which record of evidence he then uses as a basis for deciding whether or not to rearrange the fittings of the kitchen. In the first, the educational result may be seen as the artefact rather than as change in the pupil; for it is not difficult to find experience 'assessed' on examination of the artefact, without the assessor finding it necessary to see the pupil. In the second, the principal product might be seen as decisions by the pupil, derived from the physical record provided by the paper work. In such a position, the physical record is the means towards an end. But might it be reasonable to propose that in both sets of activities the common educational concern lies in the activity and its constituent processes: that is, in the action between the pupil, his teacher, and the relating media within their context? The 'design experience', on such a meta-perspective, would be the set of intentional interacting learning and change processes and consequences. Any artefact (if one were produced) would then illustrate the processes of learning, of changing, of psycho-social developing; that is, it would be illustrative or suggestive of intentional and transactional changing.

The artefact would represent a 'freezing', at a particular point, of processes which indeed continue after the completion of the artefact – and, furthermore, of processes which continue expanding in comprehensiveness. Hence, the pupil is able to look back, later, on artefacts achieved and recognise their, by now, 'shortcomings'. They can be perceived and described as shortcomings only relative to his succeeding position. That is, it might be said that the pupil has 'moved on'. He is not saying, obviously enough, 'The box has changed'. Rather, he is signifying that his perceptions and understandings of his activity (manifested in the box-as-record) have grown.

What to assess, then? Should it be the impersonal artefact? the effects of the learning-designing activity on the pupil? the further consequences of his activity (and if so, when and how?): the 'results' of installing this artefact into his home . . .? And, with the graphic record of observing and enquiring, is it possible to specify the criteria leading to some assessment of the decisions taken, and which are illustrated in the rearranging (or not) of the kitchen fittings? Or are we to consider the set of activities as artefact, with the pupil seen as graphic designer in relation to some norms of the professional field of graphic design?

The outside observer can clearly see that learning, in the broad field of art and design, is inseparably linked with 'doing', and apparently 'therefore' with making artefacts. He is surprised by the 'therefore', and disturbed that the implicit authority and power of 'therefore' might signify that any and all making is necessarily art and design education in practice. He is impressed by the seemingly unquestioned assumptions that there is a necessary connection between the making of artefacts and the development of mind; and its complementary: that *not* to be making artefacts – to be 'theorising' – is not significant learning.

And if, as is frequently asserted, the aims and the activities of art and design education are of consequence to all – pupils now and citizens later – the outside observer might comment that the making of a range of conventional products (as distinct from, say, buying and using them) is not the continuing central activity for many adults. It might however be more persuasive to suggest that the central activity – now and later – is in modelling or decision making or in acting, rather than in 'merely' artefact making. This is not to say that experience of making utilitarian objects is to be downgraded. The point is to consider the significance of the activity in relation to the permanence of the artefact produced, and, where such significance might be located. And in any case, to argue, in effect, that any and all making of useful objects *is* art and design education is possibly to perpetuate the dominance of product design (with its range of conventional products), and to contribute towards the continuation of the tradition of teaching 'essential skills' without questioning their educational ends and justification. It is also possibly to be understood by others as saying that art and design education is only for those of a 'practical mind', or especially for those so described.

In trying to perceive what 'education through art and design activity' might be said to consist in, one might start from the question: What is the relation of these local, particular techniques and artefacts to their embedding 'knowing how' and 'knowing that'? He might ask: since the artefacts (the end results physically external to the learner) in these two schools are similar, would it be worth trying to perceive differences in their achieving: might the learning activity be in the ways of their achieving?

It is worth considering the distinction between 'knowing that' and 'knowing how'. If we describe too narrowly the achieving of knowledge and the development of mind, priority may be given to the discursive intellect, placing propositional knowledge above practical knowledge. Practical knowledge – knowing how – is in the active engaging-in-the-world, which discursive knowledge cannot accommodate [1]. By contrast, 'knowing that' (something is the case) is to stand, as it were, outside the world which is then set over and against the proposition it makes true. 'Knowing how' is intrinsic to the nature of 'practical learning'. It is not of the order of propositional knowledge; the criteria of propositional knowledge are not appropriate. Practical knowledge obviously implies action rather than description and prescription. It implies practical knowing (with consequent knowledge) rather than propositional knowledge (as being prior to or a prior condition to action).

All this can be comforting to the teacher of 'practical subjects'. It can 'explain', and justify, a common mistrust of 'theory', and the not unfamiliar pejorative comment directed towards discussion of curriculum developments seen as new: 'all talk'. And, conceivably, since there is no way of accommodating the practical to the discursive intellect, this may also 'explain' the teacher's seeming inarticulateness. He may of course acknowledge that, while it is important to know *that* certain statements are true, knowing *how* to carry out particular activities – manifested through artefacts – is equally a cognitive achievement (provided our conception of mind is not restricted to the attributing of propositional knowledge), and is not to be reduced to the kind of knowledge that can be stated in propositional form.

But this should not entail, then, his apparent acceptance and assertion, demonstrated in much practice, of the proposition that the achieving of all, or any, artefacts *is* art and design education. For, in opposition to this assertion, he is frequently wary of what he understands to be developments in art and design educational practice on the grounds that 'the pupil cannot make an artefact *until* he has learned to design'. It is not that the teacher is using the word 'design' in the sense of a 'planning stage' of the route to be followed, prior to the construction of the artefact. It is rather that he asserts that there is a set of prior experiences or component exercises which lead to a point at which it is possible, and only then, to design 'properly'. It is to be assumed that his statement is derived from his understanding of his practice. But it must open to ques-

33

tion that practice in its separation of 'learning to do' and an eventual 'doing': the separation of the learning of 'the skills' from their practice. Propositional knowledge might accept the separation: the practical knowledge position cannot, since it has a place for degrees of what is describable as skilled performance.

This is more than the kind of disturbance which may be a consequence of the language that is commonly used when we say that, for instance, we are 'learning to paint', or carve, or whatever. There is a network of problematic issues here. Instead of saying that we are 'learning to paint' we might say that we 'are beginning to paint'. The two are different statements. In the first, our expression suggests that there are indeed two discrete processes: one, of learning to paint, or of learning to carve; and two, when we have completed that stage, of painting or carving proper – the first stage having been completed. It is implied that we separate 'the skills' from the act proper: that we learn the basic language and then use it, rather than there being only the action of learning to carve by carving, or to paint by painting.

At this point there is a need to outline a position concerning professional discourse and curriculum innovations. Innovators in the art and design curriculum would agree that learning is to do with action. They would sympathise with the apparent mistrust of 'talk', though in distinction from the vulgar criticism ('all theory, and no action') they might argue the need for better theory, and more of it. But the views of theory are different. Those recognised as innovators and developers would also agree with value being given to practical activity. But this easy agreement manifestly fails to undo the knot of incompatibility. A popular criticism directed towards the innovator is that his curriculum is 'too wordy'. The implication is that instead the learning should be practical. In view of the agreement between the critics and the innovator that learning *is* practical, what is the difficulty? It is worth considering that, from their perspective, the critics' position is not unreasonable.

In the implied 'instead' which is central to their position, the critics perhaps illustrate precisely the incompatibility that constitutes the failure of communication. A sense of this may be offered diagrammatically (Fig. 8). The critics' positions are to be located as A; the innovators' positions as B. The area of intersection covers areas of agreement (for example, with the proposition that learning is a practical affair; together with some shared practices). In saying 'instead', the critics speak from within A: they cannot perceive B's position. Because they cannot, they may legitimately say, 'Too much talk; too much theory'.

It is intended that the diagram shall carry the idea that the conceptions of what constitutes education, knowledge, the structure and strategies of teaching, the nature of learning, are different. The diagram presents, crudely, two general positions or two differing paradigms of practice: one, *conventional practices*; the other, *not-conventional practices* (or emergent practices).

The boundaries are, characteristically, fuzzy. This is part of the communication problem. In the case of *conventional practices*, fuzzy because practices differ: it is acceptable that constituent practices should not

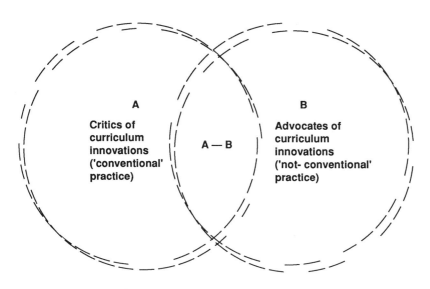

necessarily be compatible with each other. Few practitioners agree on definitions of content or on methods and procedures (even when there is philosophical discussion of such matters). The normal paradigm constitutes the taken-for-granted background. The need to discuss it is not there: when a paradigm 'works', its supporting community is not aware of anomalies and insufficiencies. Shortcomings are more easily seen by those outside of normal practice, rather than by those within.

In the case of *non-conventional practices* (or emergent practices), there is a fuzzy boundary because any emergent paradigm is constituted in open and partially open systems. The boundaries signify the distinctions.

The shared area *A–B* represents some shared practices and some shared concepts and metaphors. Because they are shared, they may also make more difficult to understand the larger areas that are different. On the other hand, if there were no shared area there might not be any possibility of practitioners working within the 'older' paradigms gaining an insight into the emergent, or of the practitioners in the 'new' appreciating not only their change of direction but also continuity.

It could be proposed that there would be no communication problem if the shared ground were not apparent: the sharing provides the communication problem. With no shared ground, the practitioners in the 'old' paradigms would be unaware of the practitioners in the 'new': no awareness would mean no problems. In any event, in many cases it might be argued that the 'old' paradigms are the necessary grounding for the 'new': a creative discontent with conventional practice would provide, for some, the stimulus towards the articulation of transformed practice.

But to revert to the critics' point. The placing of the alleged 'theory' is important: (that is, when the critics' conception of 'theory' = 'new developments' or 'design education', is 'all theory and no action'). Its location indicates a differing paradigm of practice and, consequently, of theory. For the innovators have not said (i) that learning-through-designing is 'theory' followed by 'practice'; or (ii) that learning-through-

35

designing is theory and practice, when and if these aspects are seen as mutually exclusive and discrete. They have however implicitly said that the questions, the problems, derive from and are integral with the 'knowing how'. Their 'knowing that' is of the activity: it derives from doing, making, forming, being, and then, as propositional knowledge, feeds back into action. It is not, as the critics' 'instead' might imply, that the practices often tagged 'design education' derive from some prior recipe or prescription for action.

It is possible that in condemning reflection on practice – mistakenly seen as antecedent theory – some criticism illustrates the difficulties caused by differing perceptions, made more problematic by 'translation' into verbal language. But the condemnation does not necessarily make any comment on what some curriculum developers have either said or done. The innovator and developer, from his position, cannot use 'theory' in the same sense: the discreteness and the antecedent location are not in his paradigm of practice.

This translation into verbal language is a fundamental aspect, and is concerned with the structure of verbal language and the effects of that structure. Danto says:

> It is a striking fact that philosophers have often acted as though, in order for the world to be put into language and described, the structure of the world must be antecedently linguistic . . . . It is not as though every metaphysician who has constructed reality as shaped by logical form – as having a linguistic structure at its heart – has explicitly endorsed the pictorial theory of description. But claims regarding the ineffability of reality often enough have been based on the denial that reality has the form of language, a reasonable enough denial except that to ground ineffability upon it is to commit the same fallacy, namely, to hold that reality is linguistically graspable only if it is co-structural with its descriptions . . . . But the conditions for adequate description surely do not compass parity of form, and once we renounce formal parities, the imputation of ineffability on the world's part and inadequacy on language's part becomes logically unstrung [2].

It is possible to suspect that there is a failure to observe this on the part of some who criticise developments emerging in school-based practices, especially when some of their criticism is in conjunction with, or not distinguished from, the work of some constructors of professional design problem-solving approaches. The critics do not merely point out the possibility of 'misreading' methodological constructs – which could be useful: they confuse the attempts towards sufficient description with the action. That is, there is an apparent failure to differentiate between the language of description and the action with whose modelling it is concerned. Some critics further tend to see all 'design methods' as algorithmic and prescriptive in tendency and intention, whereas the interests of school-based curriculum developers have tended to lie in questioning them. (A distinction is here being assumed between innovators and others, others who may well claim and believe that they 'follow a design process' and are, therefore, innovators.)

36

For many teachers in schools, methodologies have been vehicles, enabling questioning. The questioning has been directed towards the better personal understanding of the complexities of the structure of action in the educational field, and especially of the structure of practical knowledge. Again, this might be seen as an illustration of the critics' innocently subscribing to this fallacy, that the structure of action must be antecedently linguistic. But in any event, much of the 'all talk' criticism may be construed as a failure to distinguish between curriculum activity and professional discourse which is meta-curriculum activity.

It is also possible that some of those who have criticised the efforts of teachers attribute too great an influence, on the teachers, to theories derived from fields of professional designing. It is possible to sustain an argument that developments in the art and design curriculum were emerging without any actual or necessary connection being made, by its foremost teacher-activists, between professional design education, professional design activity, and art and design activity in general education. Simply, change in education at the secondary level has been initiated, in general, by teachers finding that conventional practice and theory are insufficient, distorting, and possibly reductive.

Nevertheless, some school-based practitioners have found that models concerned with professional designing have suggested insights pertinent to their work. As an instance of these, Christopher Jones's hierarchies of problems may be nominated [3]. Such a model has been found useful by some because its simplicity helps to reveal the relationships of the local focus of 'the designer' to the larger embedding context. A possible educational by-product, then, of theory constructing in fields of professional design may be the insights (that is all) of value that are offered to the teacher when reflecting on learning in the world of action. On such a view, there never was an intention, as some in-field critics suggested, that teachers were trying to bring into schools a model of professional design activity. It is, however, possible that there has been, and that there remains, an absence of sufficient discrimination between models of professional design activity and art and design activity in general education.

In summary, it is conceivable that the seeming incompatibility between some critics and some innovators rests on differing perceptions of what constitutes educational practice. The failure of communication is perhaps a consequence of the structure of verbal language, but further, and more significantly, it may be that the innovators are gradually articulating a different language. Such a 'new language' – in its structure, metaphors, procedures – would distinguish art and design educational developments and would distinguish them further, as it is better articulated: certainly, this represents the beliefs and aspirations of some proponents of 'design education'.

Other possibilities are suggested. For example, we might consider that the impression received – that frequently knowledge as product is identified with, or at least not distinguished from, artefact – could be construed as evidence that many teachers practise from within the intellectualist tradition. The evidence might consist in the apparent failure to recognise the category distinction. It might also be worth pursuing the observation that, generally, teachers work conventionally: they practise within a paradigm of 'normal practice'. Their aims and objectives are inherited, without a close examination of their bases. The teacher recognised as innovator, on the other hand, finds it necessary, possibly urgently necessary, to attempt to articulate a closer fit between practice and theory. The practitioners of normal practice have no such problems; and they literally may not understand what innovators are saying. The innovators and developers have, as it were, left normal practice (or perhaps have never been members) in their moving towards a contemporary sense of continuously changing actor-in-context. It is innovators who have problems.

'What is design?' is a disturbing question because paradoxically its seeming simplicity suggests that the response is problematic. We are suggesting that we should now suppose that there *is* something different (or that there may be) – new, unfamiliar, not conventional — emerging in educational practice, implied by the posing of such a question. Such a supposition may permit us to by-pass the familiar usage of the word 'design' in relatively well-established areas of activity such as graphic design, engineering design, industrial design. Similarly, descriptive and conventional titles (art, environmental education, craft, applied technology, woodwork, metalwork) that are apt to foster discussion on a school 'subject' basis may usefully be avoided, although, again, the fields of their concern must be of eventual interest. What seems unlikely to be helpful is to begin consideration of educative activity in terms of already-formed 'subjects', thus possibly being too limited by frameworks of reference provided by familiar conceptions and practices.

But the persistence of the question, 'What is design?' suggests that there is a considerable struggle going on to restructure part of the practice in the secondary curriculum, an attempt to formulate a coherent model of curriculum; and that, until a sufficiently coherent new paradigm of practice emerges, the urgency surrounding the question must continue. The issues opened up are to do with: how the institution of education might be more appropriate; the relations between well-established practices and innovatory efforts. These concerns lead to the questions: Who are the recognised practitioner-advocates of change in educational practice in this area of the secondary curriculum? What have they said, and done? What kinds of activity are implied, or made explicit? Is it possible to indicate the likely institutional consequences, in terms of their organisation, of the development of the ideas of, particularly, the design education movement in general education?

Notes and References

1 A well-known discussion of this is in: STURT, GEORGE. 1923. *The Wheelwright's Shop*. Cambridge, Cambridge University Press.
2 DANTO, ARTHUR C. 1976. *Mysticism and Morality*. Harmondsworth, Penguin, pp. 104–5.
3 See JONES, J. CHRISTOPHER. 1970. *Design Methods: Seeds of Human Futures*. London, Wiley-Interscience, p. 31.

Chapter Four

NORMAN POTTER What is Good Design?

The 'goodness' or 'rightness' of a design cannot easily be estimated outside a knowledge of its purpose, and sometimes also of its circumstantial background. This is no reason for timidity of judgement; a man must reserve his right to say 'I like that; to me it is beautiful and satisfying, and more so than that one over there that works so much better' – or, 'this is a good workmanlike solution, thank God it has no pretensions to Art'. Theoretically, a well-integrated design should come so naturally to eye and hand that neither of these comments will be called upon, but human nature isn't so simply natural and neither is human society. An optimum solution is possible where the conditions for verification can refer to absolutes: a daunting and illusory requirement in most design situations. On the other hand, a design can say to us 'here is a problem that is so well understood that it can be felt to be moving toward an optimum solution; the design is inclined in that direction'. This is designers' talk; the user of a product will not be too interested in the skill with which a designer has met his constraints. If a design is so well wrought that overtones of meaning are present, so that the work can be experienced (optionally) at many different levels simultaneously, then it is a conditions of *organic* design that the further harmonics must not clutter or deform a simple level of acceptability.

For the designer, good design is the generous and pertinent response to the full context of a design opportunity, whether large or small, and the quality of the outcome resides in a close and truthful correspondence between form and meaning. The meaning of a good garden spade is seen in its behaviour, that it performs well; in its look and feel, its strength and required durability; in a directness of address through the simple expression of its function. More complex objects, places, equipment, situations, may well exhibit less obvious dimensions of meaning. A design *decision* may prefer some determinant principle of action to a material outcome. As a social activity, the integrity of design work proceeds from the understanding that every decision by one human being on behalf of another has an implicit cultural history. Design is a field of concern, response and enquiry, as often as decision and consequence. In this sense (also), good design can both do its job well and speak to us.

Every design product has two missing factors which give substance to abstraction: realisation and use. These are the ghostly but intractable realities never to be forgotten when sitting at a drawing board. In a similar way, any discussion of design philosophy must never stray too far from nuts and bolts and catalogues and every kind of material exigency: a designer breathes life into these things by the quality of his decision-making. Thus his concern is truly 'the place of value in a world of facts' [1], and the outcome can (or should) be a form of discourse;

but not a verbal one. His work can be said to deploy the resources of a language and be accessible to understanding through the non-verbal equivalents of intention, tone, sense, and structure [2], but there are other and more directly functional levels of experience which – as has been said – must come to the hand with all the attributes of immediacy. Most of the time a designer finds it hard enough to do small things well. Any number of broader considerations must not distract him from that task, but rather enliven and give sanction to its meaning.

A product must not only be capable of realisation through manufacture, but in its very nature must respect all the human and economic constraints that surround production and effective distribution. This may seem obvious in the case of product and communication design. Similarly, it is difficult properly to evaluate a building without some idea of the cost factors and the client's briefing. Difficult, but not impossible: a clear design will generally manage to state its own terms of reference, unless disaster has intervened at some stage to distort the central intention of the work. There are many cases in which a good design will be discarded for reasons which seem arbitrary, perhaps to be replaced by some meretricious product with a better sales potential. Again, a perfectly adequate design solution, the result of much care and imagination in its development, may never reach the public at all. In this respect the artisan designer may enjoy a freedom denied to the designer for mass production (though his economic problems will limit the scale of the work), and much experimentation in form-giving will necessarily occur in situations exempt from marketing difficulties. These will include one-off jobs, limited production runs and public work (schools, hospitals, airports, for example). Much early discussion in the modern movement assumed – broadly for social reasons – that product design (mass production for the consumer market) was the centre of inertia that had to be revitalised: Herbert Read's book *Art and Industry* [3] reflected this assumption in the 1930s. Gropius's *New Architecture and the Bauhaus* [4] contained a classical statement which seemed to imply that product design would move inexorably toward the 'type-form' for the problem examined.

As things have turned out, the most interesting work has happened, of course, where it was economically possible. The domestic consumer market has gained an important component in DIY (do-it-yourself) which in itself demands a reappraisal of the designer's role in the areas affected. The mass production of building or service components (such as pressed-out or moulded bathroom service units) has hardly approached the potential seen for it fifty years ago. The notion of *place* as the focus for communal achievement has scarcely fought off the demands of *occasion* and mobility, despite moving and articulate pleas from Aldo van Eyck and others – and despite the continuing reality of place as a factor of ordinary experience, eroded as it is by communications and the rarity of imaginative work in this field. It is a mistake to see the designer's work as conjuring up new worlds at the scratch of a drawing pen: there are many fields in which the designer could profitably work with (for instance) do-it-yourself and cooperative housing agencies; and there are

40

fields in which a designer can and should respect the organic continuity that surrounds people's lives. Two examples: the interior designer is doubtful of his 'responsibility' because everyone knows that architects should design their buildings from the inside outwards. In fact, there are plenty of buildings that are simply weather-proofed and service-connected shells waiting for specific uses. However, leaving that aside, it is not a necessary argument to suppose that – given adequate social resource – the whole of our physical environment should be uprooted and totally replaced at regular intervals. This is dangerous fantasy. In fact there is plenty of scope for the adaptation of existing buildings to new uses (a so-called slum area is as much a pattern of relationships as of decayed buildings) and this is interpretative work for which the 'interior designer' could be well-fitted. Again, there are plenty of structurally sound buildings that could be given extended life with the aid of a loan and a do-it-yourself handbook. As it is, the lunacy of high-rise development has only recently been seriously questioned; in practice, land values give rise to extraordinary palaces for paperwork springing out of areas of private squalor, and the simple things – like the provision of neighbourhood amenities – are neglected in favour of drawing-board schemes which may seriously debilitate the life that 'squalor' sometimes reflects. A run-down neighbourhood may need a lot of things but the problem must be seen in more than a tidy-minded way; every problem, however complicated by planning and growth statistics, is met with concealed assumptions (and often concealed economics). Here is ground both for humility and for diagnostic sensitivity in the way a designer approaches his work.

The difficulties for product designers are not just a matter of plain villainy on the part of manufacturers; they are, in part, a consequence of capitalism. Whilst strange things do go on in boardrooms, it must be realised that a well-designed product must be sold competitively. Experimental work may be chancy as a sales proposition. As things are, a first duty of a company director is to make his company profitable (which he may conceive as a first duty to his shareholders), and a second duty is to keep work-people in continuous employment. Experiment becomes a closely calculated risk, very much at the mercy of the buyers in the retail trades, and subsequently dependent on a successful advertising policy, public response, and many other factors. In the furniture trade there are a few companies who have tried to maintain reasonable design standards, against the hope of improving them as the market 'softens' sufficiently to warrant further advancement. Such companies have relied on contract work – furniture for public buildings specified by architects or local authorities – to help carry them forward. It will be seen, at least, that under ordinary production conditions, product design cannot easily be evaluated against absolute standards, yet products meet constant criticism on such terms.

Unfortunately, it is also true that there are innumerable products that are just very poor realisations of a straightforward and entirely non-experimental design concept. They could have been marketed just as easily had they been designed with more distinction. The design capability simply was not there. Designers should be aware of property relations as a conditioning factor in the way they design (and think about design), but no designer should fool himself that given 'a better society' it would then be magically easy to design *well*. A designer who stops designing in the hope of better things may lose his ability to design anything at all; to this extent people become what they do. Here, an idealistic student might consider the partial truth in the saying 'a few are artists, the rest earn a living' – which in caricature might be said of every profession and not less of the sciences than the arts. Those who elect to put their work before everything else, which is merely one of the conditions for complete mastery in any field, must fairly expect life to present some difficulties.

The hard facts of a market economy are easy to overlook in the relatively permissive ambience of the average art or design school. Although academic life is subject to its own peculiar stresses, economic sanctions are not pre-eminent among them. Fortunately, students need not harden themselves against a perpetual winter of creative frustrations: the situation is not as depressing as some of these remarks might suggest. It is true that a designer's freedom will reflect in large measure the values of the society in which he works. Designers are not privileged to opt out of the conditions of their culture, but *are* privileged to do something about it. The designer's training equips him to act for the community, as (in limited respects) the trained eyes and hands and consciousness of that community – not in some superior human capacity, but in virtue of the perceptions which he inherits from the past, embodies in the present, and carries forward into the future. He is of and for the people; and for them, and for himself, he must work at the limit of what he sees to be good. The sentimentality of talking down, or working down, is a waste of the social energies invested in his training: thus can 'social realism' enshrine the second-rate.

If society is geared to satisfactions on the cheap, the designer has a special responsibility to straighten himself out in that respect; to decide where he stands. When real needs are neglected, and artificial ones everywhere stimulated into an avid hunger for novelty, sensation, and status appeal, largely (but not wholly) for reasons of private or public profit, then here is his own nature, his own society. He is involved, and he must decide how best to act. It should not surprise him to find a thin and pretentious reality informing the design language of the world which he inherits. A Marxist (or anarchist) analysis may be one tool to help him sort this out, but he will hardly need to put on Marxist spectacles to see that a veneer of good taste has 'reference' to certain obvious social conditions and is not the whole of good design. The design student may sometimes find that the industrial scrap-heaps, the surplus stores and the products of straightforward engineering will yield images of greater vitality than will be found in more fashionable quarters (though even here, fashion spies out the land). Such a situation is a challenge, and as such must be studied and understood.

Yet it is still no answer to live in the future; every skill must be nurtured by a commitment in depth to the present. The meaning of creativity may be seen as an equation which resolves this apparent paradox. Work that lives is rooted in the conditions of its time, but such conditions include awareness, dreams and aspirations as much as the resources of a specific technology: such work respects the past and actually creates the future. These problems, and their wider implications for human happiness, will necessarily concern students of design, because no one can make truly creative decisions without understanding; and without a real participation in the constructive spirit of his time. *This spirit must be sought out*, not necessarily by intellectual means, to be honoured wherever it is found.

Those who are depressed by the shoddiness of our environment (except in those areas of economic privilege where it is customary to buy up the past), should study the spirit of the modern movement in its development from the turn of the century to the late 1930s. Here they will find themselves in good and most various company. As Walter Gropius often explained, the modern movement was not some matter of dogma, fashion, or taste, but a profoundly wide-ranging attempt to encompass the nature of our twentieth-century experience and to meet its physical demands with a constructive response.

What may excite us most about this phenomenon is its surface appeal, the tangible achievement; a whole world of very explicit imagery conjured, as it must now seem, out of nothing – an entirely fresh start. The fact of conditions historically different from our own does not diminish the marvel of this achievement and its continuing relevance. This has nothing to do with imitating the forms of the past (near or distant): anyone who sees the modern movement in stylistic terms will fail to understand its radical nature. It is also necessary to accept that most work of today (meaning 'modern' or 'contemporary') is an enfeebled and misunderstood derivation from this earlier work, almost wholly removed from its inspiration, its most deeply rooted concerns, and the force of its guiding spirit.

The effort of zero, of the *tabula rasa*, of the new beginning, is not in principle a stylistic option (though in retrospect it may be so viewed); it is an effort consequent upon certain perceptions, for which, obviously, there will be equivalents in prophetic or diagnostic acumen, across a whole civilisation experiencing radical change – or perhaps it is truer to say, waking up to a foreshortened view of what such change might seem to imply. Earlier models, and the canons of *idle* change, the sports of fancy, become suddenly and drastically inadequate. The call is certainly to 'clear from the head the masses of impressive rubbish' and to 'make action urgent and its nature clear'; it is also to 'look shining at / New styles of architecture, a change of heart' (Auden in the 1930s) but most of all it is an effort of address toward the irreducible; that modest yet most demanding of entitlements. Is there indeed any alternative but silence, as George Steiner has remarked in another context? The possibly prophetic nature of such insights is often overlooked, especially when accusing the modern movement of a false and shallow optimism; as though a culture of utility could not be expected to ask 'what is it decently possible to assert, given the claustrophic banality of a present, and the seeming threat of a future?' Less, perhaps, an insight than an indistinct awareness, and one of two negative imperatives at work, the other being *the need to stop telling lies*.

What more active principles are involved (or indeed, derived)? It is usual to account for the modern-ness of modern work in terms of influences and precedents, the technological and social pressures, new materials and techniques, the convergent history of ideas, and so forth. It is obvious that orders of form, and forms of order, are design specifics in a practical way and experienced concretely, not as a set of abstracted verbal propositions. Yet as Viktor Frankl points out, in his book [5] written from direct experience of the concentration camps, it is curiously easy to overlook, in any analysis of human motivation, the tenacious strength of the human search for meaning. It is here that the irreducible, the without-which-not, the minimal, the verification principle, 'truth to materials', and the notion of accountability have their roots. At a different level, it is fairly obvious that failing the imitation of natural form (the dead-end of art nouveau), a verification principle would move towards number and geometry stripped of backward reference or depleted symbolism. 'Clear expression', no unseen props, and the most for the least (the strengthening of signal and the reduction of noise) have to be seen as necessary correlates to any search from zero for significant form – given a situation of survival, as distinct from options consulted on a broad wave of optimism concerning human progress.

However, it was the second broad outreach of the modern movement, involving nine more positive principles as guides to action (in fact there are a few more), that rescued a search for meaning from being merely the celebration of a rather unattractive rectitude. These are the social principles – not unwarrantably, design being a transactional art – and they prefigure certain changes in human relations which have not occurred, but may well have to if our society is to become less death-orientated. It is in this sense that the modern movement might be said to be prefigurative, and in this sense that its effort was betrayed (forgotten) in the take-over by the complicated apparatus of commercialism. These principles may be briefly stated as follows.

The first principle is that of self-determination: the search for a sub-set of self-generative principles within the situation as found; as expressed by the sayings 'a well stated problem is more than half solved' and 'a designer transforms constraint into opportunity'. As things get under way, the principle enables the job to speak up for itself with increasing confidence and fluency. Sometimes this is falsely seen, so that in fact a designer able enough to work in this way is not actually being instructed by the job, so much as providing a good fit (i.e. just being a good designer); the imposition of *arbitrary* form always throws up a lot of noise and is in other ways more conspicuous. However, it is interesting that this principle, which applies very well in a straight designer-client relationship, is also flexible enough to accommodate quite different design attitudes, including those that might be thought anti-design by those who see the modern movement in formal terms.

The second principle is that of reasonable assent; that what is done

44

should be essentially coherent, intelligible, and open to discussion. (There are problems of language here which will not detain us: from the standpoint of principle, which becomes 'generative' to the way something is done, the fuel of continuing intention is more important than the ash of dead fires.)

The third is that every part in a job should work for its living ('From each according . . .'). This implies distinction and emphasis not from 'privilege', or prior status, but from functional differentiation within the whole. This principle (aided by others) entails asymmetry, a clear structure, and certain negative imperatives mentioned earlier. (For example, in a chair, the absence of glued blocks reinforcing an unsound structural principle, or, alternatively, a structure no longer covert, but derived from glued blocks.)

The fourth principle is that objects should be designed as well as possible for use and not for profit; and that where an object cannot be designed at all unless by definition it is profitable, then the resulting compromise is against principle and not with it. The modern movement has (rightly) been accused of political naivety by supposing that optimised design was conceivable in mass production, where marketing arrangements will ensure a good product being swept away to stimulate fresh demand. Anyone who wishes to see such matters imaginatively explored should read E.C. Large's novel *Sugar in the Air* [6].

The fifth principle is that of anonymity, poignantly expressed in the effort to mass-produce objects of quality at low prices; more adventitiously, and sometimes trendily, in the way that designers like the idea of their Thonet chairs, jeans, clothes-pegs – not to mention the universal boot. The requirement in either case is that the particular should be seen as a special case of an *available* universal. The principle is also, implicitly, an attack upon the art-object so constituted by its scarcity value (for discussions of which, see John Berger's writings [7]). An extended requirement is the suppression of unwarranted detail (which in turn entails a special case of the third principle, namely that elements are distinguished from components), such that the fuss of idiosyncrasy slips below conscious regard. The human being is thus freed to enjoy a 'true' idiosyncrasy, supposedly more authentic in being less object-fixated; so that what was once merely idiosyncratic becomes genuinely individual. Thus by discovering what is uniquely true to himself (as distinct from conferred status) the road is open to self-transcendence. (See Buber's *The Way of Man* [8] for a poetic uncovering of this theme.) At a less difficult level, the principle finds expression in an allegiance to the 'set' or series (of knives, of wine glasses, or whatever) in preference to the unique and single object. The attentive reader will have noted that this principle is the most vulnerable, the most open to corruption, and the most liable to misunderstanding (old ladies deprived of their tea-cosies and sentimental possessions, reds under the bed).

The sixth principle expresses a deep desire for a new vernacular (grown out of the alienation we all feel) – seeking articulation in a popular, indigenous, locally based, and relatively unselfconscious design language; adding a sense of place to that of space, of repose and location as a

45

counter to mobility, and so on. Less wistfully, the principle develops an interest in the simple and functionally derived design solution, often with engineering overtones (*cf.* canal buildings and structures, barns, windmills, and small houses everywhere pre-1850). Local variants are usually involved – of materials and technique – and there is a predilection for small or controllable human scale. This principle has always run strongly as a current of inspiration in the modern movement, but in the early years found expression as its apparent opposite (i.e. as a paradox), namely, as an implacable resistance to sentimental craft revivals and every other evidence of a falsely imposed vernacular: the conviction that there are no short cuts to Elysium except through 'the assimilated lessons of the machine' (a view characteristically developed by Lewis Mumford in *Technics and Civilisation*) [9]. The way back is seen to be through faith and through the wilderness, and a refusal to be conned by snap answers (e.g. the candles and leathers syndrome). It is interesting, of course, that some of this antipathy can be traced to the parentage of the modern movement in the arts and crafts, and that now the movement is finding it easier to come to terms with its parents in the realm of the Alternative, the principle is gaining confidence; it is no longer so wilfully 'protecting the lost wisdom of the tribe' behind the fortifications of an arrogant modernism. However, it should be clear how the modern movement has come to be misunderstood on this point. Who was it who said that the true romantics of this age would be its most ardent classicists? I shall not waste time on the ignorant supposition that the modern movement is about high-rise buildings (or ever was, intrinsically).

The seventh principle is possibly the most important (though this is too puffed-out a word – formative is better) and it is the most closely linked to insights available from other areas of our culture: it is, of course, the search for relationship as distinct from self-sufficiency, or self-containedness, and everything that this might be held to imply at every level of decision in design. This includes, and perhaps most prominently, the complex realm of formal relationships, and how – once this principle is grasped – an entirely new way of working is disconcertingly revealed. If you had to explain to your aunt just what it is that makes 'typically modern design' different in kind to any other, this is the single principle that you would have to invoke. It is thus at once a principle of search, of reference, and of explication.

The eighth is the existential principle: that *there shall be nothing else*; and that what there is, shall be contingently respected. This most elusive of principles, is at the same time the most down-to-earth. From its employ springs the *ad hoc*, the improvised, the anti-institutionalised; and on the other hand, a healthy disrespect for the tyranny of absolutes. The joker in the pack.

Finally, the ninth principle (appropriately, that of the dance) is the translation of mass into energy and relationship. It is, in a sense, the dancing out of the seventh. This principle does not go as far as Proudhon ('property is theft') though it shakes the old boy warmly by the hand somewhere along the line; nor does it foolishly believe that the silicon chip will free mankind of its material adhesions; it is, however, the energetic principle, and as such must be assumed to be always embryonic with the hope of new life. It is also, of course, if you care to follow through Illich's indications, a holy celebrant. There are three lesser, facilitating principles – including that concerned with standard and standardization – but they will not be discussed here.

Now; if 'design' is overlooked and the preceding paragraphs reconsidered as metaphor, it should be clear that the principles translate very potently into the prerequisites for an a-political social revolution, and that this is no accident. It might also follow that a constructive art – design – can have, does have, an intelligibly expressive content. Of the two sets of ideas here, the first of which I described as 'negative imperatives', it could be said that the first collapses into a single pinched-face-personal-probity-principle, doomed to emaciation and 'the distortions of ingrown virginity' without the saving social outreach of the nine, which (on this analogy) are self-transcending. Returning now to the modern movement, the correspondence should be clear. The principles are, of course, interdependent (and much simplified) – as in the theory of compass adjustment, you have to put everything back together again before it makes sense. However, it would be inadmissible to have this discussion at all, were it not for the fact that for every principle mentioned here (including the first sub-set) there are *precise physical correlates* to be found, in the field both of object design and of design procedure generally. The notion that the modern movement prefigured certain qualitative changes in our society whereby human survival might be the better assured (under the industrial challenge) is not, on this argument, as fanciful as it might otherwise appear. It is true that I write from a declared standpoint on the libertarian left, and therefore discuss design (here) in an unorthodox way. It is also true, and one function of the discussion to demonstrate, that this modern movement in design can never usefully be seen as a fashionable option that now happens to be *passé*. It is a serious demand upon intellectual assent and practical action.

Something of this is well expressed by Paul Schuitema, the graphic designer who worked in the Netherlands and Germany in the 1920s and 1930s.

> . . . We didn't see our work as art; we didn't see our work as making beautiful things. We discovered that the romantic insights were lies; that the whole world was suffering from phraseology; that it was necessary to start at the beginning. Our research was directed to finding new ways, to establishing new insights – to find out the real characteristics of tools and creative media. Their strengths in communication – their real value. No pretence, no outward show. Therefore, when we had to construct a chair or a table, we wanted to start with the constructive possibilities of wood, iron, leather and so on; to deal with the real functions of a chair, a living room, a house, a city: social organization. The human functions. Therefore, we worked hand-in-hand with carpenters, architects, printers, and manufacturers.
>
> To reduce chaos to order, to put order into things. To make

47

things more clear, to understand the reasons. It was the result of
social movement. It was not a fashion or a special view of art.
We tried to establish our connection with the social situation in
our work . . . . The answer to our problems must be the
questions: why? what for? how? and with what? [10]

The attractive qualities of this statement should not blind us to the
fact that the modern movement has always been a minority struggle, carried on against a good deal of practical opposition, and, at best, a widely
felt social indifference. At least in its early days the conflict was capable
of clear definition.

It is necessary to stress some of the background considerations which
prompted modern design into being, because it is too easy to study the
designs that emerged as specially privileged historical monuments,
whereas the spirit that conceived them is still alive and accessible to us.
In forming our own criteria for 'good' design, we cannot, of course, escape the half-conscious assumptions which make us always the children
of our own time, but we do well to remember that our own concerns are
in some respects closer to the pre-war period than to the world of the
1950s. A whole complex of emergent ideas, values, and experimental
work was traumatically cut short by the experience of fascism, the hor-
rors of Auschwitz and Hiroshima, and by the slow aftermath of cultural
assimilation. Not only were energies dispersed in a practical way, but
their foundations were uprooted. The implicit philosophy which under-
pinned modern design was never very far from what is wearily referred
to as 'a rational view of man's conduct': the hope and even the confidence
that if technology could only be integrated into meaningful value structures, a new and fruitful way of life lay open to man's willing acceptance.
The last war brutally damaged that hope.

For those who see the world as essentially an arena of conflict between
good and evil, however, there can surely be no doubt that the modern
movement stands for clarity, sweetness, and light; order, relation, and
harmony; made accessible through the only means that are fully credible
to our experience of this century. To open up a new age of revival or
pastiche (the weakest form of wit) is merely to admit defeat in this sector
of creative possibilities. Defeat may seem inevitable, radical change may
seem a prerequisite for confidence of any kind, perhaps our civilisation
really cannot survive on its own terms; either of these realisations (if
accepted) carries a more appropriate response than backsliding into a
weakly fashionable eclecticism.

It is certainly obvious that a rational view must examine motivational
forces with a more intimate sense of their origins, and the cost of their
frustration. In the design field it is not just a matter of exchanging affective imagery for austerities that are deemed to have had their day.
Here pop must be distinguished from vernacular; the one being a bril-
liantly successful commercial racket and the other being an unavailable
option except at a stylistic level. Our civilisation has refined many hells,
but in the realm of voluntary servitude it would be hard to beat the
inanity of Radio 1 ('the Happy Sound') with perhaps a few television
commercials thrown in for good measure. A language of gesture and ex-

clamation tends always toward infantilism; a measure of its warmth but also of its inadequacy. If a new synthesis of thought and feeling is to be attempted, we must think and feel our way toward the place of design in a necessary context of social renewal. Nor must we forget that a warm heart and a rather special view of history do not make a designer. Designing is very specific: a cultivated understanding is no guarantee of a specific creativity. This is the individual problem and a central concern of my writing. For the social task we have fresh evidence all the time of man's fallibility, of his deepening technological commitment; of the nature of affluence divorced from social or spiritual awareness. Yet there is a pedantry of the spirit in dwelling too much on these things. The force of new life can break through where and when we least expect it; as in Paris in May 1968, when the impossible seemed suddenly within reach.

It should at least be clear that to speak of 'good' design is to speak of, and from, the conditions of our own time, and our response to these conditions. The intelligibility – and perhaps the existence – of a design 'language' is a problem of the cultural fragmentation that affects participation in every other aspect of our culture. Because the realisation of a designer's work is always socially contingent, his freedoms are always a recognition of necessity in a most explicit way. An elegant design solution is one that meets all the apparent conditions with a pleasing economy of means. A fruitful solution co-opts the conditions into a new integration of meaning, whereby what was 'apparent' is seen to have been insufficient. Such answers have questions in them.

Postscript in 1989

I would not like the foregoing remarks (written twenty years ago and subjected to only minor revision in 1980) to lend any false authority to the status of design as a constructive activity in Britain today. For the present, in my opinion, design has lost its way; and in doing so, some of its honour and much of its relevance. The outcome – as energy, concern, artefact – is often absurdly trivialised and barely interesting even as ephemera. The situation closely reflects, and reinforces, the current values of our society, and what I personally see as the profound philistinism at its heart. Fortunately, there are always young people coming along, and not all of them will be content with this shallow caricature of human possibilities. I hope that such young people may find encouragement in the book *What is a Designer?* [11] from which this chapter is extracted; and the future of design be enriched by their commitment.

Notes and References

1 See KÖHLER, W. 1976. *The Place of Value in a World of Facts.* Liveright.
2 See RICHARDS, I. A. 1929. *Practical Criticism.* London, Routledge & Kegan Paul.
3 READ, H. 1934. *Art and Industry: the Principles of Industrial Design.* London, Faber.
4 GROPIUS, W. 1935. *The New Architecture and the Bauhaus.* London, Faber.

5   FRANKL, V. 1963. *Man's Search for Meaning*. London, Hodder & Stoughton.

6   LARGE, E. C. 1937. *Sugar in the Air*. London, Jonathan Cape.

7   For example: BERGER, J. 1972. *Ways of Seeing*. Harmondsworth, Penguin/BBC.

8   BUBER, M. 1950. *The Way of Man*. London, Routledge.

9   MUMFORD, L. 1946. *Technics and Civilization*. London, George Routledge & Sons.

10 SCHUITEMA, P. 1966. 'A Statement', in: *Circuit* (Magazine of the West of England College of Art), Autumn 1966, pp. 1, 5. See also his article 'New Typographical Design in 1930', in: *New Graphic Design*, 11, December 1961, pp. 16–19.

11 POTTER, N. 1969. *What is a Designer?* London, Studio Vista. Revised ed. 1980. London, Hyphen Press. Revised ed. 1989. London, Hyphen Press. See also POTTER, N. 1989. *Footprints and Handouts*. London, Hyphen Press; and POTTER, N. 1989. *Models and Constructs*. London, Hyphen Press.

Chapter Five

KEN BAYNES Defining a Design Dimension of the Curriculum

In Western Europe at least, the interdependence and interrelatedness of art and design have been recognised from the very beginning. Leon Battista Alberti joined them together in 1435 when he wrote the first theoretical book on architecture, perspective and human proportion. He brought art and architecture into the wider field of knowledge and gave us the first theory of painting that rooted this art in direct visual experience. Four hundred and fifty years of further exploration should by now have confirmed the conjuncture.

But art and design are not synonymous. They are not identical. *Art* and design is only one pair. *Technology* and design is another of equal importance. Since the industrial revolution scientists, technologists and manufacturers have been as influential in forming culture as have artists. It has been one of my interests in design education to try to find a way of reintegrating this complex of influences on the environment.

A central part of our work at the Design Education Unit of the Royal College of Art was to focus on this aspect of human activity and to explain its potential in general education. What emerged was the firm conviction that design awareness is best seen as a dimension of the curriculum. Partly this was because of our frustration with the fragmentation of design in secondary schools. A child's encounter with it was likely to be incoherent and wrapped up in the preconceptions of subject areas principally concerned with other matters. But more importantly it was because we had at last come to recognise the true scope, scale and significance of design as a critical area of experience and learning in the contemporary world. Only a change in the orientation of a whole range of subject areas can do it justice. Argument for change in the curriculum must be based on an assessment of priorities. For new things to come into focus, others must move to the periphery. This needs to happen but it can only be done as a widespread cooperative venture in which specialist teachers draw on their skills and experience to shape the new studies that will emerge. Our experience with the *Art and the Built Environment* project (discussed by Eileen Adams in Chapter 11) reassures us that this can be done. To help to give a degree of focus to the discussion we prepared an agenda for the development of a design dimension of the curriculum. I will report briefly on the progress of this initiative at the end of this paper.

The origin of our initiative can be found in the publication by the Gulbenkian Foundation of *The Arts in Schools*. It was immediately clear that in an otherwise remarkably coherent report design, craft and media studies posed very great problems of explanation. They simply could not be dealt with comprehensively in a study that quite properly interpreted the arts as the aesthetic and expressive dimension of the curriculum. And yet, quite clearly, the visual arts do contribute to an awareness of design. We wrote to Gulbenkian pointing this out and they very generously agreed to fund our investigation of the problem hoping that we would join directly with teachers in attempting to clarify it.

Our original intention was very simple. It was to carry out a modest piece of curriculum development work with the title EXTENDING THE ART CURRICULUM: DESIGN AWARENESS. The thrust was to be about curriculum politics. The visual arts would assert their proprietorial rights over at least a part of the concept of design education. After about six months preparatory work we drew back from the brink. We had narrowly escaped falling victim to the inability of the secondary curriculum to move beyond subject barriers.

The most intractable problem in developing design education in schools has been that its structure and content have been determined back to front. Instead of establishing clearly the concepts, attitudes, knowledge, skills and activities that are central to design, the approach has been to interpret design through the distorting lens of specialist applications. It is quite usual, for example, for art educators to see the central issue in design as visual literacy. Their training and experience make them view it in that way. Craft teachers will construct it as a way of giving a rational preliminary to making, but then go on to say – quite irrationally – that to be able to design something you must be able to make it first. Technologists systematise it as a set of problem-solving procedures within the larger world of applied science. Home economists use it as an added ingredient in their recipes for consumer studies or textiles. No wonder it is often a concept that confuses rather than helps those who claim to be explaining it. When specialist teachers say, as they so often do, that they do not really know what design is, they are acknowledging that they are teaching a part of something without any deeper understanding of the whole. This must leave them vulnerable. And it must be distracting for their pupils.

That is why, in making a response to a document about the arts in schools, we decided first to define more clearly the nature of design and the design dimension. Only then will it be possible to work coherently with subject specialists to put their contribution into a wider framework. It will also help make clear that design, like language, is a concept beyond any one existing school subject. In curriculum terms, it is a further area of entitlement to put alongside those fundamentals to which all subjects must pay at least some attention.

At the Royal College of Art, Bruce Archer and his colleagues in the Department of Design Research have been developing a picture of what design activity is for over twenty years. This picture has passed through a number of stages that have built on but not superseded each other. From system and procedure the emphasis has moved to understanding the way designers know what they know. Now things have moved forward again: to an analysis of mental states and thought processes. A part of the future work in the Design Education Unit will be to get a far clearer understanding of the way children encounter the natural and man-made worlds and how they first experience shaping their environment.

Coming directly from this long process of analysis is the identification of design awareness and design ability as a capacity of all human beings. Professional designers – planners; architects; technologists; engineers; industrial, fashion and graphic designers – happen to have developed it to a high and economically viable degree. It is their job. The inevitably complex and specialist nature of the training they need should not be allowed to overlay the 'ordinariness' of design and its accessibility to everybody. It is a ubiquitous thing.

With this background to draw on, it is to Bruce Archer that we have looked for a definition of design on which to base our development work. Here it is:

> Design is that area of human experience, skill and knowledge
> that reflects man's concern with the appreciation and adaptation
> of his surroundings in the light of his material and spiritual
> needs. In particular it relates with configuration, composition,
> meaning, value and purpose in man-made phenomena.

He continues:

> The design area of education embraces all those activities and
> disciplines which are characterised by being anthropocentric,
> anthropological, aspirational and operational; that is, they are
> man-related, that have a value-seeking feeling or judging aspect
> and that have a planning and making aspect.

This is an admirably comprehensive statement. It sets out clearly the boundaries within which design can be located. For the teacher, however, it will need careful unpacking before it can be useful. It is worth seeing if we can take it a little further.

It is typical of human beings that they create a man-made world from the raw materials provided by the natural environment. Everywhere that there are people, they have made shelters, settlements, tools and utensils. The work of doing this is as much a part of the definition of 'humanness' as the use of language, living together in ordered social groups or the attempt to explain philosophically what life is about.

In babies the development of this need to shape the environment happens alongside and in harmony with the other ways in which children interact with their world. Just as they reach out through words and gestures, so too they reach out physically to grasp, touch and manipulate their surroundings. Their active curiosity brings them experiences through which they learn about the physical, visual and audible properties of reality. But it immediately goes further. Their experience establishes that this external world may be changed. Although, in young children, the realisation will be self-centred, it brings with it the eventual necessity for moral discussion, social action and the consideration of others.

It is from these roots that knowledge about design and skill in designing develop. They have found a traditional place in general education as part of what might be called 'life skills': homemaking and housekeeping;

53

craftsmanship and building; technology and manufacture. To a large extent these have obscured the wider significance of design. They emphasise its direct 'usefulness' at the expense of its role in widening human horizons. We are used to thinking of design and technology as practical in contrast to literature, science or art which are thought to be about knowing and speculating. This is wrong. Men and women are giving their lives meaning through shaping their environment just as powerfully as they are doing it through deductive reasoning or expressive work.

The use of technique to harness power and control the elements has been described as 'the extension of man'. At the core of this apparently practical activity is speculation about what human beings might or might not be capable of. The work of conceiving and then making a cathedral, a bridge, a ship, a town, a house, or a machine is reaching beyond physical problems into imagining and realising new possibilities for people's lives. What happens socially on this grand scale happens more intimately when families imagine and realise plans for their own lives in a home and its contents. The capacity to shape the environment not only focuses on the question 'how should human beings live their lives?' it makes possible and inevitable a continuous flow of new answers.

One of the contributions to the RCA *Design in General Education* report was an attempt to describe the relevance of design to the individual child by looking at the questions fourteen-year-olds might ask about themselves in relation to the environment.
The sequence went like this:

What is the world like?
What am I like?
How did the world come to be the way it is?
How did I come to be the way I am?
How can I look at and analyse the world I live in and
  understand it?
How can I express or represent what I feel and know about the
  world?
How do I want to live in the world?
What do I value?
Why do I like what I like?
Can I make the world more like what I like?
Can the world be made better?
Can I improve myself?
How can I plan to improve the world or myself or both?
Do I need to work with other people to improve the world?
How can I work with them?
How can I express or represent my plans?
How can I make my plans become reality?
What tools and materials can I use?
How can I use them?
Must I change my plans because of what I know about tools and
  materials?
Is what I have made a success?
What do I mean by success?

54

How do I find out if it is a success?

Do I think it is a success?

Do other people think it is a success?

Which is more important – their judgement or mine?

What have I learnt from trying to change the world?

Have I changed?

What do I value?

How do I want to live?

What is the world like?

What am I like?

The report had this to say about the sequence:

> It is obvious that the majority of these questions cannot be said to be only the concern of design. But they are all essential to design . . . the force of this combination of characteristics becomes greatest towards the centre of the range of questions. It is here that an improvement in living begins to emerge as a requirement, where plans are developed and where work is begun to bring it about by means of an adaptation of the physical environment. It is from this basis that the body of contemplative, critical and evaluative knowledge of the Humanities makes practical sense. It is from these beginnings that the force of the theoretical knowledge of Science is appreciated.

That is a daring paragraph. It takes the specific activity of design at its most intense and claims that it has relevance throughout the curriculum not only for itself but for the Humanities and Science as well. For our Gulbenkian work and the future Design Dimension Project (Figs. 9–15) we have attempted to draw on this background to propose a number of 'basic assumptions' that we believe should inform design work wherever it occurs in the school curriculum.

Basic assumptions

1 Design awareness and design ability are inherent capacities of all human beings. They can be developed by education.

2 The primary aim of design in general education is to develop everybody's design awareness so that they can:

- enjoy with understanding and insight the man-made world of places, products and images;
- take part in the personal and public design decisions that affect their lives and the life of the community;
- design and criticise design at their own level for their own material and spiritual needs;
- bring an understanding of design into their work.

3 Design awareness implies an understanding both of how the environment *was* shaped, 'why things are the way they are', and how it *can be* shaped in the future, 'how things might be'.

4 Design is about values and valuing. It is concerned with the question 'how do you want to live?' Education must, therefore, highlight the significance of values and respect their cultural and personal diversity.

55

9   The *Design Dimension Bus* is the flagship of the *Design Dimension Project*. The bus itself is an example of 'design in action' – it has been used as an INSET base, a workshop, a press centre, a project op's room, a classroom, a design centre, a dining room, a computer centre, and a layout, drafting and construction workshop.

10   Interior of the *Design Dimension Bus*.

11, 12 *Cator Park Week* in progress: fieldwork and exhibition. An important part of any project is the direct experience of designed products, environments and communications systems. Going out to see and understand why it is the way it is, and to talk to people from all walks of life, are essential parts of design research.

13 Teachers on INSET: a major part of the Project team's work is to involve teachers in developing design ideas for themselves and in presenting these to others.

14 Children presenting *Bread* Project. It is as important for children to present their ideas to others as it is for designers to communicate effectively with clients: parents can provide a useful focus for this.

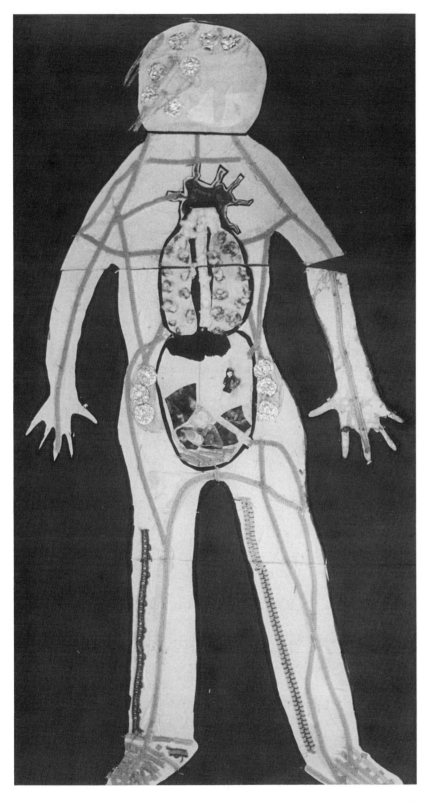

15 *Body* Project
exhibition panel.

5   Design is about compromise. The man-made environment shows the influence of many different pressures: economic, social, technical, aesthetic, moral, political. Finding the best balance is itself a valuing activity in which design has to propose the most inclusive and potentially enhancing of a range of possibilities. It is up to education to give a direct experience of this work of debate, compromise, and resolution.

6   Design studies will seek to develop those human skills that are fundamental to design awareness and design ability. It is typical of design that it depends on coherent and purposeful interaction between perceptual, analytical, propositional, communicatory, technical and manual skills. These will need to be developed in harmony.

7   In addition to language and number, the development and communication of design concepts depend on 'imaging'. This is the human ability to make and use sketches, drawings, diagrams, plans, scale models, mock-ups, prototypes and the like to represent, shape and evaluate what is and what might be. Design studies will foster people's skill in using these media for thought and action.

8   The secondary aim of design in general education is to provide the seed bed from which will come the range of future professional designers – planners; architects; technologists; engineers; industrial, fashion and graphic designers.

It will be appreciated that these 'basic assumptions' are essentially subject free. Yet it should be clear that art teachers are already centrally concerned with the issues and with the skills that handling them involves. It also happens that these basic assumptions about the design dimension relate very well indeed to recent attempts to define the required content of general education. The essential attitude of questioning and making propositions about the future can be found clearly expressed in, for example, the Home Economics section of the 11–16 curriculum document and the aims of science education in the Schools Science Curriculum Review. Successive publications on the aims of CDT (Craft, Design and Technology) teaching have explained what design is about. It has to be recognised, however, that what actually happens in workshops, kitchens, laboratories and studios is rather different. As I have suggested, with a few brilliant exceptions, the teaching of design in these areas is half-hearted and confused. Particularly, its speculative, propositional and valuing nature is not made real in the experience of children.

How can we move forward? I am very wary of proposing revolutions in education and I am fully aware that we must all work from the basis of our existing strengths and experience. This means an evolutionary approach. But it needs to be a purposeful one with a degree of urgency about it. We have identified issues that we believe should be at the top of an agenda for development.

An agenda for development

1   Misconceptions about the nature of design studies need to be identified, confronted and dispelled;

2   The scope and character of design as a dimension of the curriculum need to be extended, made more comprehensive, and better defined;

3   The teaching and learning relationships implied by the nature of design studies need to be further developed and communicated;

4   The interaction between specialist subjects contributing to design awareness needs to be more clearly understood;

5   The design aspects of initial and in-service training need to be extended;

6   Timetabling, courses and examinations need to be adapted to take account of the nature and aims of design education.

I presented this paper at the NSEAD Conference at Bath in 1984. It coincided with a plan to launch a new curriculum development project, the aim of which was to look at the role of a range of school subjects in promoting design capability. This eventually became the Design Dimension Project. Ironically, its launch coincided with my resignation from my post as Head of the Design Education Unit at the Royal College of Art. This upheaval was caused by my profound disagreement with the new Rector of the RCA, Jocelyn Stevens, who wanted to stop all involvement of the College in general education. In the event, he had his way and the NSEAD could only complain bitterly about the decision.

The Design Dimension Project, however, was successfully launched. The Department of Trade and Industry gave it backing and the London Borough of Bromley provided it with its first base. Roger Standen, General Inspector in Bromley, became the Project Director. I became its part-time Consultant while also setting up a new education design consultancy called Triangle Projects. The first phase of the Design Dimension Project was devoted to researching the proposition that design could in fact be fostered in various areas of the school curriculum. This involved work in Cleveland, Gloucestershire, Sutton, Bromley and Kingston. At the end of this phase in 1988 a considerable body of material had been assembled. It shows conclusively that it is practical curriculum politics to achieve both a base for design studies in a school and to see its significance across a range of subjects.

The first phase of the Design Dimension Project ended at a momentous time. It coincided with the establishment of the National Curriculum Design and Technology Working Party, which also takes the view that design cannot be located in any single subject in schools. This remains at the core of the work of the Design Dimension Project. In its own submission to the Design and Technology Working Party the Design Dimension team emphasised the importance of imagination in the development of design capability. They focused on speculation, imaging and modelling as the key elements which enable designers and people acting as designers to foresee the future shapes of buildings, places and communications.

Towards the end of my Bath presentation I asked the question: How can we move forward? I also suggested an agenda for development. This was related to my awareness that practice in design education often falls short of its fundamental aims and ideals. It is significant that the Design and Technology Working Party has identified exactly the same situation. The agenda I put forward in 1984 remains topical for today and tomorrow.

During 1988 the Design Dimension Project was reformed as the Design Dimension Educational Trust. This Trust has the direct support of the design professions and the Department of Education and Science. It is now based at the remarkable Dean Clough development in Halifax. Here, Ernest Hall has developed what he calls a 'practical utopia' inspired by Dartington Hall but located in the industrial north. Dean Clough mills have been brought to life again after being completely abandoned by Crossley Carpets in 1982. More than 2500 people are now employed there and the interweaving of business and the arts is complete. In this setting, it is the role of the Trust to develop the design aspect of the complex while continuing to create a national focus for work in design education.

In pursuit of this, we shall now concentrate on work in a limited number of schools, with the aim of developing further our knowledge of how design capability grows in children. This will be disseminated through in-service material for teachers produced in support of the National Curriculum. There will be a link with Warwick University for the further development of research. The Trust is working with the BBC and the Design Museum on the in-service materials, which will include video and distance-learning resources for use in a cascade programme of training.

At Bath I made the point that design capability crosses the boundary between art and science. The challenge for art and design teachers remains to provide a highly effective and widely valued input from the art side of this equation.

Chapter Six

CHRISTOPHER CROUCH Why Teach Design History?

My intention in this essay is to try and establish that it is valid to teach Design History, not merely as a separate academic discipline in its own right, but as an essential process within an education in Art and Design. In order to do so, I shall first demonstrate that because it contributes to the understanding of the nature of made objects, Design History has a role in developing a sense of cultural literacy, that is, the acquaintance of a culture with its means of communication, its history, and its relationship with other cultures. Once this idea has been established, I shall formulate a structure that can be used to interpret the function of designed objects and ascribe value to them. Alongside this a teaching structure will also emerge. I shall adopt an analytical approach which is general in its educational principles. This does not mean that I am unaware that the targeting of teaching is of fundamental concern, for what is relevant to a twelve-year-old about constructivism is bound to differ from what is relevant to students in Further and Higher Education. The essential difference in teaching the subject at these varying levels, however, is not one of quality or kind but of purpose. With this in mind, I have chosen a broad approach to Design History, establishing a set of principles and structures that can be adapted and used according to circumstance.

In general the teaching of Art History is still more acceptable than the teaching of Design History, though the two disciplines are at least sufficiently distinct for Design History to merit separate consideration. This is a good point of departure for my discussion. The Fine Arts can be seen as a means of coming to terms with the material world, a way of organising the experience of that world into a system of codes. These codes are then used to convey information to an audience in a variety of ways. Thus we have pictorial conventions that represent the illusion of space, the illusion of movement and so forth. In order for art works to be understood, their makers and their audience must have these codes in common. The work of art is created within a cultural context and uses the forms, structures, and ideas of that culture, thus addressing its audience on shared ground. In order to understand fully the meaning, and assess the values inherent in a work of art which emerges from a culture different from our own, or makes reference to experiences of which we are ignorant, we need to understand the context within which it was created. Acting as a mediator, Art History provides a means of organising and making sense of our experiences that parallels the functioning of the art work. For example, to understand fully the art of the Chinese Cultural Revolution it is necessary to understand the conditions within which the art was produced and the role that it was perceived to have. Produced in an environment considerably different in social structure from our own, with differing expectations of the function of the art work and an artistic tradition that has different roots from the European, such art can only be assimilated and valued fully if it is examined contextually. It is of course possible to approach art works at an intuitive and emotional level, but even when adopting this wholly subjective position it may be necessary at some point to justify extrinsically any insights that have been made about the work, or have been made about the world with the art work acting as mediator.

Designed objects, in which category I include the products of what used to be called the Applied Arts, differ from art works (though they are not precluded from being works of art) in having a precisely defined practical and physical function. For example, it is possible to understand a rose by approaching it through painting and literature, and this understanding would differ from that gained by approaching it with a pair of secateurs. The designed object (i.e. the secateurs) acts as a direct physical intermediary between us and the natural world (i.e. the rose): as such, not only does it act as a means of understanding that world, in the same way that an art work does, but it also acts upon that world in a way that is objectively quantifiable. It is this aspect of the designed object that often precludes students from allowing Design History a role. This is because the object is seen as the result of a linear historical process during which, through constant use modification, it becomes an 'ideal' form. It can often take a considerable time to convince people who hold such a view that they are trapped by a contemporary ideological attitude [1] every bit as strong as an eighteenth-century Classicist's.

The designed object, I suggest, could be defined as the result of the interaction of function with ideology. The object created purely as the result of technological expertise, with a precisely defined function, and without consideration as to its appearance other than that derived from its function, operates within a cultural environment that is approaching neutrality. Such an ideologically neutral environment may exist within a society as a whole, or within constituent parts of it down to the level of an individual. State mass-produced weapons are created at such a level. What is central to their design is the efficient functioning of the weapon: this supersedes any other notion as to its physical appearance. At an individual level, a broken window may be boarded up in a moment of crisis, to exclude the weather or intruders, in a way that is functional but aesthetically unpleasing. And the fact that it is thought aesthetically unpleasing demonstrates that the ideological is never completely missing.

To return to our secateurs, what would be the purpose of pruning a rose bush in a society that placed no aesthetic value upon flowers? Equally, a rabbit snare may be extremely efficient, but it would have no purpose in a Buddhist society. Alternatively, designed objects whose function is obscured, or hindered, by style, operate within a cultural environment where the ideological is dominant: any object whose appearance is subject to the whims of fashion demonstrates this. This relationship between the functional and the ideological can develop so that the use value of an object is transcended by its style. When this occurs the object starts to assume a symbolic role. (Traditionally it is at this point that the futile skirmishes between the art historian and the design historian start.) Thus Design History is necessary in the same way that Art History is necessary, in that it establishes an intellectual framework within which 'things' have meaning. It is relevant simply because it attempts to explain the way in which humankind has shaped the world. The enormous variety of objects that have been made in our past, our constant contact with such objects, and our continual production of new objects, makes an objective analysis of them much needed and long overdue.

Just as there are two component parts to the creation of a designed object, it follows that there are two aspects to the understanding of the object: an understanding of the object's function; and an understanding of the way that the form of that object is expressed. This relationship is best expressed in a question: Why, if it is possible to objectify the physical forces that operate upon objects, do objects with identical functions (such as motor cars) look so different? In order to answer this question it is necessary to separate temporarily those two qualities, function and ideology, that we have just considered to be inseparable, and distinguish what there is about the two aspects that can be definitely determined.

How can an object be analysed within the parameters that have already been set? There is a danger that once some sort of structure has been established, it acts not as an illuminator of facts, but as a form of intellectual strait-jacket. Too often, it seems to me, history of any sort is taught in a way that is dependent upon the traditions of the nineteenth-century gentleman collector. By this I mean that information is ascribed a seemingly arbitrary value, codified, piled up neatly, occasionally dusted, but rarely used, because the way that it is organised militates against any function other than that of identification. This can be seen by the high regard accorded to the ability of experts to identify style. In popular terms this is manifested in programmes about antiques and their collection. Whilst there is a need for the enumerative organisation of any material in order to make sense of it, there is a limit to what that process of organisation can achieve, in the same way that a shopping list can only indicate what objects are needed, not how they can be used. If this is the case, then what are the alternatives to a purely historicist approach in understanding objects?

It needs firstly to be said that there is an important role for the historical placing of objects, but that this should be just part of a process of understanding rather than its culmination. I wish to provide an analytical model of which the above is an integral part. The nature of the object must always be the point of departure, and if we are examining the physical nature of an object, the first consideration must be the nature of the material from which the object is manufactured. This knowledge enables us to place it immediately into some category of technological development. This also leads on to questions of ideology, which I shall examine later.

The material used in the construction of an object indicates far more than whether an object is made from something practical or unsuitable, valuable or freely available. It indicates cultural engagements. Has the material been imported? If so, this implies a network of interlocking ideas, as well as economies. Does the working of the material imply that another worked material has been brought to bear upon it, in order to alter its original natural state? If so, from where does that originate? There is a seemingly endless chain of interlocking materials, used to manipulate one another in an attempt finally to master some other natural phenomenon. At a cultural level, which could be characterised as one of subsistence, an example of this chain of material manipulation is the necessity for the hunter-gatherer to catch wild animals. A combination of materials (wood, stone, vine) makes a spear, or another material is used to work upon the wood to ensure it will break the skin of an animal, and so disable it. If both these options are unavailable materials must be manipulated into traps, snares, or dug pits. What we are also seeing here is how the use value of a material forms the use value of an object.

At a more developed level, the appearance of wool in the form of an oriental carpet in Van Eyck's *Wedding Portrait of Giovanni Arnolfini* (Fig. 16) indicates a complex design technology that enabled the physical mastery of a continent and facilitated the trading of goods from one end of it to another. This would entail the design of objects to ensure the accurate mapping of terrain, and its subsequent display in graphic or written form. It involved also the ability to transport and pack materials in such a way as to ensure their value remained undiminished by damage. And so a simple examination of the relationship of the materiality of objects can illuminate more than the objects themselves. In this way an understanding of the interaction of human manipulated material in both space (physically), and time (chronologically), emerges with a clarity that 'historic fact' can often blur.

The next stage must be the assessment of the use value of objects. Firstly, how successfully is material used in fulfilling the task that is set it, and secondly, how successful is design in using that material? This process is no longer purely historical, because it has a direct relationship with the manufacture of new objects. This relationship between the practical and the theoretical is one that is fundamental to the success of any Design History course of study. It makes sense within those disciplines that are geared towards the creation of things, that there is constant reference to the merits of objects both old and new which can be seen in use, which are used and are valued because of their success.

An analysis of a designed object should be able to demonstrate that the notions of design and technology are intimately linked. This interrelationship between material, technology and use results in the form of objects. For instance, the Roman need for efficient routes of communication meant the large-scale construction of bridges. The need to span wide rivers led to the development of a new technological approach for a traditional material, stone. The resulting technological innovation, the arch, was also a new architectural form. And so purpose, material, and form can be seen as combining to offer a new technological solution to a design problem, and the solution's value is then related to its functional

16 JAN VAN EYCK, *Wedding Portrait of Giovanni Arnolfini*, 1434; oil on panel 81·8 × 59·7 cm.
Reproduced by permission of the Trustees of the National Gallery, London.

success. This functional assessment must lead on to the question of how things are made. Whilst this must be a concern of Design History, it is an aspect that is best investigated practically. Is it necessary then to teach a history of manufacture? Unless it is directly pertinent to the evolution of an accepted design solution it would seem that it is not an aspect that needs a great deal of investigation. Providing there is an understanding of the relationships discussed above, 'knowing how' something is made is perhaps less useful than 'knowing why'.

Part of 'knowing why' is understanding the functional purpose of an object: the other aspect is its ideological purpose. The ideological is of great importance in the formulation of objects. If function could be characterised as the need for an object, then its ideological content could be characterised as the manifestation of a want. It is the ideological that often accounts for the distortions in the rational functioning of objects, because objects are frequently made for reasons that are related to ideas, before they are made to fulfil a precise physical function. The predominance of impractical shoes for women, which emphasises their assumed helplessness, is a good example of this. An ideological structure is important not only in the formulation of designed objects, but also in the subsequent interpretation of them.

Ideology can be seen as acting in three ways upon the designed object. Firstly, its function may be geared primarily towards the expression of a *symbolic* notion. Such symbolic objects are designed within a very closely defined set of codes, so that to outsiders the design is often considered meaningless and becomes purely decorative. I am thinking here of ceremonial dressing and ceremonial artefacts, where the usage and style of the objects is precisely codified. The materials used in such objects are also used ideologically. They are generally rare and thus imbued with a value because of their rarity. When materials have a function, and are rare, for example when diamonds are used for cutting materials harder than themselves, their value can be objectified. When materials are used for their aesthetic quality, and when their rarity enhances this quality, then obviously their use is ideological. With this in mind, how is it possible to determine at what point an emerald assumes the correct colouration? An emerald can be considered as too light, or it can be too dark; it has no practical use as it is a soft gem, and yet it can be used as an indicator of wealth and status. It is objects which are closely formed through ideological pressures that need careful contextualisation in order to be understood, because outside of their cultural context they become meaningless.

The second way in which ideology affects the formation of an object is by determining a role for an object which has a pragmatic function within the context of its manufacture. In this case of ideological influence we see more clearly than in the previous examples the meaning and purpose of the designed object, without necessarily having to understand the complete context. A church building falls into this category. Even from outside the culture of Christianity it would be possible to determine the function of a church as a meeting place, and a meeting place with a set of regular functional rituals that demanded fixtures such as the pulpit, the choir stalls and the altar. All these could be understood in terms of general function, but it is its position within an ideological structure that gives a church its full meaning, as the positioning of the church and the alignment of the nave and altar are all predetermined by an intrinsic set of functional demands and values. This phenomenon also encompasses the notion of ascribed value that occurs within the closed terms of an ideological interpretation – a good church building is one that satisfies the requirements for a good church building.

Thirdly, ideology interacts with function in a way that modifies only superficially its form, elaborating (or not) a functional item in terms of decoration. It is this aspect which is most common and which is readily exploited at all levels of design. It is possible to determine a set of physical parameters for the efficient functioning of an object, be it a building, a motor car, or a pen. The designer having done this, and having established an acceptable level of physical performance, the object can then be embellished with whatever set of codified imagery is required, or constructed out of whatever materials the ideological necessity determines. This can be seen in Rolls Royce and Skoda motor cars, which are essentially the same mechanical contrivance, using similar technological means of construction and propulsion. However, in contemporary Britain a Rolls Royce has a value both as a commodity and as a symbol of affluence that far outweighs its production cost in both materials and labour. The Skoda has not. Such instances are so common, being fundamental to the smooth running of our ideological system, as to be unremarkable. Because of this familiarity with a set of values, objects produced within our own culture are often misread by students as being ideology-free. This can lead to further problems in the interpretation of objects from unfamiliar cultures, which are sometimes dismissed in such prescriptive terms as 'old fashioned', and 'ugly'.

Having examined the nature of the formation of the designed object, it is also important to examine the way in which the object is interpreted. I hope I have established a relatively value-free system of analysis that relies upon a contextualisation of the object, both physically and ideologically. But just as the object itself is *created* through an interaction of function and ideology, so too is it *evaluated*. An essential part of understanding the success of an object is to look at how its possession or its use is perceived by others. At a crude social level this is manifested in consumer obsession with brand imagery and the value that it is perceived to have. Thus the object has a value to its owner, and because it has value to that individual, it also has an ideological value within the cultural group in which the individual finds him or herself. This ideological value can be objectified, because the worth given to the object reflects a quantifiable cultural consensus. This does not mean that there is a fixed sense of value, but rather that anything valued within a system of thought, whatever that system may be, is worthy of study. Thus it is possible to identify and define two kinds of value: *use value*, where the object is fundamental to the fulfilment of a necessary, or functional task; and *ideological value*, which is ascribed to objects whose desirability is determined by groupings within a society.

69

Interpreting the value of objects is dependent for the most part upon the ideological position of the interpreter. As an example of what I mean, take the hoary old notion of decoration and its suitability for objects of use. In his *Pioneers of Modern Design* [2], Nikolaus Pevsner talks of the 'barbarism' and 'atrocities' of *trompe l'oeil* decorative effects, and refers in one case to 'unpleasantly realistic flowers'. What he demands as a prerequisite for successful decorative design is the 'integrity of the surface', and argues that William Morris's *Daisy* wallpaper is successful in part because of its consciously two dimensional style. This, argues Pevsner, is a result of the remorseless logic of the protomodernist tenet of 'truth to materials'. That the depiction of daisies is considered not only a suitable wall decoration, but a correct one, solely when non-illusionistic, is an example of the difficulties of implementing a fixed system of thought. One is forced to ask at what point in the development of Pevsner's argument does the use of the daisy as an image cease to be appropriate? The multiplicity and complexity of cultural interactions eventually make any form of dogmatic interpretation based on a notion of an absolute appear ludicrous.

If this is the case, what alternative do I have to offer as a means of analysis? What I envisage as a suitable basic structure necessary to teach Design History, is a set of formal devices that enable the dissection and evaluation of a chosen style, or object. I have no wish to influence control over the content of what is studied, rather the way that it is examined. I have mentioned a number of issues that could justify the teaching of Design History: they are part of the overall ideological stance that I consider gives purpose to the study of the subject. It should be clear however that the following structure stands whether or not the discipline itself is valued.

1   All objects are the result of the interaction of function and ideology.
2   The materials used in the construction of objects can be objectively assessed in terms of practicality, and can be seen as having a further subjective, or ideological purpose.
3   The use of an object can be objectively assessed, and its function can also be related to its immediate cultural or ideological environment.
4   The form of an object is the result of its use or purpose. It can be determined by objective means, and also by ideological demands.
5   An object has an objectively quantifiable past, and may be placed chronologically.
6   Objective questions that can be asked about the object are: What information does the object convey? How does it convey it? Why does it convey it?
7   The meaning of an object is dependent upon the ideological context within which it is being interpreted.

This scheme is a means of analysis that can be used at whatever teaching level is required, because its mode of questioning, and the questions it asks, are free from any ideological values that could interfere with an objective assessment of the object. The questions that the above structure supports can only be properly answered by direct relation to the object and its environment. To separate the two is to destabilise, and even deprive, the object of meaning. In this way a coffin becomes a blanket chest, and the *Laocoon* a hatstand.

In conclusion I wish to put the ideas I have examined into a context which indicates the power of Design History to interpret and help shape the environment. The relevance of a cultural literacy, the familiarity that a culture has with its processes and their relationship with other cultures, cannot be underestimated. It ensures a social cohesiveness which in itself guarantees an environment of stability. If aspects of a society's cultural life are valued and given prominence, an important arena is created within which social development can take place in an informed and reasoned atmosphere. It is within such an environment that Design History's role is important to both manufacturer and consumer. Manufacturers need to create objects that ensure their economic survival: consumers need objects that improve the quality of their lives. It makes economic (functional), and moral (ideological) sense to create objects whose worth does not become devalued. It is rare that the possessors of quality objects (be they sable brushes, an Aga range, or a Mercedes Benz) wish to change them. They are valued because they work well, are pleasurable to look at and have a seemingly infinite life span. Design History can help supply young designers with the ability and motivation to create objects of sophistication. It can also help educate an audience of consumers to understand the processes which go into the designing, manufacturing, and marketing of objects. A worker needs and values efficiently designed tools in order to function properly. So too, in a world of finite resources, where luxury for the North means economic enslavement for the South, our society needs objects which enrich it at a price that everybody is prepared to pay.

Notes and References

1 By *ideology* I mean that form of thought that reflects a social consensus or belief. It stems from social knowledge, as opposed to that knowledge which reflects nature, existing as it does, independently of thought.
2 PEVSNER, N. *Pioneers of Modern Design.* Harmondsworth, Penguin, 1968; pp. 40–56.

Chapter Seven

PETER DORMER Frontiers of the Invisible

That marvellous philosopher of design and craft David Pye wrote in his book *The Nature and Aesthetics of Design* [1] that craftsmen and craftswomen are frontier people; they work on surfaces, and surfaces are at the frontier of the invisible. This brief essay is a note about the nature of the intelligence involved in craft skill and, in particular, the skills involved in creating expressive surfaces. What the visual and the tactile arts are good at is expressing sensation. The ideas, the intelligence all occur in the craft skills which enable the artist or craftsperson to express the sensation. The craft is the idea.

It is the unwillingness to recognise the centrality of craft skill in any visual work – but especially contemporary fine art and, increasingly, applied art – that accounts for the muddle in both the teaching and the professional practice of fine art and applied arts. In particular, the art departments of the polytechnics and the art and design colleges have failed to define an ideology for applied art; practitioners of crafts in art schools have become ambivalent about what it is they do, and who they are to serve. In this essay I propose that the concept of skill and the concept of service be brought to the fore in the re-evaluation of the purpose of teaching and practising the applied arts.

Skill

For the fine artists within the citadel of the *art world* and the applied artists clustered just beyond the citadel's walls, words such as 'skill' and 'craft' are troublesome. Both words are still regarded by many practitioners and educators as tyrannical terms. This is surely where professionals in other spheres of cultural activity would tend to disagree and, instead, argue that the possession of a skill gives an individual the possibility of economic autonomy as well as creative choice [2].

Certain artists prominent in the years after the Second World War attacked the orthodoxies of teaching skills in art schools and argued for a more self-expressive approach. David Bomberg was one of these propagandists. According to Roy Oxlade, Bomberg found academic drawing *sterile* [3]. And one knows what Oxlade means when he adds that the art school taught 'diluted attitudes' of representational drawing. Such drawing was disappointing less because of the illustrative work it produced than for its 'drabness of attitude'.

It is the dilution which produced the drab attitudes, especially when each succeeding generation looks merely to the work of its immediate teachers and not the founders. The ideas wrapped around the baton of convention are swiftly degraded by the time the thing has been passed on a few times.

Drabness and dilution into sterility are not the preserve of fine art academicism. A example of dilution happened in twentieth-century pottery. Bernard Leach brought together a number of ideas and influences gained through studying Oriental and traditional English wares. His synthesis – known now as the Anglo-Oriental tradition – rejuvenated studio pottery but the 'tradition' was quickly degraded. People copied Leach. Then people copied the people copying Leach, and so on. It seems likely that to retain the integrity of a skill – and a skill is a body of knowledge – one must keep returning to original sources.

Citing pottery sheds light on another Bomberg issue. Oxlade explains that Bomberg was ambitious to make works that caught the representation of form as a *felt* thing. There is another good potter, Bill Newlands, a much regarded educator (now retired) at the London Institute of Education, who campaigned to get clay workshops into secondary schools in the early 1950s because he wanted children to understand form and mass and weight. He wanted to reconnect their imaginations with the weight of a thing, as well as its look. Newlands believes that art education is too two-dimensional, too graphic.

But what these condensed observations from Bomberg and Newlands suggest is not the disavowal of traditional skills but a symphony of different ones kept lively by returning to good first sources. Without wanting to be sophistical, one might argue that Bomberg's true rejection was of conventions, not skills.

One of the modern fallacies which has damaged the faith in skills as bodies of knowledge which give you freedom, as opposed to tyrannical rules which close down the mind, concerns the issue of gesture and expression and the sustained modernist rejection of the skills of representational art. Consider a painting by Rembrandt (or one of his highly skilled imitators or pupils). Look at the eyes – in a good portrait we see and, through our imagination, feel their pellucidity, the wetness, and the jelliness. But if one touches the painting one feels only old, encrusted paint on dry canvas. The 'wetness' of the eye is not real to your fingertips, only to your imagination.

Fashion has meant that skills of illusion take second place to the immediacy of expressionist gesture. Part of the argument hung on illusions as deceptive, whereas the expressionist gesture was immediate and therefore more honest. But, ironically, in dismissing the art of the illusory surface, we dismissed much of the artist's power or to express feeling and help us understand what he or she had discovered.

One of the contemporary art world's favoured artists, an expressionist, is Georg Baselitz. He is an interesting example to discuss. In my view a limewood sculpture by Baselitz is a poor dumb creature compared with one by Tilman Riemenschneider (Fig. 17) [4]. Baselitz paints and carves crudely, with scant interest in illusion. He does not transform a surface, he only leaves marks upon it. The mainsprings of Baselitz's work are aggression and egocentricity. He has said that he does not want to improve anything, but only to be first.

> Whenever I start a painting I set out to formulate things as if I were the first one, the only one . . . .

17 TILMAN RIEMENSCHNEIDER OF WÜRZBURG, *Altarpiece of the Holy Blood*, 1499–1505, limewood, height approx 900 cm; [detail]; St Jakobskirche, Rothenburg-on-the-Tauber. Reproduced by permission of Yale University Press.

The aggression in his work may be expressive of some kind of modern agony but equally it seems remarkably self-indulgent. Either way, who can really tell? What is clear is that the Expressionism which Baselitz offers us is a literary interpretation of suffering, not a visual one. The marks are only cyphers waiting for words to complete them: without the theory and the explanation they are bereft of any ability to move us. In carefully constructed representational painting or sculpture, on the other hand, the pain, suffering and inhumanity are made clearer, sharper and more poignant the finer the craftsmanship and the more acute the observation. This does not mean that literalness is the answer. Literalness without a transforming metaphor is as dead as expressionistic lumpenness. Anyone seeking to transform a material into a visual metaphor which is to act as a bridge between one human experience and another must have a moral imagination as well as intellectual and physical skill.

Mere mark making holds no great interest for ordinary (but intelligent) people who prefer and enjoy art and craft that celebrates recognisable natural or human-made forms. Yet the association of gesture with expression of feeling has led to the notion that gesture is an unknowing, untutored, primal act. In dictionaries of contemporary art Jackson Pollock is often quoted as saying he was interested in expressing what he felt. But, to take a topical example, the wholly non-primal, highly skilled, very deliberate paintings of Lucian Freud are as gestural, as expressive and as felt as Pollock or Bomberg. When I read about Bomberg's desire for the felt mass and form I thought straight away of Lucian Freud's paintings where the sitter has a small dog to hand. These Freud dogs are painted in such a way that you know, you feel, the living, shifting weight of a muscular, lively animal.

I cannot believe that skill necessarily gets in the way of expression. For example, there is a lot of interest in a potter/artist called Rosa N. Q. Duc, a recent graduate from the Royal College of Art. She models animals, including dogs and horses. I bought a piece of her work and its sense of volume gives me a lot of pleasure but an Alfred Munnings painting of a horse, in all its anatomical knowledge, would give me the same and very much more. One is soon troubled in a piece of Rosa's work by the lack of knowledge about the legs of a horse, say, or the way a head sits on a body. The lack of knowledge turns the spontaneous gesture into a blurted guess.

Calligraphy is where gesture, feeling and skill come together. It is an area of craft that is mostly ignored by outsiders and too readily dismissed by the art world. But with the work of the late Irene Wellington and one of her pupils, Anne Hechle, we see that the calligrapher's art is an interpretative one – it seeks to match the shape of words to their meaning. Calligraphy, especially in its extended sense of including 'illuminations', demands a formidable grasp of composition and a good colour sense. Many of Irene Wellington's works are very complex and include illustrations. But a taste of the skill and knowledge that makes possible the gesture in calligraphy can be gauged by such commentary as this from Anne Hechle:

Irene's early training with a quill gave her a spontaneity which

75

she was able to carry over into the manipulation of a steel pen. Because the quill is a more flexible and sensitive instrument and it releases ink more readily than a steel pen, the strokes it makes need to be anticipated earlier, and can be maintained later; this allows for a greater 'catching in' of the white spaces. Also, the freedom of the flow of the ink makes for a discovery of speed of movement, and within that a personal rhythm.

Part of the ambience in art teaching since the Second World War has been the unwritten orthodoxy that all skills are equally 'valid' or 'relevant' (although relevant to what is hardly ever spelled out). So the term 'mark making' rapidly grew in currency because it was a *democratic* term. It meant that close observational drawing was of equal merit to collaging with used bus tickets. Currently there is still a reluctance to admit to hierarchies of skill and conceptual complexity. The plea is made that one thing is *not* better than or more difficult than another but simply different. But this really is not true.

Skills are bodies of knowledge and some are harder to grasp than others. In pottery, for example, throwing well on the wheel is a harder skill to acquire than hand-building vessels with coils of clay or with slabs. And modelling mass to make naturalistic representations in clay is a harder skill than either. Within painting and drawing, matters are clearly more complicated. Representational drawing, modelling form in three dimensions, and understanding colour are all areas of intellectual as well as intelligent learning. Without intending to be too crass, I suggest that the popularity with which a variety of forms of expressionism (especially those forms which are practised in ignorance of what is known about colour, about anatomy, about perception) are pursued within art schools testifies either to the relative ease of the process, or ignorance of the teachers, or both. You do see students in a frightful mess which tutors are too unskilled themselves to help sort out. People like things easy and most skills in painting, as in the applied arts, are hard work. And hard work is painful.

The intelligence of rendering surfaces

Carving in wood or stone, modelling in clay or working and bending metal are manifestly different activities to painting. In painting, given the two-dimensional nature of the process, nearly everything is illusion. The painter remembers the surface he is seeking and tries to conjure it up in his paint: the clay modeller, the wood carver, the stone mason are all struggling with a real material with which each has to work. Great knowledge of the material is needed.

The kind of knowledge demanded of a craftsperson, such as a wood-carver, results from two different but related inputs, the one balancing the other. The two inputs are knowledge of the material and knowledge of the surface that is desired. Skill lies in having both. To carve a piece of drapery you have to know how a piece of silk falls (as distinct from a length of cotton) and you have to remember its qualities in your head and your finger tips. But, supposing you are carving wood, in order to

76

get the wood into the texture and form of drapery you have to know the character of the wood. It takes a lot of time, a lot of quiet, even humble work – unfashionable work in these days – to know the character of a material such as wood.

There is a good account by Michael Baxandall [5] of the kind of knowledge possessed by the best of the German Renaissance sculptors in limewood. Baxandall asks

> In what terms are we to think of a piece of wood as having a character to be respected?

First, wood is more complex than stone. Stone tends to be inert and homogeneous, wood does not. Limewood is a hardwood and hardwood has a more intricate structure than softwood. The carver must understand these intricacies. Limewood is light and it can be carved across the grain; it is also elastic. Limewood is, however, liable to great cracking and splitting because of the tensions between the solidwood and the sapwood. There are also internal and contradictory movements within the wood as a result of its particular fibrous and cellular structure. In limewood the shrinkage and fracturing process is not entirely cured by seasoning and Baxandall describes wood sculptures as remaining slow-motion mobiles for their entire existence.

In learning to work at the frontier, the craftsman must cope with the inner nature of the material. Baxandall explains that first the carver removes the hardwood (most wood sculptures are hollow), second, unlike a stone carver, the wood carver avoids large solid masses – these are unstable. In carving in thin shapes the carver hopes to avoid the contradictory tensions in the wood but, as Baxandall implies, the real craftsmanship, the working with wood, implies almost a listening out for the internal workings. Of the Renaissance carvers Baxandall suggests that the better carvers

> played on the internal mobility of wood, following or defying its currents, in ways that give them a special means of expression.

Contemporary gestural art and craft are different. The difference lies in the nature of the act – attacking the surface, or working with it; defying the material or watching out for it. Not all gestural art is unskilled or unknowledgeable. The very best work is that which is fluent, fast and done with an immediacy born out of great knowledge – but then one can argue that the quickest, most fluent and significant gesture has in reality taken the longest time, namely years of apprenticeship.

Anne Hechle has remarked that calligraphy, a gestural art, is one of the riskiest of crafts. You have to get it right first time and the fluidity and confidence required to construct a letter has to be practised: calligraphy is a performance art, it is like singing or dancing, you cannot erase out the movement once it has been performed. But calligraphy is not a craft of abandoned sweeps: the sweeps of the quill or the brush or the steel nib are thought through with practice.

The ability to work materials expressively and figuratively has been greatly diminished in the applied arts by the 'lazier' techniques of assemblage, fabrication and collage. Mass-manufactured expressive surfaces and stable, inert sheets of plastic have made it easy for artists and craftspeople to make compositions without the need to work a material. Renaissance craftsmen did not have so many instant surfaces available – everything had to be carved, formed, painted or woven. The act of making these surfaces gave the craftspeople a tremendous sensitivity towards textures. Indeed, one has only to list, as Baxandall does, the names of the cloths that the Renaissance craftworkers were familiar with, to make one's fingertips alert with nostalgic anticipation – satin, damask, camlet, velvet, silk, taffeta, tabby and brocade.

Various art-crafts have succumbed to the ease of fabrication only to find it is not enough. For example, from the late 1970s to the early 1980s there flourished in Europe an avant-garde in jewellery design – the 'new jewellery' movement – but it ran short of energy because of its over-reliance upon simple fabrication and montage techniques. Artists just went to the suppliers, chose manufactured materials, and put them together. Within a few years, after everyone had made all the possible combinations of plastics, papers and found materials, these craftspeople were forced either to begin working materials again or to take some other occupation.

However, of all the skills, those of carving provide a sublime achievement in creating expression and aesthetic sensation. The combination of brain, hand, imagination and sensuous awareness that creates the expressive surface is an example of a very special kind of intelligence. If our culture lost this intelligence, it would take decades of persistent work and enquiry to resurrect it.

The pain of practising craft

The reluctance of art students to learn and of art tutors to teach skills has, I think, some of its roots in the discovery that the least directed work – abstract expressionist painting being a prime example – is, superficially, the most pleasurable, combining as it does the sensation of 'doing work' with the satisfaction of 'getting results'. Moreover, the student has, it appears, a considerable freedom because there are no criteria by which he or she can be said to fail. Abstract expressionism took the pain out of painting. It gave a licence to all followers of expressionism to ignore all other skills in art because, happily, anything that hurt your head could be considered irrelevant.

The association of pain and creative work is significant in two ways. There is the discipline and rigour needed to acquire through practice the skills with which to work. There are also, in some applied art processes, the rigours of the labour itself. There is no ignoring the fact that pain is a very important matter in any discussion about skill and labour. And pain, it seems obvious, is something that any pleasure-seeking society shrinks from. In really *hard*, physically *hard*, work such as doing repetitive tasks in a clothing factory or restaurant – whether skilled (fitting sleeves on jackets) or less skilled (washing up) – exhaustion and boredom turn labour into pain. The worker's world diminishes because it is blighted with painful work which dominates also the non-working hours in the form of recuperation.

78

Work is often painful where there is the lack of freedom to stop doing it or vary its content and conditions. But many men and women, especially potters or weavers or stone masons who have established themselves as independent craftspeople, happily engage in hard labour as a part of their overall craft. And this is interesting because, of course, it points to an important part of the ideology of craft, which is that even the physical labouring can be tolerable or even pleasurable if one is doing it through choice and as part of the process towards some other, higher goal over which one has direction and creative responsibility. Provided that one is not being forced to work under the strain of compulsion, the creative autonomy that skill can give is one of the blessings of studying for and becoming a craftsperson.

The considerable attraction of doing handicraft and applied art work – wheel-thrown domestic pottery, hand-built furniture, weaving, calligraphy – is the opportunity it gives a person for creative, self-directed work. And, with regard to those parts of the work which are not *creative* but are preparatory, administrative or regulatory (pugging clay, emptying a kiln, setting up a loom), the fact that these tasks are a part of a process over which you maintain control takes some of the pain out of the labour. Even more pain is removed from the labour by knowing that these tasks are directed at enabling you to practise higher skills – the ones that give you both creative choice and economic independence.

There are two elements in the attraction of pursuing *obviously* skilled work: distraction and criteria. Most work, voluntarily entered into, offers distraction because if the effort is made to do it well then there are criteria to be upheld and met. One knows what a clean floor should look like, one knows what a good piece of thrown pottery should look like. If one is a stone letter-cutter or draughtsman one knows what a good piece of Trajan lettering should look like – and, importantly, so do other people.

Some of the criteria are in the nature of rules – there is a right and wrong way to prepare clay or, even, to build a painting (disregard the practice of working from light to dark and you can get into trouble). But some of the criteria are not rules but guesses – hoped for aspirations – the intelligent moving towards the right profile to a pot or the right expression to a face. Nonetheless, it is the framework of rules and aspirations which provides the thickening and the complexity to an activity and makes the work a distraction, an absorbing occupation.

The ability of the craftsman or the artist to do skilled work thus gives two kinds of autonomy of direct benefit to the possessor. First there is the selfish pleasure of distraction offered by the complexities and challenges of the craft. Second, because other people take pleasure from work that makes sense to them and displays a skill they can share in, albeit vicariously, they are more likely to want to buy the work: this gives the craftsperson the possibility of economic autonomy.

There is also the communal aspect of skill to consider. The demonstration of skill, whether it is in the carving of a Renaissance sculpture or a piece of Grinling Gibbon or the ecstatic composition of an Odilon Redon is, in itself, a public pleasure. People relish, are awed by, take delight in the demonstration of the virtuous. It is one of the reasons why there is a gap of indifference between the 'lay' public and the modern museums – the latter do not contain sufficient examples of anything that is clearly *virtuoso*. To borrow from the vocabulary of art critic Peter Fuller, the demonstration of skill is one of the elements of a shared visual vocabulary. Skill is also, primarily, the means of revelation. By his skill Lucian Freud makes a bridge between his autonomous observation and that of each individual observer.

Of course, one must be careful not to confuse our pleasure as observers with the pleasure of the maker or the artist. Certainly in the past much craftsmanship was done to high standards but under severe constraints – the labour was intense and poorly paid, the hours long. One of the things Ruskin taught us was that just because an artefact gives us pleasure we cannot infer that it gave its creator pleasure. However, the position in the late twentieth century is that both crafts and art are largely middle class activities carried out through choice in the context of relative wealth and well-being.

It then becomes rather telling that so much of the quite massive art and craft 'industry', both in teaching and in professional practice, has deskilled itself – almost as if the hard work, the 'pain' of developing skills and acquiring knowledge is too much for the protagonists.

Notes and References

1 PYE, D. 1983. *The Nature and Aesthetics of Design*. The Herbert Press.
2 Admittedly, skills can become degraded from help into hindrance if they are rendered sterile by unimaginative teaching.
3 OXLADE, R. 1988. 'Nôtre-Dames of the Mind', in: *Modern Painters*, Vol. 1, No. 1, 1988, pp. 13–19.
4 BAXANDALL, M. 1980. *The Limewood Sculptors of Renaissance Germany*. Yale University Press, See also DORMER, P. 1988. 'Baselitz', in: *Modern Painters*, Vol. 1, No. 1, 1988; pp. 82–3.
5 BAXANDALL, *op. cit.*

Chapter Eight

JOHN FULTON Design in Primary Education: the Name of the Game

Writing now, about design in primary education, is rather like commenting from the field of play about a game for which the rule book has just been rewritten. So far we know only the half-time score. We players on the field must act, in the meantime, as our perception of the game demands. Our ability to read the game is compounded of our existing knowledge, our training off the field and the feedback which we receive from other players. The following notes should be thought of as part of that feedback from a veteran player who finds the present state of play too exciting to become a mere spectator.

The current version of the game seems to include the popular pastime of making assertions about schools and what should go on in them. Apparently anyone can play. If, here, I make some assertions of my own I do so in the hope that they will be relevant. I shall value the criticism of those who offer scholarship where I do not, and of other players whose experience leads them to read the game differently. I wish to acknowledge the beliefs, and no doubt the prejudices, which enable me to welcome the recent appearance of government interest in design in primary education and to greet, both enthusiastically and critically, the interim report of the working party on design and technology in the national curriculum [1].

Government interest in encouraging awareness of design in education goes back, in my experience, to the immediately post-war period with the introduction of posters for schools, inspired I believe by the late Gordon Russell, and issued by the, then, Council for Industrial Design. They arrived regularly in the junior technical school where I taught. The series on teapots was typical. I remember little of the didactic notes which accompanied it, except that teapots should pour properly and empty efficiently when inverted on a draining board, but I have a lasting impression of the quality of the photographs and the stout paper on which they were printed, which helped to raise our aspirations during post-war austerity.

It is beyond the scope of this essay to undertake a detailed review of what has subsequently occurred in primary classrooms. It is worth saying, however, that at any time since the war it has been possible to point to good examples of work in aspects of art, craft, design and technology in some primary schools. For the greater part such work was described as 'creative activity' or 'art and craft' and usually the design and technological implications of the work were not emphasised to the extent which is now advocated. Certainly the opportunity to engage in activities related to design and technology has not been available to the majority of pupils, still less has it been a sustained requirement for all.

Nevertheless it is fair to say that a major contribution to primary education in this country after the war was made by the twin strands of the 'Child Art' movement. One strand of influence, stemming from the findings of Post-Impressionism, emphasised the importance of individual perception, the other emphasised craftsmanship and respect for 'natural' materials. The eager response of pupils, their vastly improved confidence and enjoyment were, at that time, adequate testimony to the effectiveness of a new teaching style.

Instead of regarding children's work as merely unskilled striving after adult imagery, informed teachers were now able to understand that the characteristics of pupils' work owed at least as much to how children saw and thought as to their degree of manual dexterity. The wide range of styles in adult art and design enabled teachers to identify and to respond to potential in their pupils, much of which had become evident for the first time. New understanding about differences in perception and the integrity of mind at different stages of development made possible more challenging teaching and more active learning.

Teaching methods followed the example set by charismatic leaders in the field. The influence of their teaching styles extended across the curriculum and were widely imitated. However, only some teachers understood the principles upon which they were based or shared the perceptions which lent authority to their actions. Today, in a world which has undergone a rapid shift towards technical sophistication and specialisation, such leadership is less prevalent and less widely credible. We are, as a profession, still some way from agreement over a reasoned case for what Peter Fuller, in his article 'Art in Education', called 'a continuum of aesthetic teaching, rather than a series of often oppositional systems' [2]. Nevertheless it is to learning from teachers and pupils over many years and to my own experience as a parent and teacher that I owe the convictions which I am attempting to clarify here.

I shall first consider some of the changes in adult life which might legitimately alter the content of the curriculum to include design and technology, and how these shifts in expectation are most likely to be met. It is not difficult to account for the present interest both in design and in technology. Given a world in which manufacturing and marketing are international, it becomes important for a nation to be seen to be in possession not only of goods and ideas which others wish to purchase but also of a lifestyle which excites their interest and long-term confidence. To achieve and maintain a response to these requirements demands a high level of design with all that it implies for design education. No government, in planning a national curriculum, could afford to ignore the force of that demand.

Furthermore, technology is rapidly being drawn away from the traditional structures and constraints of craft-based mechanical engineering by the urge to realise the dramatic new possibilities opened up by the advance of electronic controls and synthetic materials. Until now, designers have often secured good form and function by understanding, and turning to good advantage, the characteristic limitations of natural or traditional materials. The escape from traditional constraints, which new technologies facilitate, presents a major challenge to design. Without the demands of natural or traditional materials and without the legibility of formal mechanical logic, technology cannot so readily rely upon recent models for guidance. While 'fitness for purpose' will remain an important guiding principle, catchword criteria such as 'form follows function' and 'truth to material' may be much less useful than before.

The role of the designer has changed and design education and criticism must articulate and perhaps rediscover criteria which have the durability to survive radical change of the kind just described. These may be found in a better understanding of the ways in which people interact with the modified environment. Research into those factors which nourish the human spirit has always been a major preoccupation of artists and has provided some of them with their most rewarding employment. Understanding the responsibilities of artists who adopt this role may need to be re-established as an objective for education in art and design.

Future design will draw heavily upon our store of information and inspiration from nature. Knowledge of what are already referred to as 'human factors' becomes increasingly important in the make-up of design teams. Successful designs are increasingly the outcome of teamwork which draws widely and unstintingly upon available knowledge across a range of disciplines. In their introduction to *New American Design* by Hugh Aldersley-Williams, Michael and Katherine McCoy write:

> The availability of extraordinarily versatile plastics and flexible
> control technologies now raises the question: if it can be
> anything, what should it be? The designer is now more than ever
> the interpreter of the meaning of the object to the user, the
> mediator between people and their object/information
> environment [3].

Ralph Caplan, in a foreword to the same volume, writes:

> The elimination of constraints always appears to be liberating,
> but the experienced designer will not rush to shout, 'Free at
> last!' In design, as in life generally, if we have no constraints, we
> have to invent them [4].

We have a rapidly increasing capacity to construct the artefacts, forms and environments we choose. Choice of this magnitude implies increased responsibility for which our education must be geared to fit us. It can be argued that our education system, up to now, has successfully produced capable specialist designers, though it could hardly be argued that it has been equally successful in educating industrialists or indeed the general public in a critical awareness of design. We need these 'neglected' groups to be better informed and to play a more responsible role than in the past. Specialist designers will need to be less isolated from other disciplines during their training and in their professional practice. All need to acquire the kinds of insights and attitudes which are established early and reinforced by successful interaction throughout all the years of schooling. 'Down to earth' practicality, as well as a capacity for creative divergence, needs to complement academic educational objectives. Hence the need to recognise opportunities for design-related activity during early years at school.

In spite of many profound and well-documented changes which have occurred in design training, both in further and higher education and in secondary schools over the post-war decades, it was not until the early 1980s that government interest, specifically in design in primary education, emerged. Following its earlier reports [5] on the later stages of design education, the Design Council set up a working party in 1984, funded by the Department of Trade and Industry, to make recommendations with respect to design-related activities in primary schools. This may be seen to be a logical, if rather belated, recognition of the fact that any further improvements would need to be built upon good foundations at the primary stage.

The Council's report *Design in Primary Education*, which was published in 1987, sees design not as a separate subject but essentially as an activity which crosses subject boundaries. Its extensive recommendations are based upon an acknowledgement of the fact that art, craft and technology make a major contribution but, the report says,

> It is central to our argument, however, that design-related
> activities are found throughout the activity of the primary
> school [6]

and goes on to cite examples from language, mathematics, science, environmental studies, dance and drama. The working party makes the vigorous assertion that

> The skills of designing and making are every bit as basic as those
> of literacy and numeracy [7].

This is no small claim and its intention is underlined by the chairman's writing, in the first paragraph of the foreword, that the report stresses

> the importance of design, both as a part of all our lives and as
> having a distinctive contribution to make towards children's
> education [8].

We have already seen how advances in technology have wrought changes in the ways in which we think about the importance of design in education. I should now like to consider some of the more permanent themes which need to be borne in mind when considering how we teach design, and its concomitant, technology, to children of primary school age. It is important not to lose sight of what we know about different perceptions and the integrity of mind at different stages of development.

I wish to argue that the word 'design' denotes an activity which is characteristically and uniquely human. It depends upon an ability to see existing circumstances analytically and to envisage the possibility of changing them. It extends into an ability to rehearse alternatives in the mind, and later to select and take appropriate action. Design has enabled our species to adapt to conditions in which we would not otherwise have been able to survive. To those who are tempted to think of design as an extra which can be applied to a product, like icing to a cake, I wish to emphasise that the most persistent problems have always been those where design failures result in loss of life. Homo sapiens arrived late on

84

the evolutionary tree, only after his predecessors had refined the use of prehensile hands and stereoscopic vision. It is not surprising that we exhibit a characteristic appetite for adventure which leads us, even as we test the security of our present position, to be already on the lookout for another to which we may leap to secure a new grasp. So much are our eyes and hands our means of access to knowledge that we still urge our children to 'see' what we mean and to gain a firm 'grasp' of what we seek to teach them.

Technology is at least as old as design. André Leroi-Gourhan, in the Introduction to *A History of Technology and Invention* edited by Maurice Daumas in 1962 [9], reviews the prehistorical evidence and concludes that

> technical ability as it exists in man was present in rudimentary
> form in the series of prehensile mammals.

He adds:

> It is paradoxical that the hand preceded the brain; it is equally
> paradoxical that in a certain sense the tool preceded intelligence.

This is a useful reminder that in considering technology in education we are not to think of it as a new phenomenon. Nor do we need to worry over the apparent paradoxes which exercise Leroi-Gourhan, since our position is that it is the hand and other sense organs which inform our intelligence and provide it with some of the models it requires in its approach to language and design. Design, even at its most primitive, implies imagination and the power to exercise the kind of choice which we associate with intelligence.

Moreover, it is a characteristic of technology that innovation adds to the total range of machines and processes available and that it extends, rather than replaces, earlier forms. Many of the older technologies continue to be valued and used because of the particular qualities which they impart to the product. I shall argue that familiarity with some of these early forms may be as important educationally as knowledge of the most recent, particularly for younger pupils, who are still developing the foundations of their language and their capacity for design.

Richard Gregory in *Mind in Science* [10] writes that

> The immense importance of technology in moulding how we
> think has implications only dimly appreciated.

He goes on to point out the limitations of a psychology based only on our biological origins and suggests that what is amazing about man is how far he has escaped his origins through the effect upon him of technology.

> These considerations are at least as important as our biological
> background for understanding man and how the first
> mythological, philosophical and scientific ideas were conceived
> and developed.

Gregory then explores the idea that most abstract notions of philosophies and theories of mind stem directly from technology.

Bruce Archer and his associates in the Design Education Unit of the Royal College of Art have identified a distinctive capacity analogous with that for language and for mathematics. This was first termed 'modelling'

[11] (1978). Subsequent use of the term 'cognitive modelling' [12] (1979), and the addition of the term 'imaging' [13] (1982) suggests that this thesis is being further refined, perhaps towards a theory of what Ken Baynes, a member of the original unit, has recently called 'design intelligence'.

I incline to the view that attempts to divide our capacities for thought into discrete categories are likely to remain speculative. This is because, so far at least, we can know little about thought except through the action, actual or symbolic, which it generates. It is nevertheless clear that we can, and do, think in any language, medium or modelling material with which we are familiar.

Jerome Bruner describes thought as vicarious action which human beings uniquely use for manipulating representations and models rather than acting directly on the world: thought reduces 'the high cost of error'.

> It is the characteristic of human beings and no other species that we can carry out this vicarious action with a large number of prosthetic devices, that are so to speak, the tools provided by the culture. Natural language is the prime example, but there are pictorial and diagrammatic conventions as well, theories, myths, modes of reckoning and ordering [14].

Drawing and picturing earn their place on Bruner's list precisely because they add to the range of thought which is possible. Our tendency to attribute only to verbal language the kind of potential which resides in all such 'prosthetic devices' may have contributed to our relative failure to develop that potential. It may have led us also to lose sight of the contribution which such devices make to the teaching of language itself.

In our own time it is possible to see how deeply language rests upon technology. It does so not only for its sophisticated systems of storage and transmission but for the metaphors which enable language to function. We may say, for example, that the very fabric of language is fashioned from the warp and weft of our technical history. Our sentences are 'packed' with concepts which we can 'construct and convey' largely because we have experiences upon which such ideas can be 'modelled'. These are stilted examples but ordinary language is littered with less obvious metaphor.

Our ability to manipulate models in the mind is, as we have seen, at the core of our capacity for design. Even more important, perhaps, is the possibility that it lies at the core of our capacity for language. Our theoretical knowledge of this process is limited, though effective teachers of young children have long known of the importance of creative activity with materials. They know that useful vocabulary cannot be learnt unless pupils share a range of experiences which call for discriminating observation and precise language. In practice this means social activity involving the selection and use of a range of materials.

Children draw. This activity has been well documented and, perhaps because it is both inexpensive and convenient, provision is made for it in most primary schools and in many households. The outcomes are easily retained for study. Children also model. The crayon with which a child draws may be balanced on one end to 'stand' for a man, a tree or a tower: on its side it may be pushed along the floor to 'act' as a train or a boat. Where other materials or objects are available they too are explored for their modelling potential. The outcomes, the models, are often short-lived, not so easily stored and therefore less readily available for prolonged study.

Those of us who have been privileged to observe children's activity with materials for many years are led to conclude that drawing may be a less singular activity than it seems. When a child first discovers the mark-making property of graphic materials, this is not the only phenomenon which is enjoyed. All materials are examined, looked at, touched, grasped, moved, poked, smeared, heaped, struck or – as confidence rises – attacked.

Actions which are rewarding or which lead to approval or pleasure are repeated, as they are in the early stages of drawing. Eventually, however, the modelling potential is discovered. A group of tightly scribbled marks may be named as members of the family or a spoon made to 'sail' past a pepper-pot 'lighthouse'. Neither the marks, the spoon nor the pepper-pot are required to resemble what is represented, provided that they can, together, function in terms of the game proposed. We learn to use and to read drawings and models much as we learn to read language, by becoming familiar with ways in which relatively meaningless units can be arranged into patterns capable of carrying ideas. Often the aptness of a model is to be found in how the parts relate to each other. Often the important relationship can be seen in the gestures which accompany the model or which have contributed to the making of a drawing.

The model is useful in showing the pupil and the teacher what the pupil thinks. The meaning of the constituent parts is derived from their function in the context proposed. For example a trace, in paint, of a circular gesture may function as a 'frying pan' or a 'roundabout' in the different contexts which a child may propose during the act of painting. Primary teachers, particularly those who are experienced in teaching infants, know the importance of this capacity for seeing relationships and meanings. We call it 'recognition': the knowing again which validates our vocabulary and our expanding model of the world.

The continuing process here, of which the drawn image or model is a handsome by-product, is the refinement by the pupil of his working hypothesis about how events in the observed world may be characterised and rendered coherent. Sometimes the clarity of a child's perception, the aptness of the model or the potency of the image can evoke in us an aesthetic response. No harm lies in that, provided that it does not lead us to treat the child as artistically gifted or to dismiss the activity which led to the model as merely a charming episode. What appears to us to be poetry is, for the child, a necessary account of his or her experience. We are entitled to take pleasure in the creativity exhibited in the model but effective teaching demands a more challenging response. To our pupils' use of ordinary language we call upon our skill in reading and listening and upon our knowledge of literature to help us to respond.

We need to ask ourselves what skills can help us here, where our pupils use the language of modelling.

First we must learn to read drawings and models, in the terms which our pupils propose, so that we may respond both appreciatively and critically. Second we must gain for our pupils, and for ourselves, familiarity with the best examples of the ways in which artists, designers and technologists use this language. To fail to meet these requirements would be to leave ourselves in a position exactly analogous to someone attempting to teach a language which he or she cannot read to children who have no books.

I have attempted to show that modelling and drawing function for children in ways significantly similar to those of language. If ordinary language is the structuring of ideas in words, drawing is the structuring of ideas in line, tone and gesture, and modelling is structuring thought in terms of the properties of the other materials used. Ideas, even our own, are known to us only to the extent that they are structured in some such accessible terms.

Pupils can be taught to structure their thought in everyday language by the practice of speaking and writing. They also learn to structure their thought as they act upon tactile and visual materials such as paint, wood, metal, clay or textile. Because of the distinctive 'terms' which each medium makes available each offers different advantages and disadvantages. Each is therefore capable of generating a different set of ideas and perceptions. The materials which function as media in this way are not interchangeable. Translation from one medium to another is possible but pupils can be expected to achieve this only when they have adequate experience in both media. Even then translation is always at the expense of some adjustment to the advantages and disadvantages which were derived from the original medium.

As they gain familiarity with ordinary language pupils demonstrate that they can develop ideas, in the mind, for example by telling stories or constructing imaginary dialogue. Similarly, given familiarity with a range of materials children will already have shown ability to think in terms of pictures and models. As we have seen, the capability to see and to model in the mind's eye and hand constitutes a mode of thinking from which we derive our capacity to design and to understand design. It is this ability which design education undertakes to develop to the highest possible level. It is also an ability less readily recognised and encouraged by government in the past than in the present.

Many primary schools already give a reasoned priority to a progression of work with materials in a variety of art, craft and design contexts. What is often lacking is an awareness of the need to reinforce the technological and other insights which pupils gain through their involvement in this work. This awareness is absent because it has not hitherto been expected, nor has it been provided to any significant extent in the initial training of primary teachers. It is necessary, now, to develop further in-service and initial training to meet this expectation. The primary school curriculum, actively taught through design-related activities, provides endless opportunities for such reinforcement and development.

Notes and References

1 NATIONAL CURRICULUM DESIGN AND TECHNOLOGY WORKING GROUP. 1988. *Interim Report*. London, DES.
2 FULLER, P. 1985. *Images of God*. London, Chatto & Windus, pp. 194–99.
3 McCOY, K. and M. McCOY. 1988. 'Design in the Information Age', in: ALDERSLEY-WILLIAMS, H. 1988. *New American Design*. New York, Rizzoli, pp. 16–17.
4 CAPLAN, R. 1988. 'The Original and the Good', in: ALDERSLEY-WILLIAMS. *Op. cit.*
5 DESIGN COUNCIL. 1976. *Engineering Design Education*. 1977. *Industrial Design Education in the* UK. 1980. *Design Education at Secondary Level*. London.
6 DESIGN COUNCIL. 1988. *Design in Primary Education*. London, para 3.8.
7 *Ibid.*, paras 9.3, 4.8.
8 *Ibid.*, FAIRBAIRN, A. Chairman's Foreword.
9 LEROI-GOURHAN, A. 1962. 'Introduction to Birth and Early Development of Technology', in: DAUMAS, N. (ed.) *Histoire Generale des Techniques*. Paris, Presses Universitaires de France. English trans. 1969. New York, Crown Publishers Inc., pp. 12–16.
10 GREGORY, R. L. 1981. *Mind in Science*. Harmondsworth, Penguin, p. 43.
11 ARCHER, B. 1978. *Time for a Revolution in Art and Design Education*. RCA Papers No. 6. London, Royal College of Art, p. 6.
12 ARCHER, B. and P. ROBERTS. 1979. 'Design and Technological Awareness in Education', in: *Studies in Design Education*, Vol. 12, No. 1, Winter 1978, pp. 55–6.
13 ARCHER, B. 1982. *Cognitive Modelling, Rational Thinking, Language, Designerly Thinking and Imaging*. An internal paper. London, Royal College of Art.
14 BRUNER, J. S. 1972. *Relevance of Education*. London, Allen & Unwin, p. 20.

Chapter Nine

ROBERT CLEMENT Developing Craft Activities in Schools

Differentiation between craft and design subjects

The place of the crafts in schools is made complex by the variety of subjects that offer craft experience and the variety of functions attributed to the crafts by the different subject teachers concerned.

The past decade-and-a-half in education has seen the emergence and establishment of Design Courses and Design Faculties within many schools, and the different concerns and interests of teachers of Art, Home Economics, and CDT (Craft, Design and Technology) have been focused and brought together in an attempt to find common ground – especially in their teaching of Craft and Design. Although these developments can only be applauded, they have brought with them many problems. Some of these are rooted within the complex and varied nature of the subjects involved. As a group of subjects they have nothing like the homogeneity to be found in other traditional groupings such as the Humanities, Sciences, Languages, etc. There may be considerable varieties of approach within each of the subject areas concerned and between them they offer a complex range of educational discourse.

There has perhaps been too much emphasis within the 'Design Education' movement in England and Wales upon the establishment of a design rationale or process to which the constituent subjects should *conform*, rather than a search for ways to rationalise and balance the different contexts within which the teaching of craft may take place.

Many Design Departments have concentrated on trying to establish what the different crafts have in common in relation to some generalised notion of design. Teachers of Art, Craft, and Home Economics need to focus more upon the content and context of their teaching of the different crafts, to establish what is taught through what process, and what different skills are acquired through encounter with different materials. The present emphasis upon the classification of crafts by material areas undoubtedly leads to much repetition both of process and concept in craft.

Something of the dilemma of classifying the crafts by their materials can be revealed when we consider, for example, the different contexts within which the teaching of ceramics may take place. Ceramics may be taught on the basis of acquiring skills to make such things as pinch pots, coil pots, slab ware, pressed mould dishes, etc. It may also be used as an extension of drawing in which the children are encouraged to use clay as an expressive medium, making three-dimensional images that have a personal meaning. Clay can be one of the media used to extend basic design concepts, as a vehicle for exploring such qualities as surface, form, pattern, etc., and for modelling natural and man-made forms both observed and analysed. More rarely it can be related to three-dimensional problem solving, as in the designing and making of clay forms to satisfy given functions or requirements. Where a group of teachers of different subjects are seeking for some kind of balance across their various contributions to craft teaching it is more useful to look at the different kinds of context within which they work, rather than the materials they use.

The three dominant processes used within craft teaching could be described as follows:

Visual Enquiry: where the work in craft grows out of exploration of the visual world, either objectively through observation of things seen and translation into media, or analytically through an exploration of the visual elements that contribute to our perception of the world, e.g. colour, structure, surface, pattern, movement, etc.

Acquisition of Skills: where the work in craft follows upon the student being taught a number of basic skills or processes – which once learnt can be applied to the making of things.

Problem Solving: where the work in craft is determined by problems set or defined. These can range from experimenting with materials to exploring general principles, or work where clear-cut problems of function are set before the children.

Within these general classifications of process in craft teaching there are such contributory factors as the teacher's general attitude towards the best way to motivate children to make things – ranging from those who see craft as acquiring and then applying skills at one extreme, to those at the other who believe that children are best motivated by ideas and concepts and that these will lead to the acquisition of skills as and when required.

There is a need for teachers of Craft, whether within Design departments or operating in separate departments, to review in detail both the content of their work and the context within which they teach their craft in order to ensure that what time is available for craft is used constructively, and that there are no unnecessary repetitions of concept and process from one material to another. It may make more sense for teachers to identify and balance their different approaches to the teaching of *craft* rather than pursue that common ground implied within the design education movement, where all too often what has been achieved is the lowest common denominator rather than factors of quality!

Integration of 2D and 3D work across material areas

In many Art, Craft, and Design departments or faculties there have been serious attempts to find a pattern of working whereby the work of designing and making is supported by a programme of two-dimensional work within which the children explore concepts or elements that feed into the making activity. These programmes in the main have been simplified versions of the kind of Basic Design Course pioneered at the

Bauhaus which had a significant influence upon work in the English Art Schools through such teachers as Maurice de Sausmarez, Harry Thubron, Victor Pasmore, Kurt Rowlands *et al.*

The syllabuses of many Art and Design departments refer to the need for children to acquire a basic visual vocabulary which may be applied to making in a variety of materials. The content of such programmes is usually an introduction to the standard visual elements and may include such areas of exploration as colour, tone, surface, structure, pattern, form, etc. It has been rather assumed that basic visual concepts such as these can be acquired in much the same way as basic manual skills and the rotation system used by many Art and Design faculties has led to their being taught as discrete areas of 'visual' knowledge.

It is rather ironic that the teaching of these basic visual skills is usually restricted to the first two years of secondary schooling in much the same way that the traditional teacher of woodwork puts his students through two years of basic operations in order for them to acquire sufficient skills to go on to making real things in wood. There is no doubt that children aged eleven and twelve are not a particularly suitable audience for this kind of work. The *abstract* nature of much basic design teaching and the assumption that children of this age can make that intellectual jump from theory to practice has led to a great deal of rather low-level pattern making in materials.

There is no doubt that children can apply such elementary visual skills as the basic design system teaches but only if acquisition of the visual is immediately related to a real task. There is nothing more depressing than to put a class of children through an intensive six week programme of colour theory, only to discover that they can't apply it to making a painting! In these circumstances it would be more useful for that group of teachers involved in crafts education to look more closely at the different kinds of process they offer through their teaching as a signpost to how best they might relate to each other, rather than seeking a common programme of basic design.

What is common to all craftsmen and women is not a collection of rather low-level visual skills: it is more likely to be a common concern for the ways that craft-making grows out of the following processes:
1   Through drawing, an examination of that range of visual information offered by the natural and man-made world.
2   Through analysis and selection, a focusing upon those aspects of the real world which both motivate and inspire the individual craftsperson.
3   Through exploration of materials, some understanding of how they may be used to support the making of artefacts that have both quality and personal meaning (Figs. 18–24).
What that group of teachers involved in the business of craftsmanship need to discuss and explore is not what elementary visual skills the children might need to acquire, if and when they are allowed to make things, but rather those common elements of observing, analysing, information collecting and material manipulation that are present in the work of all good craftsmen.

92

18 *Lighthouses*, weaving, 9 years; Thornbury Primary School, Plymouth, Devon.

19 *My Friend*, ceramics, 17 years; Plymstock School, Devon.

20 *House*, ceramics, 15 years; Axminster School, Devon.

Day-to-day work in schools

The day-to-day practice of the teaching of craft is largely determined by the pattern of timetabling and organisation adopted by individual schools. There is a considerable variety of practice, much of it influenced by the way particular schools choose to organise their subject groupings. In some schools Art, CDT, and Home Economics are autonomous Departments – in others they may be grouped together to form a faculty with such various labels as 'Art and Design', 'Design', 'Creative Design', etc. In some schools they are part of a larger grouping within a 'Creative Arts' faculty and may work alongside Music, Drama and sometimes Physical Education. Some schools choose to separate Art from CDT and Home Economics and to form separate faculties of 'Expressive Arts' and 'Craft and Design'.

Although there should in theory be a better working relationship between the subjects when they are grouped together, this is not necessarily reflected in practice. It is as common to find good teaching of the crafts and reasonable liaison and consultation between autonomous departments as it is within the more formal groupings. Much will depend upon whether the teachers concerned have moved beyond a simple classification of the crafts by their material labels (woodwork, metalwork, needlework, pottery, etc.) towards some serious discussion about the different experiences their crafts offer. Many faculties have foundered where they have been established for the wrong reasons – as an administrative convenience, because the studios and workshops are physically related in a new building, because these subjects are seen as being 'practical', or because it is assumed that they are all 'creative' in the same generalised way.

Similarly, in theory, the block timetabling of the 'practical' subjects together should lead to a better management of the teaching of craft. It is comparatively rare to find those subjects using the flexibility that block timetabling allows: establishing lead sessions and team teaching, alternating or changing the subject emphasis as a programme or theme develops, linking areas of work, alternating groups between teachers as new skills and concepts need to be fed into a project, etc. It is more common to find within block timetabling an unimaginative rotation of children from one material area to another, each section working with the same size groups for the same length of time. The common pattern of the half-termly shift from Art to Pottery to Wood to Metal to Textiles (needle-work) to Home Economics assumes a unanimity of working methods across the materials that doesn't exist; it also assumes that all the areas have the same value and that the crafts can be taught without reference to each other as separate pockets of skills.

This 'democracy' of skills has been forced upon some schools for those philosophical reasons already touched upon. It can also be the consequence of inadequate allocations of time to this group of subjects, which

21 *Seascape*, weaving, 13 years; St Thomas High School, Exeter, Devon.

22 *Baby's Head*, ceramics,
16 years; Plymstock
School, Devon.

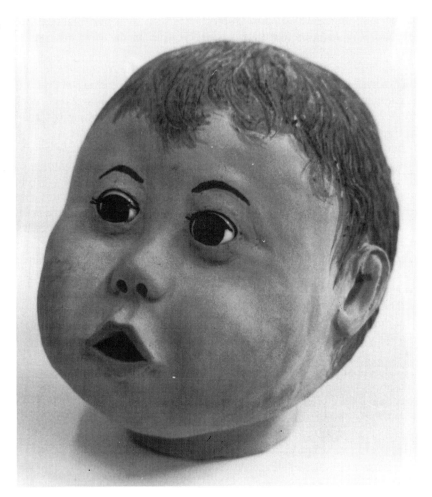

is more often than not a reflection of the status these subjects have within
the overall curriculum of the school.

Some problems stem from the establishment of the principle that boys
and girls should have equal access to all the practical areas – not a principle that anyone would wish to challenge but one not matched by those
improvements to resources and staffing that would make it sensible in
practice. A direct consequence of this was an almost immediate cutting
by half of the time that children used to be able to spend in any one
craft room when the crafts were subdivided into those suitable for boys
and those that were the prerogative of girls! The average allocation of
time to this group of subjects is six periods in a forty-period week. When
that has to be subdivided between art, ceramics, wood, metal, textiles,
home economics and technology, an equal sharing out of the time can
result in very inadequate time being spent in any one area of experience.
It is difficult for children to gain any real knowledge or grasp of one of
the crafts when in each of their first three years of secondary schooling
they may have as little as eighteen hours' experience of work in that
craft.

96

A direct consequence has been the tendency of more traditional teachers to restrict their craft teaching still further to the acquisition of what limited skills can be taught in the time available. Bearing in mind that in any of the craft areas the majority of children in any one year group will opt out of that subject when it comes to choosing 4th and 5th courses, there is a need to question the practice in many schools of teaching the children limited basic skills in several craft areas which they will never have the opportunity to pursue further.

Faced with these problems, teachers of Art, CDT, and Home Economics have adopted a number of ploys to try to make the most effective use of what can be regarded as unsatisfactory time allocations. The most common one is simply to reduce the number of areas available through a limited option system from year to year. In the first year the children will have a 'taste' of each of the craft/material experiences available within the school. In the second year they may through guided choice reduce the number of areas to four, and in the third year to two or three. This is at least preferable to their spending three years flitting from one workshop/studio to another.

In some schools there is a conscious attempt to set up a logical sequence from one art or craft area to another that makes for some kind of logic, in that skills and concepts acquired with one teacher are used and built upon by the next teacher the child works with. For example, an Art module, in which the children explore colour and surface qualities, may be followed by a module in textiles where some of those principles may be applied. Although this is possible in the transfer from one workshop/studio to another it is difficult to design a logical programme of this kind of linking right through the year, simply because not all the craft areas relate so directly to each other as in the example given.

23 *Boots*, ceramics, 13 years; Estover School, Plymouth, Devon.

97

Other schools have attempted to relate the craft areas thematically, so that in any one term or half term the children in different craft areas may be working on similar themes. It has often proved difficult to find themes which are equally relevant to all the areas involved and which do not trivialise the level of work in some areas. The most successful seem to be where the teachers concerned have been able to agree upon a sequence of themes that are both demanding and general enough for each craft area to use on its own terms. In one school, the children in the first year move from the study of surface appearance, to structure, to movement in a variety of materials. The structured use of visual source material, work sheets and some lead sessions and team teaching help to make this progression understandable to the children, as does the conscious use of sharing and critical sessions at the end of each 'theme'.

In another school the assumption that all the craft areas can share the same concerns is challenged. Two modules a week are set aside for shared or combined work, and teachers of the different subjects can choose to opt into this shared time or remain out of it. This has the advantage of bringing together for the shared work those teachers who have some understanding of and commitment to the principle, while allowing those who are doubtful recruits to continue more confidently with their separate and more specialist concerns.

In comparatively few, usually smaller, schools different subject teachers have been able to establish common principles for the teaching of the crafts, so that project or thematic study does not present the children with conflicting attitudes and methods of working as they move from one workshop or studio to another.

Whatever system a group of craft teachers adopts, the crucial factor is always how well the teachers resolve that conflict between the need for children to have on the one hand a general understanding of the principles of making and designing, and on the other, sufficient time to develop skills and confidence to engage in craft with some authority. There seems little point in children being required to learn low-level skills in a variety of materials during their first two/three years of secondary schooling. If the children are not progressing much beyond square one in a wide range of craft activities, it would seem more sensible to accept the fact that experience of every material is not essential and that more might be gained by giving them experiences of some quality in fewer areas.

If the balance is right – between making which is determined by process, visual enquiry or problem solving, between materials which are either resistant or plastic – it would seem more sensible to accept the fact that craftsmanship is more likely to flourish where the children have been given the skills and confidence to operate well within some craft areas rather than inadequately across a wide range.

Chapter Ten

TOM HUDSON Creative Technology

Two major changes are required if we are to instigate a serious development of technology education in primary and secondary schools. First, we must pursue a system of education that is in keeping with the main patterns of twentieth-century culture, reflecting the most dynamic aspects of creative ideas and poised to engage new developments. This should be pragmatic, methodological and open-ended. It should also be capable of producing a truly creative mode of teaching sufficiently flexible to evolve new techniques and ideas and not based upon outworn academic attitudes. Second, it is apparent that we shall have to change our whole concept of administration and execution of education in order to permit such creative developments.

There is no doubt that creative forms of education are going to be demanding on both teacher and pupil. But we have for too long pursued too-limited objectives, satisfying ourselves with a simple-minded practicality operating at the lowest common denominator of productivity and creativity. We have also accepted for too long the debased conventions of an educational system that has hardly changed since the Renaissance – fragmentary, historical and one-directional. The teacher, as well as the child, is a victim of a system that limits the concept of education to a few vocational years in an individual's lifetime – a poorly administered, institutionalised concept of vocational training that is really a form of status allocation confined to the formative years.

In an age when the growth and dissemination of information, the expansion of ideas, and the vast mental production of humankind is transforming the world, the teacher is too often left disoriented, practically and emotionally confused. If we are to develop an education conducive to a really contemporary and informed practicality, as well as an emotionally secure and unique individuality, the teacher will have to develop more integrated concepts and be able to adapt rapidly to changing patterns of process and method. Evolution controlled by self-conscious humanity is likely to become a faster process, for good or evil, for construction or destruction, than the nature-dominant systems of recent history. It is vital that we begin to balance our more destructive tendencies with a greater development of intuitive, constructive creativity.

Minds trained on present educational principles generally operate at the level of scribble: uncoordinated and wasteful, we struggle to concentrate, often failing to solve problems because we cannot even conceive of the implications of what we do, and cannot comprehend the relevance of results. Any education should at least lay bare the problem, demand commitment and sensitivity towards consequences, and be a specifically creative process not only producing desirable end-products but also eliciting critical attitudes and value judgements. Today, almost all teaching is inordinately generalised: we move from generalisation to specialisation, from breadth to narrowness in the worst sense. If we comprehend even the simplest notions of post-Freudian individualism we must reject the present methods based on subjects rather than ideas, on role and performance rather than self.

At the moment we pay lip service to individual psychological development: we mouth platitudes about collective or social orientation and achieve little of either. It is in fact impossible to achieve either one adequately within the present pattern of education. What is required now is a reassessment of our provisions – a very precise analytical scrutiny of educational processes, assessing their timing, staging and creative merit. If we believe at all in the simple Darwinian concept of evolution we should reject the present timetabling system – the pitiful fragmentation of time – which makes generalised and so-called liberal education a prescription for butterfly-minded mediocrity. The average adolescent can in fact work for very long periods on an idea, and journey deeply into the nature of a problem. On the other hand, we can achieve certain things by very rapid processes, by specially processing information, and by integrating procedures. These same procedures – group and team methods – will dispel the belief that a good staff/pupil ratio always means the fewest possible students per member of staff.

It is extremely important that future education in technology will pay as much regard to the aesthetic as the functional: in fact, it would be better to think in terms of a single, aesthetic-functional problem. By this I do not mean seeking the art-craft product, or the machined product with art overlay, the usual superficial incorporation or application of an 'art' style. Let there be an end to the restyling, pseudo-functional game that results in Tudor electric light-fittings and conventional tables clad in 'contemporary' tiles: let us deal with fundamental problems.

It is wrong to believe that children cannot cope with functional design problems – that they must be limited to low-level craft applications. It is wrong also to inflict on them the worst kind of 'step-by-step' pedagogic processes in which any possibility of a sum, equation or synthesis of experience is highly improbable. 'Lineal' education is often unnecessarily over-simplified, excluding any comprehensive understanding of problem and situation. This approach inhibits those who are capable of conceptual creative acts, which – given the right conditions and training – means most people. The functional problem in design education should always be a Gestalt, with the child dealing with a totality, permitting him or her the possibilities of conceptual comprehension and comprehensive conceptualising.

Individuals have distinct preferences for form and material: these are instinctive and highly subjective – outside of fashion. Individuals also exert preferences in other ways: they respond differently to scale, precision, colour, etc. A great part of education should be carried out from positions of strength – that is, from the basis of pupils' preferences wherein they may demonstrate their greatest abilities. But in developing their experience in breadth one would include training in alternative materials, forms and processes, and this is the reverse of the present convention that proceeds from breadth to specialisation. One should also create a balance between work in two and three dimensions, and develop the capacity to move easily from one to the other. Many technical processes are very limited, and once the pupil's mind is 'cued' to the appropriate action he or she should be directed to purposive, creative thinking – through the technique as medium – instead of being confined to the equivalent of 'scribble'.

The teacher's rationale of the pedagogic process should be openly revealed to pupils. Even quite young children should be informed in this way. I always took it as a gratuitous insult that no-one confided in me the principles of the education I underwent – probably because it was so devoid of principle that no exposition was possible or credible. If the teacher explains general motivating principles, he or she may then encourage a balanced dialogue by asking Why? and How? when dealing with particulars. In the workshop this means an end to the stereotype exercise carried out *en masse*. It also discourages the teacher-oriented or teacher-directed problem. The 'exercise' has a limited value as the means of achieving predetermined ends, but is of little use creatively. The 'experiment', on the other hand, is one of the fundamental processes of our culture, and if its use can be extended beyond the confirmation of an hypothesis, towards pragmatic open-ended research, it becomes a journey of discovery leading to confrontation with the unknown.

Technical education should certainly utilise whatever scientific knowledge is available, and apply scientific methodology to its own processes when necessary, but when dealing with creatively-based problems we should experiment in a non-repetitive way – thus more experiments and fewer exercises. Experimenting with materials and processes should always push beyond the limits of probability, and engage a-formal as well as formal problems. By this I mean that materials should be exploited beyond their limits – experimenting towards the destructive as well as the constructive, not merely 'going along with the nature of the material'. This romantic attitude towards materials can be too respectful. For example, woods and metals are materials that lend themselves to machining, yet their essential characteristics are often lost in the geometric sections of production forms in which they are supplied. A constructive understanding of these characteristics may therefore demand destructive and a-formal experimental investigation. The compartmentalised attitude towards materials is also insupportable: experiments should not only be qualitative and comparative in relation to a particular material, but also involve materials in combination. The development of synthetic materials has widened the range for possible analysis and synthesis, and has also vastly increased the range of possible geometry.

Too much design education (like education in general) is concerned with subject and methodology and not enough with ideas. The reverse, however, is more productive: if ideas are meaningful and excite discovery, then appropriate processes evolve in a fruitful way. I prefer commitment to a creative idea because it demands its own quality of process and production. By this I mean that if we were discovering new forms or new methods of fabrication I should not worry too much initially about qualities of craft or construction – they will automatically ensue. One is always trying to find more precise equivalents for one's ideas, but the concepts and ideas come first, and demand tools and processes that are then utilised relative to problem and personality.

I noticed when I carried out research with children of 4–5 years of age that the 'idea' was always the predominant factor in creative production. A box became a 'house' by an act of preference and selection: it could also become a 'ship', a 'basket' or any other container because the child

25   Creative technology: joined materials, however crudely assembled, become creatures of the child's imagination.

103

understood the basic structure and 'simple' function of the form. Similarly, a child would take two pieces of wood and, holding them together in a cruciform, assert that this was an 'aeroplane', again the affirmation of the structural concept. As the child grows in experience, exploitation gives way to a desire to develop the idea, and hence his or her command of processes (Fig. 25).

Technological understanding evolves in parallel with comprehension of the idea: technology in this sense is the business of fabricating the idea. A 6–7 year old child can discriminate between very sophisticated types of form, as well as having a real and intense concept of inherent structure. Types of aeroplane, ship, etc., are recognised because of visual character even before functional implications are understood. The child will want to demonstrate this knowledge and will try to invent an enabling technology to fit tail fin, engine, mast or sail. This aptitude should be the basis of a continuous structural enlightenment and development, both practical and theoretical, to elucidate the whole appearance and principles of the child's environment, not merely train him or her in the production of artefacts. This inherent structural empathy should be the basis for later developments.

There are countless ways of engaging creative involvement in basic technology: here I would like to suggest merely the simplest and most obvious principles. The first one is that pupils should have access to materials in variety, so that they appreciate from the outset that technologies are suggested by material properties and cannot be conceived as abstract, unrelated disciplines. Materials for study can be different in type, characteristics and/or form. One could experiment with soft, hard and differently structured woods, from beech blocks to bamboo canes, concentrating on the special properties associated with each species and exploring possibilities for combination. A very productive approach is to have a limited problem tackled by a group of individuals avoiding repetition. They could join 'like' forms together – that is, inventing as many ways as possible of joining two pieces of square-section wood, or round section to round section, or sheet to sheet. Initially this could be confined to simple identical forms, but could then be varied using (i) more complex forms; (ii) greatly enlarged scale; (iii) different species of wood; and (iv) large variations in relative scale (Figs. 26–28).

There are very many permutations of development using only 'like' forms. The formal possibilities of conjugating the geometry of 'unlike' forms are infinite – square section to round; round to sheet; sheet to square, and so on. As with 'like' and 'unlike', one can progress from dealing with 'simple' to 'complex' forms by using both industrial and invented profiles. There are many different rectilinear and curvilinear sections available in wood, and of course there are hundreds of fabricated and extruded sections in metal and plastics, from simple I, L, T, U and H to very complex ones. Pupils should therefore invent their technology while they are learning, and be given only simple demonstrations and instructions sufficient to use tools and equipment effectively. In this the physiological aspects should be stressed – position, poise, action, pressure, rhythm – relative to the form, action and character of the tool. One

104

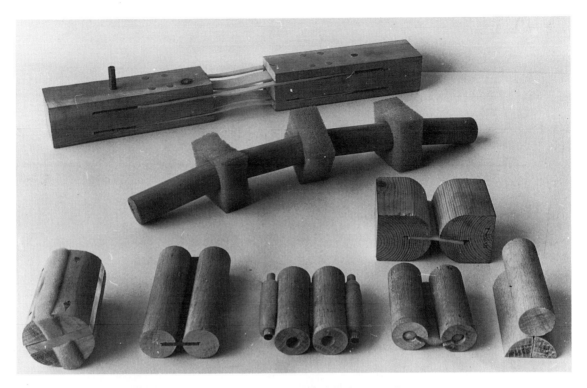

26, 27 Invention of technology: devising unconventional methods of joining different materials and objects without relying on customary technology.

28 Invention of
technology: devising
universal methods of
joining characteristically
different materials (here
hand-formed in wood and
milled in mild steel).

should also relate the pupil to a wider concept of orientation – the individual and tool oriented to bench, vice, room, building – a relationship
featuring the self at the centre of an expanding geometrical world
dominated by man and man-made systems of construction, seeking to
dominate the physical nature of the universe by creative concepts.

Pupils should be encouraged to invent and define their own problems.
Constructing with simple forms – say, square section to square section –
they might produce not only diverse results but also new possibilities.
Their results should be criticised, analysed and categorised, paying particular attention to the relative functional/aesthetic characteristics of each
experimental solution. The limited range we find already exploited in
technology will be dominantly functional, but pupils will invent many
others – some equally functional, others more aesthetically pleasing, and
innumerable combinations of the two. Any pupil will be capable of inventing variations of standard joints, or of taking a joint he or she has
evolved and using it as a basic structural or organisational system. Square
to square will eventually lead to a three-dimensional grid; but then this
may be deformed, allowing comparison of regular-symmetrical and ir-
regular-asymmetrical systems. More sophisticated problems arise indi-
vidually – for example, the jointing of linear cube, plane cube and solid

cube, a sculptural engineering problem and a very creative game. I am often astounded at the inventiveness of children with no previous (taught) ability and technical experience. In fact if one does not witness new forms and ideas emanating from the workshop there is something seriously wrong. I personally expect daily to feel surprise and envy.

There is no need for design experimentation of this kind to result in utilitarian objects (Figs. 29–30). It is sufficient if the so-called 'non-functional' product is a functional structure – that is, that it is integral and functionally effective in its own structural terms. This applies equally to working with more a-formal possibilities – perhaps using wood with string, rope, elastic, rubber, or wire. It may be surprising that pupils rarely investigate the implications of colour without teacher encouragement. The local colour of wood should be stressed again and again, and actually exploited by revelation in structural systems. In technology we should have problems that *begin* with colour, not merely end with it as decorative overlay. But the critical point is that work should not be limited by mathematical or numerical processes, and certainly not restricted to chromatically-neutral, Pythagorean solids. The main aspects to be considered are the *range* of forms chosen or created, and the character of the *language* of their construction. The first involves material, scale, aesthetic quality; the second deals with systems of organisation. Young pupils will evolve regular and irregular, symmetrical and non-

29 Creative machine processes: inventive deconstruction of the cuboid.

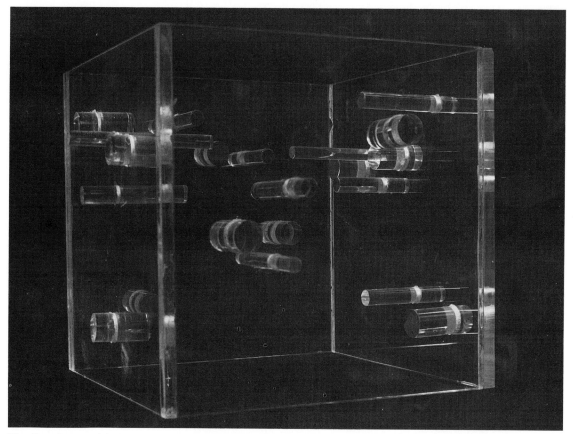

30 Creative machine processes: inventive reconstruction of the cuboid.

symmetrical, rigid and flexible, fixed and variable, geometrical and non-geometrical constructions that can be applied to very different environmental situations – inside, outside, spatial, aerial, fluid – and operate not only statically but move sequentially, mechanically, electronically. The personal development of language and idea should be the key concept, featuring equally the invention of forms and images 'in the mind' and 'in practical construction'.

If we introduce this positively creative, experimental attitude, cutting away preconception, then we may expect personal vision and individualised pragmatic developments. There is the whole world to consider and select from. Instead of the senseless reproduction of preconceived forms for the sake of technique – pipe-racks, book-racks, stools and chairs – let motivation be based on personal predilection for problem and predicament. For example, instead of requiring pupils to design and make stools, we may start with an investigation of the varied ergonomic problems associated with the human form in different environmental and social contexts. If 'sitting' is regarded as a significant activity – perhaps in the sub-contexts of 'working' and 'relaxing' – then some pupils might consider this problem. If in the evolution of the problem they invent the 'stool' or, more likely, varieties of alternative forms for the stool, then they have not only viable end-products but also the results of a creative *design* process that can continue in teaching/learning as a comparative *critical* process. Selection, assessment, critical scrutiny, objective rationalisation and subjective comprehension are all part of the problem.

Individual research, leading from individuated problem-identification to personal solution, is tremendously important in inculcating intellectual and creative courage. In this field of experiment and acquisition of experience with materials and structures the work of the designer is in many respects similar to that of the three-dimensional artist: both must find solutions that incorporate functional efficiency and visual simplicity in aesthetically satisfying structures. However, design is different in one critical respect: many developments with materials can be better carried out by working in groups than by means of the kind of isolated activity *traditionally* (though not necessarily productively) associated with the artist. The majority of people ultimately work in group organisations, yet in both general and specialist education little work has been devoted to this phenomenon.

This, as a field requiring serious research, is second only to the question of developing a machine creativity. Precision of working and of finish are exciting qualities to which most pupils respond, since they seem to reflect the techniques and standards of a desired adult world. Certainly all pupils should have opportunities to work in an industrial idiom, allowing that aesthetic as well as functional ends may be pursued. Some will respond to the powerfully expressive qualities of machine-formed materials. There are those, in fact, who may *only* be able to give full expression to the meticulous care and precision of their ideas through the processes of machine forming.

It is unnecessary, and in any case impossible, to train pupils in all processes: no designer could ever afford the time to become proficient in all those for which he or she will design. The basic convention of teaching – that of demonstration and practice – is also unrealistic for most design-educational purposes. 'Learning by doing', applied to a range of *representative* technologies, is much more advantageous, providing it is sufficiently exploratory and does not devolve into mere exercises. This 'learning by doing' was an important aspect of the Bauhaus at its best, but it should be borne in mind that Bauhaus technologies were elementary as compared with those of today. Using simple diagrams, which initially demonstrate machine principles and which detail aspects of the processes involved, we can expect pupils to be able to design for *sophisticated* machines they have never encountered.

The capacity to think and create across the whole range of possible forms and technologies is imperative for future designers and makers at all levels of origination and production, and sensitivity towards these processes is vital also for the buyers and consumers of their products. All citizens should be able to share a common visual, aesthetic, constructive, functional language – each contributing creatively. A great wealth of new ideas, new forms, new systems and new technologies can flow from this. We can make design education into the life-enhancing force it ought to be, with technology its *creative*, rather than merely *manipulative*, essential discipline.

Chapter Eleven

EILEEN ADAMS Teachers and Architects: Collaboration in Education

Learning to See is the title of a research project, funded by the Royal Fine Art Commission and the Architecture Education Trust. It started in April 1988, and my involvement has been to direct the study, collate its findings and prepare a report to the Secretary of State for Education to aid his deliberations on this area of the curriculum. The research was completed in 1989. The focus of the Project's work in schools, which continues, is on *environmental experience*, which develops:

aesthetic and design awareness;

a feeling response to place;

discriminatory and critical skills (developing capacities for judgement); and

design ability (concerned with shaping the environment and dealing with change).

It is an area which links art, design and environmental concerns, and as such does not always find a ready-made niche in the school timetable. However, as far as the National Curriculum is concerned, it can be incorporated as part of Art and Design, Design and Technology, and Environmental education. But perhaps that would be to deal only with the 'formal' curriculum – what teachers think they are teaching. I would also wish to include consideration of the 'informal' curriculum (what pupils learn from each other) and the 'hidden' curriculum (what they learn from just being in the school environment).

My first experience of environmental work was as an art teacher at Pimlico School 1974–6, working on the *Front Door* project [1]. Many art and design teachers will be familiar with this as having been a pilot scheme where teachers, planners and architects worked together to devise a course of design studies based upon exploration of the local area. Architects and planners view change in positive terms, seeing it as a fact of life to be exploited and controlled. Problems are there to be tackled, to be solved, to be surmounted or ignored. As a teacher I had seen problems as inhibiting factors. However, the architects viewed them not as constraints but as spurs to action; and this attitude deriving from our subject-matter was applied, from the outset, to curriculum reform.

Subsequently I was co-director of the Schools Council curriculum development project *Art and the Built Environment* [2]. This had two main aims: to develop environmental perception through art-based approaches to study; and to develop discriminatory and critical skills in relation to environmental appraisal. I was surprised to find that many teachers did not see the built environment as a marvellous resource, inexhaustible and ever-present, a source of stimulus and excitement to be explored and understood through the eyes of artists, critics and designers. Less still were they prepared to view it in critical or design terms, where pupils were required to make value judgements about environmental quality and, if appropriate, put forward proposals for change. It was not unusual to meet teachers who 'did not believe in the environment' or 'did not have access to an appropriate environment'. Many felt negatively about the man-made environment, preferring, it seemed, the romantic escapism of tree roots and sheep's skulls.

In the early 1970s there was a growing interest in environmental concerns, particularly the urban environment, given greater attention after the publication of the Skeffington Report in 1969 which advocated greater public involvement in the planning process [3]. However, the 'natural' environment was still more favoured in schools as a focus for study. Environmental education in schools was approached from a scientific, geographical, historical, or sociological basis. Teachers engaged in environmental study were content to use the environment as a source of stimulus or reference for observational work. In primary schools, sketches were framed, triple mounted, and hung on the walls, or used as illustrations for project work or creative writing. In secondary schools, sketches and photographs were placed in portfolios as reference material

31 *Art and the Built Environment*. Seven-year-olds at the Alderman Davies School in West Glamorgan made observational studies of the bandstand in a local park. The children's attention was taken by the structure itself, as well as associated natural forms and people. A rumour spread that there were lovers in the park, and they appeared in many drawings.

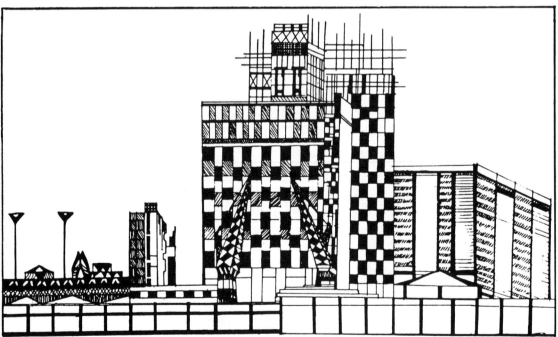

32, 33, 34   *Art and the Built Environment*. Secondary project work, 1979. Analytical and constructed pattern studies of the urban environment: *Battersea Power Station*; *Covent Garden Market*; and *Study of Street Furniture*.

from which expressive work in a variety of media would be developed later on. There was evidence of the environment being used as a stimulus, for reference material, being 'raided' for ideas, with the focus mainly on natural form. Many art teachers assumed that 'environmental study' was the geography or biology teacher's responsibility – indeed, if a post of special responsibility for environmental studies was created, it was usually a geographer or biologist that got it.

Even today environmental education is usually handled by these specialists. It is presented in terms of problems to be solved – pollution; diminishing resources; disappearing wildlife; the exploitation of the Third World; the energy crisis; the disappearing ozone layer; poverty and hunger. The urban environment is treated as a desecration, and the city as anathema rather than the cradle of Western civilization. There is still a need to generate a more positive and creative attitude towards the built environment and to value urban life and urban forms.

During the 1970s the study of architecture in secondary education – where it existed in comparatively few schools – was confined to historical study of the development of architectural styles. Where pupils studied art history, it was likely to be the history of painting. Not all art teachers or advisers were aware that their brief was for art *and* architecture education. Critical studies had not yet acquired its current significance. Teachers tended to see criticism in negative terms: they were uncertain how to handle critical study in relation to the environment, and found it difficult to understand how it might play a part in their teaching. Similarly, design education was seen more and more as the province of the craft and technology teacher, and environmental study played only a small part in their work, although the design examination syllabuses included substantial environmental components. The Royal College of Art study *Design in General Education* [4] revealed that design education in schools was confined to product and graphic design, with the emphasis on making things. There was little evidence of critical study and none at all of environmental design.

The *Front Door* project was set up as an experiment in direct response to these findings. At that time two art inspectors were particularly influential in promoting environmental work in schools: Dan Shannon, through a series of DES (Department of Education and Science) short courses dealing with architecture and planning matters; and Ralph Jeffery, a prime mover in setting up *Art and the Built Environment*. Dan Shannon was particularly interested in bringing teachers into working contact with architects and planners; and Ralph Jeffery had a particular interest in critical study. Various curriculum documents and examination syllabuses seemed to support this area of study which encouraged critical, designerly thinking: yet there was still resistance among teachers to tackling an area of study where they felt a lack of both personal confidence and professional competence. The emphasis in art education was still on expressive work, and the model of the artist was very much to the fore in determining what was taught and how it was taught in relation to environmental work. For many art teachers the experience of their own training – many of them as painters – had a profound effect on their practice, and the challenge of extending this into unfamiliar territory threatened their role identity.

It was very difficult for teachers to adopt different attitudes without stimulus, encouragement and support from outside their number. To provide such a catalyst for change many architects and planners, as environmental designers, were encouraged to work with teachers to develop critical and design aspects of environmental study. Their own work calls for discrimination and judgement in relation to environmental matters and they are constantly concerned with the management of change. Support for the importance of art and design in environmental education and for the involvement of architects and planners was to be found in the DOE (Department of Environment) report *Environmental Education in Urban Areas* [5]:

> Urban environmental education should help people perceive, understand, analyse and finally improve their built environment. It should be centrally concerned with aiding people to participate more effectively in shaping their local environment. It is not a pure subject in its own right, but should draw on environmental aspects of traditional subjects ranging from the natural sciences through geography and history to art, architecture and planning. It should include visual and design components and should involve direct experience as well as academic study [Conclusion 2].

114

The aesthetic and emotional responses formed one of the most important and neglected areas. Our total lack of attention to visual education, to teaching people to see, was reiterated time and again by those interviewed; they found this one of the most worrying features of our education system and one that had disastrous consequences. The fostering of a sense of place and an awareness of roots was seen as particularly vital today when so much experience is second-hand. Pleasure, curiosity and a sense of wonder, where appropriate, should be actively encouraged. [Conclusion 12].

A number of agencies were influential in making such interprofessional collaboration in education possible: European Architectural Heritage Year; the Schools Council; the RIBA (Royal Institute of British Architects); the Royal Town Planning Institute; and the Regional Arts Associations. Architecture workshops and urban studies centres also helped to facilitate this. Many local authority architecture and planning departments made time, information and other resources available to schools to help them develop environmental education. However, art and design departments were not generally at the front of the queue to take advantage of these resources.

There has been the danger that the growing popularity of issue-based learning has tended to emphasise the socio-economic and political reality at the expense of the aesthetic and design concerns, and has neglected the importance of individual perception, the subjective view and the affective response:

> . . . the city as we know it, the soft city of illusion, myth and nightmare is as real, maybe more real, than the hard city one can locate on maps, in statistics, in monographs on urban sociology and architecture [6].

The prevailing emphasis on quantitative analysis has made it very difficult to introduce qualitative studies, emphasising appraisal, valuing and judgement-making. However, environmental quality and environmental impact have now become issues in themselves. Interest in such matters in royal circles, in the media, in the establishment, in government and in bus queues all points to a reawakening of interest in this significant area of our life experience – the environment where we live, work and play; what it looks like; what it feels like; how we are affected by it; and how we affect it. Both Prince Charles and the RIBA at least agree on the need for a more informed and critical public. HMI (Her Majesty's Inspectorate) were saying this years ago:

> . . . the essence of the contribution which art makes here lies in judgement and decision . . . .
>
> . . . the forming and informing of these judgements by practice and enrichment is a principal aim of art in school.
>
> . . . pupils might be expected to have a critical awareness of their environment, its quality and style (or lack of it), of design in the home, of dress and adornment and how things might be improved.

The principal skills developed by the practice of art lie in the

115

wales working party news

West Glamorgan

35, 36 *Art and the Built Environment Bulletins.* Analytical study (Wales) and Critical study (London).

Schools Council Project/Art and the Built Environment
WORKING PARTIES PROJECT
Bulletin 1 — London

ability to communicate visually and the power of discrimination – the recognition that as the Newsom report put it, 'pupils are people who have the capacity to form a right judgement.'

Tradition and precedent is less useful now as a guide in a situation of accelerating change, and therefore there is more need for an enhanced and constructive sense of judgement. Whether we respond for example to new consumer products, to fresh artistic manifestations or changes in the environment with concern, self-confidence and good judgement, or on the contrary, with a vulnerable lack of awareness depends in part on the quality of the educational process [7].

The long-term aim of the *Art and the Built Environment* project was to enable people to take a more creative and participatory stance in shaping their environment in the future. This has now re-emerged as a concern in current DOE initiatives such as the *Estates Action Programme* and the *Community Refurbishment* schemes, where residents are encouraged to take more control in the shaping and management of their surroundings. It has re-emerged in the environmental lobby as a concern for conservation, rehabilitation, renovation and heritage. It has re-emerged in renewed efforts of institutions and pressure groups such as the Royal Fine Art Commission, the Civic Trust, English Heritage, the Royal Academy, the Town and Country Planning Association and the Royal Town Planning Institute to increase levels of interest, understanding and concern in both the professional and lay public. It has re-emerged in government rhetoric as the need for greater personal responsibility for the environment and engagement in citizenship. It has re-emerged as a concern of the media in countless television programmes on inner-city revival, modern architecture and environmental design. It figures in so many competitions and award schemes – the BBC tells us *It's My City*; Kodak calls for *Conservation*; and Shell is urging us towards a *Better Britain*.

So what has all this to do with art and design in the context of environmental education? It has everything to do with it, especially if we have a broad view of our task and we relate it to general education concerns. It has everything to do with developing awareness, understanding and concern for aesthetic and design quality. If we balance the upsurge of public and official interest in environmental matters with the unparalleled attention currently being paid to education, those involved in art and design education need to be aware of the importance of their subject in areas that are currently under close scrutiny. These are: *Aesthetics*, which involves sensory experience, consideration of form and appearance; *Criticism*, which involves making judgements about quality; and *Design*, which involves shaping and controlling the environment. All of these deal with relationships between people and places, which involve emotional significance, symbolic meaning and cultural understanding. All are quite properly the province of the art and design teacher.

Work in schools covers a wide range of concerns. These include developing a greater degree of environmental awareness, building up a vocabulary relating to aesthetic and design experience and, as a result,

118

encouraging an enlarged emotional response to promote a sense of place. Art and design is important here in developing a sense of possession and identity in relation to the environment. It is used as a means of intensifying experience, influencing perception, enabling pupils to reflect upon and rework that experience in order to make sense of it. This work encourages and emphasises critical study, where pupils are helped to form value judgements about quality and to attempt to explain or justify these. It therefore involves the use of both visual language and words. It also initiates design activities, where pupils conceptualise possibilities for change, using imagination and fantasy to create new realities.

Its study methods seek to respond to two questions: How can we extend pupils' environmental experience? And how can we deepen their understanding of the environment? Art and design is used as a means of intensifying experience, concentrating attention, as a means of perception, of analysis, of reflection upon that experience, as a means of reworking that experience in order to understand it. It is used not only to respond to what is there, but to consider what might be, to explore meaning and value, and to involve pupils in the creation of meaning through valuing activities.

These ideas bear close scrutiny, but of course they will be short-lived unless there are attempts to institutionalise them. This has been happening in many ways: through initial teacher education and in-service provisions; through curriculum development initiatives such as inter-professional working parties; and through examination systems – current GCSE and BTEC syllabuses accommodate the work both within and across specific disciplines. But built environment studies must be explicitly acknowledged by, and accommodated within, the National Curriculum. They will feature in at least three areas – not just geography but in art and design and design and technology – and may therefore provide one of the most useful means of connecting subject areas in an educational system newly committed to cross-curricular activities. A key factor in built environment studies is that they are multi-disciplinary.

The demands made on schools far exceed the narrow range of studies they were originally set up to deal with. The need now is to view schools as providing a particular focus for education and teachers as having special responsibilities. But we should understand that other individuals and agencies within the community have important contributions to make. What is lacking is an effective mechanism to permit their involvement, and some means of dealing with this for the foreseeable future.

Architects and teachers working together have provided a variety of models for inter-professional collaboration in education which can possibly be extended to other areas of the curriculum and to wider community involvement. Health education, arts education and links with industry, besides design education, have much to gain from this. Architect-teacher collaboration has exploited community resources and created new ones in establishing new working relations between schools and the communities they serve. It has extended responsibilities for general education from schools to a wider range of agencies and people. This particular collaboration in art and design education can illuminate

119

other forms of inter-professional partnership and has implications for other areas of curriculum development.

However, architect-teacher collaboration must be established carefully and constructively. It is no good *exhorting* schools and teachers to recognise the importance or necessity of built environment studies in schools, attempting to add something else to an already overloaded timetable and imposing an increasing list of demands on the school curriculum. There is nothing to be gained from making teachers feel inadequate, threatening their subject-identity, or presenting architecture as a difficult and mysterious area of understanding. The need is to change public attitudes to the built environment, and towards change, through de-mystification and positive action – to create relationships, systems and strategies to influence attitudes and practices within education. A start has been made: there *are* models of architect-teacher collaboration to follow, demonstrating the contribution art and design can make to environmental education [8].

Architects' involvement in education has enabled teachers to tackle areas of study previously inaccessible to them, and has been particularly influential in encouraging the development of critical and design studies. Architects' *attitudes* to change and dealing with problems mean that they are apt to take a more positive stance than teachers, many of whom see criticism as negative and problems as obstacles. Architects' *experience* of design, designerly thinking and designerly modes of working affect both the content of studies and the methods employed. This has reinforced the model of the teacher as the good learner, who knows the questions to ask and can demonstrate how to learn. Architects' *knowledge* of the environment has created a new vocabulary for many teachers and pupils to describe their experience of townscape and architecture. This has enabled them to deal with the complex sets of relationships between structure, spaces and people, using architects' *expertise* in understanding and analysing built form and space, in devising criteria for judgement, and in dealing with change.

However, there are also potential dangers in architect-teacher collaboration. There is the danger of meddling in a field that is not your own. There is a danger that architects might usurp the teacher's role in the classroom, and create a greater dependency on the involvement of the architect rather than confidence on the part of the teacher to deal with built environment studies. There is a danger of continuing to promote inter-professional collaboration as a series of isolated projects which will not impinge on the system sufficiently to bring about significant change. But the benefits greatly outweigh the drawbacks. Attitudinal change does not come easily from *within* a system but is more likely to come from an *external* agency and requires encouragement and pressure from outside. I can think of no other body better equipped to exert pressure for change in built environment studies in schools than the architectural profession.

It seems obvious that architects have a crucial role, but I am not sure if it is possible to pinpoint motivation, on their part, for involving themselves in general education. Rod Hackney, former President of the RIBA, talks about opening the debate to promote better architecture; developing a more aware, articulate, critical and demanding public so that we can achieve better architectural standards; developing a community-oriented stance, changing roles in the architect-client relationship; and encouraging participation in the design process.

What can be said is that architects have been encouraged to review critically their ideas and their own work in the effort to extend and enrich the educational experience they offer to pupils. They have been obliged to review their professional role through greater access to the lay-person's view of the environment and their work as designers. A greater understanding of the perceptions of non-professionals has enlarged professional concern for the social effects of their work. Each group has become more aware of the constraints and problems with which the other has to deal.

The nature of the relationships established between architects and teachers has varied from single experiences of working together on a course or short programme in school or study centre, to meeting infrequently for discussion on the preparation of teaching materials, to long-term involvement in curriculum groups. Only where there has been long-term commitment, and provision for evaluation and dissemination, has there been a significant influence on educational practice. We might consider the following strategies in an attempt to capitalise further on such efforts:

1 Working contacts

Individual contacts between architects and teachers should continue to be encouraged whenever possible, not just through official projects but through informal contacts, architecture workshops, urban studies centres and community groups.

2 Curriculum development

There is a qualitative difference between curriculum innovation and curriculum development. In the former, excitement and experiment are key elements in initiating new approaches to study. However, curriculum development requires periods of consolidation, reflection and evaluation, leading to dissemination and wider acceptance of novel practices and ideas. The degree of implementation differentiates between innovation and substantive development.

3 Coordination

Individual initiatives and small group efforts are all very well, but a coordinated effort at national level is necessary to legitimise and institutionalise the work in schools. However welcome individual initiatives may be, it has become increasingly evident that a greater degree of communication and collaboration is now necessary between groups to build on the accumulated experience of all those involved in environmental education concerns. There is a variety of agencies involved, each with its

37 *Art and the Built Environment.* Secondary pupils at Priory School, Portsmouth, preparing a design for a play area.

own bias. There needs to be a greater degree of collaboration between them to make the fullest use of limited resources and to develop the work coherently. There is no equivalent in built environment education, for instance, of the nature conservation lobby in education, currently exercising a powerful influence on environmental education in schools.

4 Research in higher education

It is evident that there is a need for a much more vigorous approach to testing and refining the experience thrown up by architect-teacher collaboration. Further thought needs to be given to evaluation programmes and dissemination procedures. This can be done effectively in a higher education base, which can develop a theoretical framework and provide opportunities for critical reflection and the creation of an educational rationale.

5 Teacher training

A more effective use of architects' time than a series of individual contacts in schools is their involvement in initial and in-service training courses for teachers, though it is desirable for architects to have some experience of working in schools if they are to offer appropriate advice. The aims should be to influence teachers' attitudes towards the environment with regard to critical and design studies; and to help them come

122

to grips with methods of learning that will extend their knowledge and deepen their understanding of the environment. The need is to heighten teachers' interest in the environment and motivate them to use it in their teaching.

6 National curriculum

It may well seem that our concerns have been provided for in the National Curriculum. However, policy requirements will need continual monitoring in practice. The requirement for built environment studies may in theory be satisfied in a number of different curriculum areas. This should be accepted as an opportunity for the art and design teacher to make positive contributions across the curriculum in all subject areas concerned with environmental study. The National Curriculum provides a framework but does not specify content. To originate this, teachers will have to engage in curriculum development programmes to confront areas of study beyond their own, and develop appropriate teaching strategies. This is where collaboration between teachers and environmental designers will be of particular value.

7 Local authorities

At local authority level it may not be the question of extra resources that we need to consider, but the better use of what we already have in terms of people, time, information, materials and services. There is a need for greater flexibility and interdepartmental cooperation to provide for a shared concern and a shared responsibility for education.

8 DoE/DES collaboration

The DoE and DES should develop a joint approach to environmental education and work out a coordinated policy to promote long-term research and development.

9 Long-term funding

There is a need to identify and allocate resources to fund long-term development of built environment studies. Relying on small pockets of pump-priming funding for short-term projects is wasteful in terms not only of money, but of experience and expertise that cannot be channelled into long-term development. Urban studies centres and architecture workshops have been inevitable casualties of such funding arrangements.

I return to my very first remarks when I say that these nine points are some of the concerns of the *Learning to See* project. It provides an opportunity to reflect on the experience of sixteen years of development, to document some of the work of teachers involved in built environment studies, to tease out key issues relating to the establishment of this area of study in schools, and to consider how it might be developed in the future. Inter-professional collaboration must surely play a key part.

Notes and References

1 'Front Door Project'. *Bulletin of Environmental Education*, 96, April 1976.
2 ADAMS, E. and C. WARD. 1982. *Art and the Built Environment*. London, Longman.
ADAMS, E. and K. BAYNES. 1982. *Art and the Built Environment: Study Activities*. London, Longman Resources Unit.
ADAMS, E. 1982. *Art and the Built Environment: Working Parties*. London, Longman Resources Unit.
CITY OF BIRMINGHAM POLYTECHNIC. 1983. Two monographs derived from the work of PGCE and DPSE students, Department of Art.
3 SKEFFINGTON REPORT. 1969. *People and Places*. London, HMSO.
4 ROYAL COLLEGE OF ART. 1979. *Design in General Education*. Design Education Unit.
5 HALL, PETER. 1979. *Environmental Education in Urban Areas*. London, DOE.
6 RABAN, JONATHAN. 1974. *Soft City*. London, Hamilton.
7 DES. 1987. *Curriculum 5–16: Discussion Papers*. HMSO.
8 ADAMS, E. 1983. *Teachers, Architects and Planners: Collaboration in Education*. Unpublished MA thesis, Royal College of Art.
ADAMS, E. 1984. 'Curriculum Development in Art and Design Education: a Personal View', in: *Journal of Art and Design Education*, Vol. 3, No. 3, 1984, pp. 333–45.
ADAMS, E., E. BERG and R. MASON. 1986. *Art Education and Environmental Education*. UNESCO/INSEA.

Chapter Twelve

DAVID WILLEY The 'Making' and 'Conceiving' Traditions in Architectural Design Education

In preparing students for the professions there is continual tension between the poles of training and education. Training focuses on the student's acquisition of identifiable skills related to the pursuit of the profession itself. In education general principles are the focus of attention and the intention is to prepare the student to cope with the (probably changing) context in which professional skills have to be exercised.

In architectural design education a second tension can be identified which could be easily confused with or subsumed into the professional dichotomy. This tension arises because architectural designing possesses a critical conceptual component whilst also enjoying a distinctive technological basis. Buildings have to be assembled from a wide range of materials of various properties to resist structural forces, the weather and man's occupation. The acquisition of the detailed knowledge needed to make choices about these technologies can easily be construed as training. Teachers have to resolve how to communicate the conceptual content of architectural design whilst at the same time retaining its technological foundation. This paper will explore connections between the technical and conceptual elements in architectural design and articulate their consequences for design teaching.

Reflecting the division outlined above, architecture can be characterised as two clear and distinct design traditions; building as *concept* and building as *construction*. On the one hand the building is seen as the realisation of a set of ideas about the philosophy of beauty, symbology and the nature of space, human interaction and place. On the other building is an assembly of materials that are jointed, finished and positioned to protect and promote human activity. These traditions can be characterised as the *conceiving* and the *making* traditions. Few architects would dispute the central position which both traditions hold: concepts must be built with care and only appropriate constructions made. However it is very difficult to combine the traditions as co-equal partners as each architect has a natural tendency to be either a conceiver or a maker.

The conceiving tradition has been well documented by and is to some extent the product of historians, whose academic concern is the world of ideas. Schulz articulates this tradition by stating that a building's form manifests its task [1]. He places social, cultural, functional and physical needs at the heart of his theory, and these the form reveals and reflects. Technology exists only to enable the form. It performs no symbolic or generative role in itself. Thus in a work of architecture a design concept is perceived through the clarity of the plan and section of the building.

That clarity is attained through the degree of articulation of the concept in plan and section. The articulation allows the building to be comprehended as a whole and as a collection of related parts. The nature of the relations allows the concept to be expressed. The concept reveals the social, cultural, functional and physical requirements which necessarily created the need to build.

A substantial proportion of the conceiving tradition has also espoused an additional tenet, namely that aesthetic ideas are paramount. Pevsner expresses this view with remarkable clarity in the opening paragraph of his *Outline of European Architecture*.

> A bicycle shed is a building; Lincoln Cathedral is a piece of architecture. Nearly everything that encloses space on a scale sufficient for a human being to move in is a building; the term architecture applies only to those buildings designed with a view to aesthetic appeal [2].

Such a view not only maintains technical issues at the periphery of design as simple enablers of form but also relegates social, physical and functional issues. This antipathy to all but the visual issues is one reason why it is rare to find an architect who encompasses the two traditions. For a conceptual designer, concerned primarily with the aesthetic issues, the sources of form will be found in visual and aesthetic preoccupations rather than in the exploitation of new materials and technologies.

The aesthetic tradition remains active after having come to some prominence in the Post-Modern projects and buildings publicised in the 1970s and early 1980s during the recession in the building industry. The Post-Modern movement has caused a massive shift in emphasis towards the visual appearance of buildings but without providing any theoretical insight as to how that appearance is to be achieved. Peter Eisenman, one of America's leading architects and theorists, was asked at a conference about the art gallery that he designed for Ohio State University. He confessed that he had no idea how it was to be lit, that he did not care about the presentation of the art or the art itself, so long as the art could adapt to his building [3]. A less extreme expression of the aesthetic tradition can be found in the work of Rob Krier where the themes for his work are all derived from aesthetic and cultural concerns. He is devoted to developing the perimeter block, the courtyard house, the urban wall of the street and the square [4].

In the making tradition the building's technological means, its materials, erection and performance, are the focus of attention. They play a dominant role during the process of taking design decisions and will supply themes for the architect's innovative and conceptual contribution. This tradition is not well documented and therefore plays only a minor role in the literature of architectural history and theory [5], although it holds a strong position amongst the general body of practising architects. The use of structure and materials, the building's ability to modify climate and the needs of erection and maintenance are placed at the heart of this theory and the form is the manifestation of the employment of these technologies. Within the making tradition there is also a distinction between architects who see technology essentially as a set of interacting

126

systems and those who perceive it as an assembly of parts. The form may be the result of either the direct satisfaction of technical problems or the enabling of a concept in such a way that all sizes and shapes have been determined for technical reasons.

In traditional forms of construction each element of a building served several functional, technical and symbolic purposes whereas modern construction generally provides elements which all fulfil individual purposes. The traditional load-bearing wall contained both structure, thermal storage and a weathertight skin, whereas in a modern framed structure the weathering skin will not carry any loads or provide any thermal storage. Thus technical requirements and their satisfaction have become more apparent during the twentieth century and have become capable of playing a dominant role in the experiencing of the building.

The making and conceiving traditions should also be seen as responses to two different aspects of the architect's work. The conceiving tradition produces buildings which can be understood by the public (or at least by critics, historians and patrons) as a contribution to a set of developing ideas about the role of buildings in our society. Such an understanding requires no technical knowledge. The ideas with which individual architects are engaging are spread well beyond architects as a group and are shared by a spectrum of society. Thus the conceiving tradition provides the essential link between the architect and the cultural milieu. The making tradition concerns the architect's special means. It focuses on those technical issues in which the architect has specialist skills and knowledge. This knowledge is, by definition, not public or widely shared, and has little to do with public understanding of architecture.

There is, however, a difficulty in sustaining the argument that making is and will always remain the architect's private concern, for over the past century our society has come to value technological advance. The Modern Movement can be characterised as a response to changing technological means and their aesthetic consequences. The Post-Modernist dismissal of the Modern Movement over the last two decades has also seen the dismissal of technology as an issue in much architectural work, and in this sense at least Post-Modernism has lost touch with one of the potent sources in our culture.

Three case studies will be examined which illustrate ways in which technological concerns give rise to building designs. The first is William Henman's Royal Infirmary at Belfast, the second is Mies van der Rohe's Farnsworth House, and the third is the self-build housing at Lewisham designed by Walter Segal.

Throughout the closing decade of the nineteenth century there was a sustained burst of hospital construction activity and a good deal of professional interest was displayed in the design issues raised [6]. William Henman was the first architect successfully to incorporate a mechanical ventilation and humidity control system into a hospital in his design for Birmingham's General Hospital which was completed in 1897 [7]. The overall planning of the building (Fig. 38) followed the conventional pavilion form based on air movement provided by good cross ventilation. A series of ward pavilions were linked by long corridors.

127

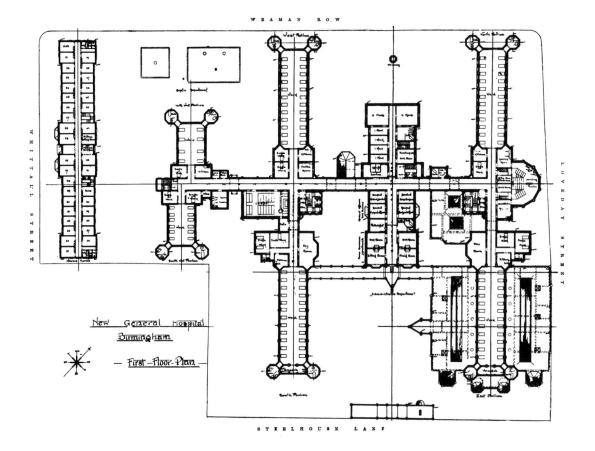

38   WILLIAM HENMAN, *Birmingham General Hospital*, 1897, First Floor Plan. Reproduced by permission of *RIBA Journal*.

There were large windows on both sides of the wards and a space between each ward block sufficient to encourage the free movement of air. With the use of mechanical ventilation it is important to control air movement, so at Birmingham the windows were fixed closed. Henman's design for Belfast Royal Infirmary, completed in 1903, also employed mechanical ventilation and humidity control [8]. However, Henman recognised that the elimination of the need for cross ventilation had also removed the *raison d'etre* for the pavilion plan and he replaced it with a compact plan to minimise both the duct length for the air and the amount of walking about for nurses and doctors. The wards were placed side by side and lit from above (Fig. 39). The conventional pavilion form and Henman's Belfast design share a preoccupation with the supply of clean air: the result is an architectural form based on the resolution of this technical issue.

In the Farnsworth House, designed by Mies van der Rohe and completed in 1950 (Fig. 40), the relationship between technical issues and the design's formulation are much more difficult to decipher [9]. Briefly the building was erected as a weekend cottage for a Chicago academic, Dr Edith Farnsworth, and it was to be occupied in the main by her alone. It was built on the flood plain of the river Fox on a well wooded site. Van der Rohe designed two podiums raised off the ground and the

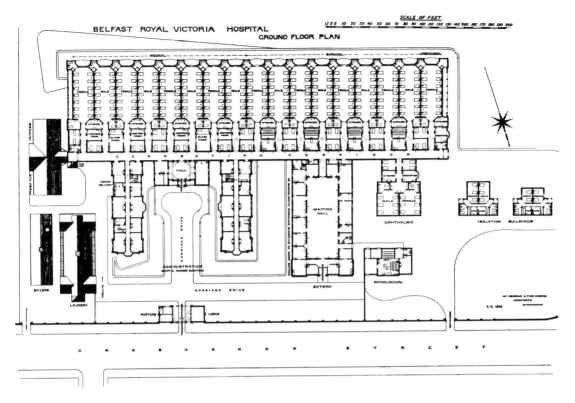

39 WILLIAM HENMAN, *Belfast Royal Victoria Hospital*, 1903, Ground Floor Plan. Reproduced by permission of RIBA *Journal*.

40 MIES VAN DER ROHE, *Farnsworth House*, 1950, Reproduced from *Mies Van der Rohe: The Villas and Country Houses*, New York Museum of Modern Art. © Hedrich Blessing, Chicago

129

higher of these he enclosed with glass plate to create a volume which was divided internally, but not closed off, by a screen of wardrobes and the kitchen, bathrooms and boiler-room. His concern for the correctness and quality of construction of the house ended in a litigious dispute with the client over the building's cost. The construction consisted of a steel framework comprising the plates for floor and roof. The two plates were then supported off the ground by six steel columns plug-welded to the outside edge of the plates. The steelwork was sandblasted to remove any trace of the welding operation and then painted white.

It is not possible to argue that the plan arrangement of the Farnsworth House is a direct response to technical issues. The lack of interruption to space and the diminution of the division between inside and outside space are clearly the most important aspects of this house, and are derived from concepts about the universal nature of space. However, van der Rohe in his work in general attaches enormous importance to the detail of construction. In his buildings, detail transcends any simple desire to realise a concept. Two definitions of architecture which he sometimes employed illustrate his attitude to construction and his building's detailing.

Architecture begins when two bricks are put carefully together.
Architecture is a language having the discipline of a grammar.
Language can be used for normal day-to-day purposes as prose.
And if you are very good you can be a poet [10].

When clear construction is elevated to an exact expression, that is what I call architecture [11].

In both these definitions the making of the building is the starting point, and they are therefore in sharp contrast to Pevsner's aesthetic definition. The definitions do not provide any clue as to what 'carefully' or 'clear' or 'exact' could mean. Van der Rohe evidently believed that his use of the steel frame and glass wall was enough to create a building which represented the epoch: that of mass production, efficiency and precision.

In detailing a building an architect can have at least four concerns: construction processes; weatherproofing; integration (of structure, enclosure and services); appearance. In the Farnsworth House, at least, it would seem that the architect's interest lay mainly in the appearance of the building. The structural frame is white and blemish free. The building's enclosure was not designed to be easily or quickly built as there were almost no tolerances included in the details to accommodate even small errors in the positioning of the columns and mullions. Problems caused by the deflection of structural members under load appear to have been catered for by making those members larger than their direct load-bearing role would have demanded. The final appearance and quality of the house is derived from the choice of materials, their treatment, positioning, and jointing. In the Farnsworth House the construction gives an appearance of great simplicity. That simplicity was achieved through exercising close managerial control of both materials and construction tolerances on the site.

Walter Segal's designs for self-build housing in Lewisham (Fig. 41) represent a third approach to making as the cornerstone of an architec-

41 (*above and below*) WALTER SEGAL, *Self-Build Housing, Lewisham*, 1980. Reproduced by permission of *Architects' Journal*.

tural philosophy. The flat-roofed houses are raised up off the ground by timber frames which rest on small pad foundations. The frame is clad in timber. Segal, in outlining his approach, assumes a technological basis.

> I have been thinking about the ways in which technology and priorities are defined. There is no need to use the complete potential of the Western world in high technology for purposes which can be answered with medium and low technology [12].

> For many years I had the desire to find a way of building which used the products of industry in such a way that the shapes and dimensions that were given to these products were unchanged, in other words, you were using the products in their market sizes, and fitting those into a plan of structure [13].

The simple form and small scale of the Lewisham houses, their capacity for modification and adaptation, the role of the occupiers in building and planning their own homes all demonstrate that Segal's primary concern is not with the appearance of his work but with its effectiveness in securing amenable shelter.

These three examples all focus on technological means as a central concern in creating architecture. Segal in particular was concerned with the simple assembly of his buildings. There is, however, a literature which treats technology as a cultural artefact and the role of architecture as the expression of the cultural significance of that technology. Pawley has argued that architectural history can be viewed as a process of technology transfer in which buildings have embodied and expressed technologies established elsewhere [14]. In this perspective the Modern movement was an expression of the late nineteenth-century technologies of glass, steel and reinforced concrete. Subsequently there should have been further changes; the use of aluminium alloys and monocoque structures following the Second World War and later systems spun off from space exploration. The transfer of these technologies has yet to occur. Pawley does not recognise that during the twentieth century the construction of buildings has ceased to be the culminating achievement of a society. Aircraft construction, space exploration, computing and television for the first time create technologies which have little bearing on buildings and so rob the expression of a building's technological means of its earlier cultural significance.

Building is no longer at the cutting edge of technological developments within our culture. That role belongs to information technology, bioengineering and space exploration. Concorde is a more potent symbol than the Lloyds building. Perhaps in recognition of this, Mateo has argued that technology should not be employed to express technological values but according to its character as a discipline. He hopes then to 'eliminate all fortuitousness in the form and dimensions of objects' [15]. This view seems close to those of Segal and van der Rohe yet still tries to raise technical consideration above the apparently simple issue that a building is made, in time and space, of solid materials. Making should be valued not because it brings a discipline to design or because it symbolises cultural values but because it is *making*. To build well, whether

132

it is a sandcastle or a palace, is necessary and deeply satisfying. It needs no other justification.

The making tradition has rarely figured in the mainstream of architectural debate. Its status in British architectural education has also been far from secure, especially since the decision in 1958 to close the part-time non-degree route to architectural qualification, severing the close link between the student and the ideals and preoccupations of practice. Academic culture has thus become the dominant source of the student's system of values and intentions. Within the constraints of an academic course the conceiving tradition is both easier to teach and to staff. For example it is generally accepted that it is difficult for a career academic to maintain an intimate knowledge of building regulations, fire precautions, innovative materials and new erection techniques without regularly building on a substantial scale. The time needed to design, document and supervise major construction, with all its normal demands and crises, is almost never available to the academic. In addition, or perhaps as a result of these difficulties, the making tradition has been under particular strain as evidenced by an international student competition and the HMI report on *Public Sector Education in Architecture*.

The *Hockney-Caro Gallery* competition which ran during 1985 was open to all architectural students and received 952 entries from 190 Schools of Architecture in 36 different countries. In reviewing its results Farrelly noted: 'The business of lighting, probably the most critical single issue in art gallery design, was all but ignored by the brief and so by most of the students' [16]. It is striking that Madge, in reviewing the same competition, laments that each competition entrant 'allows the scheme to develop from a self-imposed series of arbitrary accidents' [17], but he does not expand on an alternative strategy and fails to mention any technological issues at all.

The competition was set by James Stirling, arguably Britain's leading architect and much involved in museum and gallery design. It may be that competitions are a poor barometer of the state of architectural education as they simply reflect the student culture's view of the assessor's preoccupations. Such a simple dismissal of the results of the competition is not possible, however, when set against the report by HMI on the public sector schools of architecture [18]. (There is no evidence to suggest that the university schools of architecture differ from their public sector counterparts in any substantial way in their ability effectively to teach technical issues.)

The report catalogues the collapse of the making tradition in architectural education. Paragraph fifteen states:

> Collaboration between schools of architecture and related
> disciplines tends to be limited to the occasional special project.
> . . . .There is a tendency in this situation for students to lose
> sight of the technological factors and other specialisms that shape
> and form their work. At one college . . . students were forthright
> in their opinion that their future role would be that of creative
> aesthetic designers with little need for a knowledge of
> technology.

Later, in paragraph nineteen, the report points out:

> The treatment of technology is a controversial and unsettled issue
> in almost all schools . . . there was evidence during the survey
> that an unacceptably high proportion of students pass through
> the courses without acquiring, or being required to demonstrate,
> a knowledge of fundamental principles of building science,
> economics and practical construction technology.

Paragraph twenty-six goes on to show at least part of the reason for the lack of fundamental knowledge when it states:

> Throughout the degree and even to some extent in the diploma
> the schools appear to protect their students from what tutors
> perceive to be the stultifying effects of too early an exposure to a
> realistic consideration of technology and economics in design
> work.

These three comments from the report indicate the seriousness with which the Inspectorate viewed the lack of commitment in the Schools to technological issues.

The Inspectorate would have found support for their view in the preface to Reid's book on the technological basis for building:

> I was asked to give a course of lectures – on fire safety, as it
> happened – at a leading school of architecture in London.
> Discussing the timetable, the tutor in charge of technical teaching
> warned me that technical lectures were poorly attended and not
> compulsory. But it did not matter I was told. Building
> technology was only common sense and did not lend itself to
> formal teaching anyway – far better the student years be left
> unfettered by technology, allowing a freer design expression to
> develop at the drawing board. Anything lacking in technical
> knowledge would soon be made up, once in practice [19].

It appears that many teachers and students have failed to distinguish between the training-education and making-conceiving dichotomies. Thus making is identified with training, and together they are rejected in favour of the long term benefits to be found in engaging with educationally valuable conceptual issues. Or more simply it would appear that most teachers accept that aesthetic considerations should be dominant.

Most schools of architecture in Britain divide their courses between the design studio and lectures, and typically the division results in the students giving their time about equally to the two parts. Technological and cultural studies are usually based on the lecture courses, while the creative and integrative study of design takes place in the studio using a design project as a vehicle. A typical five-year full-time course will begin in the first year studio with simple exercises introducing students to notions of construction, environmental control, function and aesthetics whilst encouraging them to develop graphic skills. This will generally culminate in the third term with the design of a small building such as a house. As students progress through the years of the course they will tackle increasingly complex buildings and the studio projects will also occupy longer time periods. Generally in the third year at least one project takes the whole of one term, the first four or five weeks being devoted to the production of a sketch design to which constructional and other technical studies are applied in the latter half of the term. A student in the fifth and final years will spend at least two terms, possibly three, designing a thesis project where a full range of social, cultural, physical, functional and technical issues are expected to be addressed.

Few courses are consciously designed from the standpoint of either the conceiving or the making traditions. Some courses have been seen as having a technological bias, requiring students to have a science background on entry, and including a large amount of mathematics, structural mechanics, physics and economics in their lecture courses. Other courses are seen as 'design-based' and are focused on the studio portion of the teaching. Applicants for these courses may be asked for a mixture of arts and science subjects in their background and be required to submit a portfolio of artwork before being accepted. However, despite major differences in lecture course content there is little evidence to suggest that either type of course offers significantly different studio design experience.

An important indicator of the distinction between the conceiving and making traditions is the place taken by technical issues in studio projects. In the conceiving tradition technical issues are included in the final stages of a major project to ensure that the design is realisable. In the constructing tradition technical issues will figure as generators of design solutions. The *Hockney-Caro Gallery* competition, with its concern for the dialogue between the abstract and the representational, is a good example of a *conceiving* project. A comparable *constructing* project might be an aeroplane museum, to ensure that issues of large span structure dominate and that parallels between aeroplane and building construction are inevitable.

It could be argued that a healthy school of architecture should encourage both traditions to exist and compete. Students would then be free to choose and develop frameworks, attitudes and theories for themselves. For the schools of architecture the principal problem in shaping a course would be to find a way to sustain both the making and the conceiving traditions. However, it is as difficult for both traditions to be contained in one course as it is for both to be encapsulated within one person.

A *making course* would be characterised initially by studies of comfort conditions with special reference to light and heat, and by an examination of some limited range of materials such as wood, brick, glass, reinforced concrete and steel. Later the implications of choices of technical system would begin to dominate. Those main choices are between structures which are framed or load-bearing, constructions which are lightweight or heavyweight, environmental controls which are energy-consuming or conserving, and building life spans which are short or long. Design techniques would concentrate on realistic model making to emphasise the three-dimensional, constructed nature of architecture. Design projects would always require descriptions of the building at large scales to allow detail to be examined.

A *conceiving course* would be characterised initially by studies of drawing, both freehand and constructed, and of aesthetics: form, mass, space, surface, proportion, contrast, rhythm, texture and colour. Later, the cultural significance of architecture would be developed with theoretical and historical studies aimed to highlight the symbolic role of buildings within our society. Design techniques focus on graphic communication and white cardboard models emphasising conceptual issues and the spatial and formal arrangement of the building. Design projects always require statements of intention and diagrams illustrating principal concepts.

The two traditions do not sit together comfortably. The working methods which have to be employed in each tradition are very different. A conceiving project requires periods of contemplation and reflection early in its development whilst, say, studying precedent, when the student will be sketching and doodling apparently aimlessly. In a making project technical issues will need to be precisely explored graphically at an early stage. In the latter stages a making project will be concerned with large-scale drawings, while a conceiving project will be moving towards high quality rendering of the building in its context. To ask students to switch from one mode of working to another as they move from one project to the next creates discontinuities in their learning, with students having to spend the early part of each project readjusting to the changed methodology and focus of attention. In this situation staff frequently lament that the students are unprepared for the course they are teaching.

Despite the attraction of offering both traditions to students and allowing them to draw their own conclusions, the need to offer a clear and coherent course suggests that one tradition should dominate. Perhaps because of the recent history of schools of architecture, the making tradition demands the central role in architectural education for at least four reasons. First, the making of a building is a necessity for it to become a reality and to demonstrate its qualities. Second, as the Farnsworth House illustrates, to 'make carefully' can transcend 'making real'. Third, a building's form can be derived from a direct response to technological issues, as Henman's work demonstrated. Fourth, making is the architect's particular skill. Placing *making* at the centre of a course will require a number of changes. First, the amount of technical knowledge understood by architectural graduates should be increased. Second, technical issues will need to be placed at the generative heart of projects. Third, teachers in architecture schools will have to shift their perception of their educational aims.

Although this paper has concentrated on two designing traditions and their consequences for architectural design education, the success of a particular course can depend at least as much on its methodological focus as its curriculum content. The course devised and implemented by Mies van der Rohe at the Illinois Institute of Technology, Chicago [20], had a constructing bias. It was also based on a step-by-step approach in which well-understood truth was gradually revealed to the student. Indeed, van der Rohe ended his inaugural address as Director of the Department of Architecture by saying

136

Nothing can express the aim and meaning of our work better
than the profound words of St. Augustine: 'Beauty is the
splendour of Truth'.

This approach can be sharply contrasted with the aims of design
educators who focus on the development of the students' own creativity.
To foster this creativity in students requires that

they do not remain in a closed, familiar labelled world but that
they want to go beyond embeddedness in the familiar and in the
routine, and to relate to another object, or to the same one more
fully, or from another angle, anew, afresh . . . [21].

Creativity in this view is not a question of course content but of course
style. The learning methodology of the course, its openness, its valuing
of the students and their contribution, its commitment to always seeing
things afresh, can be used as the means to support and develop students'
creative and conceptual skills whilst the course content is solidly
grounded on *making*.

Notes and References

1 SCHULZ, C. N. 1963. *Intentions in Architecture*. Allen and Unwin.
2 PEVSNER, N. 1963. *Outline of European Architecture*. Harmondsworth, Penguin, p. 15.
3 BROZEN, K. 1988. 'Performing Architecture', in: *Blueprint*, No. 50, September 1988, pp. 73–4.
4 BERKE, D. and K. FRAMPTON 1982. *Rob Krier: Urban Projects 1968–82*. Institute for Architecture and Urban Studies/Rizzoli International Publications Inc.
5 But see, for example: BANHAM, R. 1960. *Theory and Design in the First Machine Age*. London, Architectural Press. See also: BANHAM, R. 1969. *The Architecture of the Well-Tempered Environment*. London, Architectural Press.
6 See BURRDETT, H. C. 1891. *Hospitals and Asylums of the World*. 5 vols. London, Churchill.
7 HENMAN, W. 1894. 'Hospital Construction', in: *The Builder*, p. 439. HENMAN, W. 1897. 'The Construction of Hospitals', in: *Journal of the Royal Institute of British Architects*, pp. 333–343.
8 HENMAN, W. and H. LEA 1903. 'Royal Victoria Hospital, Belfast: its Initiation, Design and Equipment', in: *Journal of the Royal Institute of British Architects*, pp. 89–113.
   HENMAN, W. 1904. 'The Plenum System of Ventilation', in: *Journal of the Royal Institute of British Architects*, pp. 630–639.
9 FUTAGAWA, Y. 1974. *The Farnsworth House*. Global Architecture 27, Tokyo, A.D.A. Edita.
   LOHAN, D. 1976. *Mies van der Rohe: Farnsworth House*. Global Architecture Detail, Tokyo, A.D.A. Edita.
10 ROHE, M. VAN DER. 1969. *Architectural Record*, September 1969, p. 9.
11 BLASER, W. 1977. *Mies van der Rohe: Principles and School*. Basel, Birkhauser Verlag, p. 15.
12 ELLIS, C. 1980. 'Do-it-Yourself Vernacular', in: *Architects' Journal*, Vol. 172, No. 51, 17 December 1980, pp. 1185–1205.
   ELLIS, C. 1982. 'Segal's First Half Century of Practice', in: *Architects' Journal*, Vol. 175, No. 14, 7 April 1982, pp. 32–36.
13 SEGAL, W. 1982. 'View From A Lifetime', in: *Royal Institute of British Architects Transcripts*, Vol. 1, No. 1, pp. 6–14.
14 PAWLEY, M. 1987. 'Technology Transfer', *Architectural Review*, Vol. 182, No. 1087, September 1987, pp. 30–39.

15   MATEO, J. V. 1986. 'Technics and Projects', in: *Quaderns*, No. 171, October – December 1986, pp. 2–3.

16   FARRELLY, E. M. 1985. 'Take Courage: Stirling Rewards', in: *Architectural Review*, Vol. 178, No. 1061, July 1985, pp. 60–70.

17   MADGE, J. 1985. 'National Character Denied', in: *Journal of the Royal Institute of British Architects*, Vol. 92, No. 9, September 1985, pp. 41–44.

18   DEPARTMENT OF EDUCATION AND SCIENCE. 1985. *Public Sector Education in Architecture*. HMSO.

19   REID, E. 1984. *Understanding Buildings*. London, Longman Scientific and Technical.

20   SWENSON, A. and P. C. CHANG 1980. *Architectural Education at IIT 1938–78*. Chicago, Illinois Institute of Technology. See also BLASER, note 11.

21   SCHACHTEL, E. G. 1959. *Metamorphosis: On the Development of Affect, Perception, Attention, and Memory*. New York, Basic Books, p. 241.

Chapter Thirteen

DAVID YEOMANS Modelling Structural Form in Design Education

'Structures' is a discipline shared by Architecture and Engineering. It is concerned with ensuring that built artefacts have adequate strengths in order to resist the loads that come upon them, and that they are sufficiently stiff so that deflections under those loads will not render them unstable – in other words, it is the discipline that militates against the sudden catastrophic collapse of architectural and engineering structures. For many engineers the problems are well-defined: the forms of their structures will be largely determined by external constraints, and their task will be to produce efficient designs within those constraints. In contrast, the architect manipulates a quite different set of relationships. The form and plan of his or her building are determined by many factors besides the structural, but even so the architect cannot exceed the limitations imposed by structural needs. This clearly requires an understanding of structure, but a different kind of understanding from that of the engineer. The architect does not need the same degree of analytical knowledge, but must understand the relationships between structural and spatial forms.

In teaching engineers the usual practice is to present students with a set of analytical techniques. Comparatively little attention is paid to the means by which the forms which are analysed may be generated. When teaching structures, the training is biased towards the production of stress analysts rather than structural designers. In contrast, the teaching of architects has always been based on developing design skills. Analytical techniques are taught so that students may have the tools by which to 'prove' the validity of their design proposals but this leaves the students with little guidance on how structural forms are developed. Without this the student may be left with an extremely inefficient design process based on little more than trial and error. The designer must, therefore, have some appreciation of the constraints imposed by technical limitations, and develop an ability to take these into account as a part of the design process. Simply concentrating on limitations would be a fairly negative approach, developing a feeling for the restrictions that exist rather than the possibilities that do not yet exist. We should be aiming to develop in the student a feeling for these technical possibilities, enabling him or her to handle them imaginatively in design.

Described here is a model-making exercise that has been used with some success to introduce students to the relationship between structural design and architectural form. This exercise has been developed from an original idea described by Bruce Allsopp [1]. Its purpose is to link the traditional teaching of structural analysis in lectures and the manipulation of structural ideas in the studio design exercises that the students will be tackling later in the course.

Teaching structural analysis

To illustrate the need for such a course one needs to consider the way in which structural analysis is normally taught. In order to analyse the structure of a building to determine its capacity to carry the loads imposed upon it, it must be subdivided into elements which are capable of mathematical description. The simpler the mathematical tools at our disposal, the simpler will be the mathematical model that can be built to describe the structure. A building is therefore divided into walls, columns and beams, each of which is isolated from the elements around it. The loads upon each element are found and its ability to support these loads calculated. A logical and sequential process of analysis follows from this which will be familiar to the practised engineer but which may not be assimilated easily by the architectural student whose acquaintance with complete building is limited.

Classes in structural analysis normally begin with the individual elements, and experience has shown that many students have difficulty in relating these to a complete building – either because they have difficulty in separating the building into its 'constituent parts', or because they cannot visualise the way in which the loads may be transmitted from one part to another within the building. In an existing building this is a problem of analysis, while for a proposed building it is a problem of design. In part, this exercise is an attempt to begin to form those links between the two concerns: with the part and with the whole.

Although exercises may be designed to develop either design or analytical skills, those that are aimed towards design skills, and which are suitable for use early in a course, often use models which make no attempt to resemble real building structures [2]. Instead they are aimed at understanding some fundamental properties of structural behaviour, and they have the distinct disadvantage of an uncertain translation between models and real structures. They may be very useful in developing an understanding of the fundamental behaviour of individual elements, as in the exercises described by Hilson [3]. These models are not built of the same materials as the real structure. It would hardly be useful if they were because the behavioural effects do not scale down easily. For example, Hilson suggests the use of balsa wood and paper to represent a steel plate girder. This is because the buckling characteristics of paper model the buckling characteristics of steel plate sufficiently well to provide a qualitative understanding of the structure.

The exercise described here, however, uses real structures as a basis for teaching in the belief that an important element of structural understanding is a recognition of the behaviour of building materials as well as building structures. This is because the materials of a structure limit the forms that are possible and result in specific sets of relationships between the building and structural form. It is, therefore, an exercise which develops analytical rather than design skills, in that the student must be able to analyse the structures that are being studied. But it is also one which develops an awareness of the relationships that will later be used in design. It is presented to the student in a way that introduces several skills.

Model making

The essence of the exercise is that students are asked to select a building from a given list and to make a model to illustrate its structure. What then is the exercise intended to achieve? A design exercise must address the development of a number of skills at the same time. To illustrate a structure the students must first recognise the tasks that the structure has to perform. At the same time, it would be unrealistic to assume that this is the only skill the exercise develops. There is more to it than just recognising what the loads are and where they act. It must include an appreciation of the way that the plan, and the nature of the spaces required, influence the form of the structure. Secondly, this naturally involves seeing the structure as a three-dimensional whole rather than as a series of two-dimensional components. Thirdly, it means recognising that elements of the structure may be performing more than one task. Fourthly, the students need to be aware that there may be more than one way of providing a structure for any given task, and this implies making a comparison with similar kinds of building. The other side of that coin is that a given structural device may be used in a variety of different situations: the buildings for the exercise should be chosen to bring out these points. Therefore it is useful to see how these issues may appear in different kinds of building.

1 In a simple bridge truss each member serves a single function so that little abstraction is required. Sometimes the structure may itself be an abstraction, as when an arch bridge takes the form of a bending moment diagram (Fig. 42). In structures like this the relationship between structural depth, overall shape and their relation to the load distribution can be discussed together with ideas of structural efficiency and choice

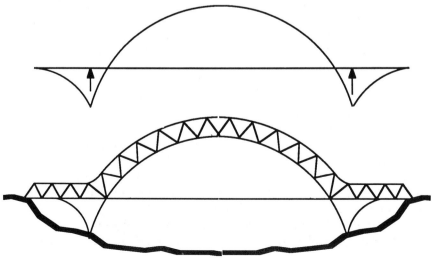

42 Structure as bending moment diagram. (Above) The bending moment diagram for a uniformly distributed load on a simply supported beam with cantilevered ends. (Below) These principles evident in a sketch of the type of arch suspension structure adopted for the Runcorn Bridge, Cheshire.

141

of form within a relatively simple set of functional requirements. A much greater degree of abstraction is needed where structural members act in more than one way. This may occur in buildings which superficially appear quite simple and is dealt with below (point 3).

2 The second requirement of the exercise is that students begin to appreciate the relationship between structure and architectural form. This is associated with the influence of properties of materials upon structure and building form: materials limit the forms that may be built with them. Masonry, for example, is limited to structures which are entirely in compression. This kind of relationship can be illustrated by a simple model of Gothic cathedral structure (Fig. 43). The model comprises a 'kit' of wooden pieces, which may be assembled to represent one bay of the cathedral structure. The pieces are loosely jointed so that loading produces movement in the structure and the structural action can be illustrated. Alternatively, pieces may be omitted to show the nature of the resulting instability. A modular design has been adapted so that a

43 Gothic cathedral structure: model kit.

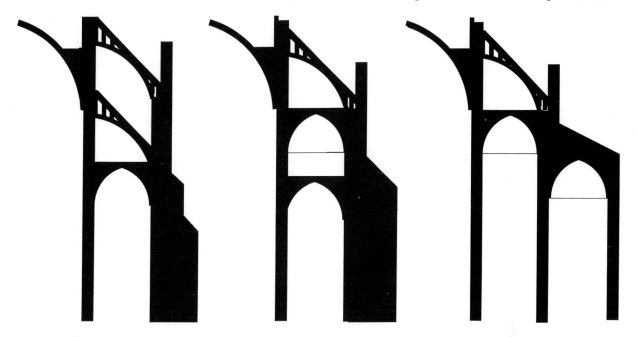

number of different sections may be built, varying in height [4]. By this means it can be shown that: (a) the width of the building must be increased with the height to maintain its stability; and (b) there are alternative ways of achieving this increased width which result in different architectural forms (Fig. 44).

3 While a bridge carries a simple set of loads, and there is usually a clear distinction between the functions of each member, this is not true of many structures. The brick walls of a normal house, for example, act in compression to carry the loads of the floor and roof. They also resist the wind loads on the house by virtue of their in-plane stiffness. One might represent this by a series of vertical members stiffened by diagonal bracing, or by a thin sheet material. In the latter case the resulting model would bear more visual resemblance to a timber-framed wall than to a masonry wall. In this case the model might substitute a series of linear elements for what in practice are solid planes. Note, however, that while all external walls will be providing stability (because wind loads may come from any direction), only one pair of walls may be carrying vertical load because the roof and floors will normally span onto one pair of walls, or possibly an internal wall will be carrying vertical load only and not contributing to the stability of the building.

4 In the simple shed wind resistance may be provided for by diagonal bracing members, which would also be visible once the cladding was removed. It is possible to make a feature of this structural necessity. The *Centre Beaubourg* in Paris has its structure exposed on the outside [5]. The most noticeable component of this may be the vertical columns that carry the weight, but the X-shaped bracing between them that provides stability has been used in every bay. Norman Foster has also used this device on a much more modest building: his earlier factory at Swindon had exposed bracing in this way. But much the same function can be

44 Variations of Gothic structure showing different arrangements of aisle heights and buttressing for the same nave.

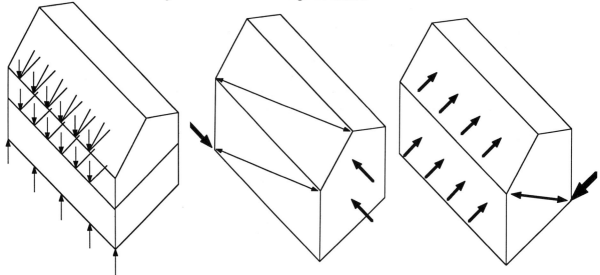

45 A possible structural arrangement for a simple house. (Left) The loads from the roof and floor joists are carried by the front and back walls. (Centre) The same walls resist wind loads on the gable end. (Right) The wind loadings on the roof surfaces and the walls below are transmitted to the ground by the end walls.

served by brickwork – just as in the house, though here the brickwork need not support any vertical load but simply act as wind bracing.

These alternatives show two design possibilities: separation of enclosure (i.e., wall) from structure, or the combination of enclosure and structure in the same element. Even so, the load-bearing structure may be separate from the structure that provides bracing and so give stability to the building. In traditional brick house construction, the walls provide all three functions: enclosure, strength in supporting the floors and roof, and stability in resisting wind loads (Fig. 45).

In order to draw the students' attention to the relationship between structure and architectural form, the building list is divided into groups, each group having variations upon the same basic theme. Students are, therefore, making a choice from within a group of buildings which illustrate a particular structural device or architectural form. Usually the buildings are in groups of three. Students are asked to make a model of one of the buildings in the group, but also to explain how this building differs from the others. These may be chosen to show how the same form can be achieved with quite different structures.

Domes are a good example of this. The *Dome of the Rock*, Jerusalem, originally had a series of timber ribs arranged radially. These were curved to the shape of the dome. A number of eighteenth-century domed buildings also used timber structures, but these were often trusses whose structural shape only loosely followed the external form. The *Radcliffe Camera*, Oxford, is a good example. The dome of *St Paul's*, London, uses a masonry structure, but it is a brick cone and the dome that we see is supported off this on timber false-work. The dome of *St Peter's*, Rome, is a true masonry dome, with a series of iron chains round it to contain the outward thrust. By carrying out this kind of comparison, students begin to see structures within the context of the architectural requirements. More particularly, they see that the relationship between the two is not rigid, but may be manipulated by the designer.

5 The buildings in some groups may have been selected to show a single structural device used in a variety of ways. The dome is also a

useful example here, because it exists both as a structural device and as a visual form. The *Pantheon*, Rome; *Hagia Sophia*, Istanbul and *Perigeaux Cathedral* are all masonry domes but each has come to terms with the structural limitations of the masonry dome in a different way and to cover quite different shapes. A thin shell of unreinforced masonry cannot be used to form a complete hemisphere because only a small part of the hemisphere can be built without the masonry of the shell cracking. The *Pantheon*, however, achieves a hemisphere internally by combining the thin masonry shell with heavy walls, which are corbled out below the springing of the dome proper to complete the desired internal space (Fig. 46).

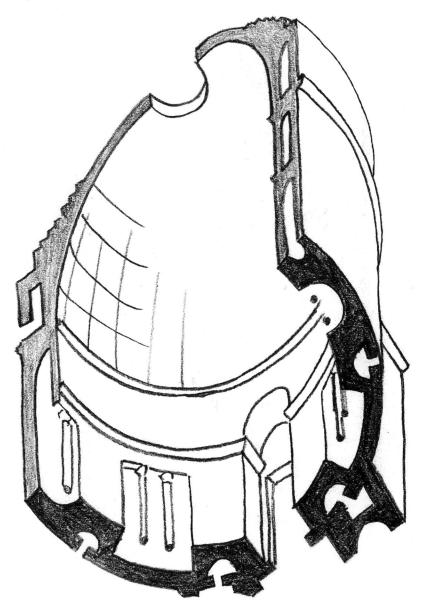

46 *Pantheon*, Rome.
Worm's-eye cut-away
axonometric sketch.

47 *Hagia Sophia,*
Istanbul. Bird's-eye cut-
away isometric sketch.

The walls that support the dome of the *Pantheon* are circular and although some development of the plan is achieved by niches formed in
them they remain, through structural necessity, basically circular. In
Hagia Sophia the circular dome is first carried by pendentives which,
together with the dome, cover a cubic central space and bring the weight
of the dome down to four corner points. The cubic space is then
developed along one axis by carrying the outward thrust of the dome on
a series of semi-domes (Fig. 47).

At *Perigeaux*, a number of domes are arranged to roof the cross-shaped
plan and the structure of the dome itself is far less important as a gen-
erator of space. Instead, the dominant feature of the interior is the
grouping of columns and arches that support the domes (Fig. 48). In
these three buildings the same basic structure has been used to produce
a variety of interior spaces. The differences in structure are in the
arrangements of the supports.

Describing the structure

Students are asked to select a building from a list of examples and to
make a model which illustrates its structure. The examples offered may

48 *Perigeaux Cathedral.* Perspective sketch showing spaces below the domes and pendentives and the supporting columns.

loosely be described as 'historic', but range from Greek temples to concrete cooling towers. References are given to sources which provide the student with basic information on the building and possibly some description of its structural behaviour. The student has to abstract from the overall fabric of the building those elements that are structural, i.e. those elements that are carrying loads. These may be floor loadings, the weight of the roof covering or the horizontal loads caused by the wind. The action of the structural members then has to be illustrated by means of a model which may involve a second stage of abstraction, so that the model which the student makes may bear very little visual resemblance to the original building. When we look at a building the structure is often not apparent and may be only a small and visually insignificant part; and it is this that will be modelled. Sometimes a visually simple form is structurally much more complex, in which case the model will need to reflect this complexity.

147

Some elaboration of this idea is useful: understanding it is an important part of the student's later ability to design successful structures. In a simple steel- or concrete-framed factory shed, the structure is immediately apparent from the inside of the building. Outside all that is seen is the cladding – a skin which, if stripped off, reveals the skeleton underneath. If this were done the result would be a series of columns to support the roof where the structure comprises inclined rafters and horizontal purlins that carry the roofing material. In this case revealing the structure by stripping away the cladding is fairly simple but in most building types it is more difficult. A two-way spanning concrete slab is a good example of visual simplicity disguising structural complexity. It is in effect a grid of intersecting beams and the model will need to demonstrate this.

What methods are appropriate to illustrate the structure if a simple model of the building will not do? In some cases the structure may be apparent in its outward form. While a steel-trussed bridge is a simple display of structure, a model of its visual form would not be a complete explanation. To show the structural action, one might choose to represent tension members by thread, and compression members by some stiff material like balsa wood. A fine explanatory model of the *Forth Bridge* was illustrated in Arthur Mee's *Children's Encyclopaedia*. In this, each of the double cantilevers was represented by a man sitting on a chair supporting heavy weights at arms' length with the aid of wooden struts. Such a model gives an immediate 'feel' for the forces in the structure, which this exercise is intended to develop.

Some students show considerable ingenuity in demonstrating structural action by introducing movement into their models where, for example, the removal of a critical member produces a collapse. The mechanism of collapse thus shows the function of that member. In this way one might demonstrate the function of chains containing the outward thrust of a dome. In a less dramatic form, 'elastic' materials might be incorporated to show the effect of loading upon a structure by displaying large deflections.

It is also important to be aware that the model is an abstraction and that it is being used to explore rather than duplicate the structural behaviour of the building. This should be made clear to the students at an early stage, so that they may be aware of what aspect of the structural behaviour is to be represented. An arch is often represented as an inverted chain, taking a form that depends upon the distribution of the loads supported. In this way the shape of a bridge may reflect the mass of material used in its construction, but it fails to account for the way that the structure responds to the loads that pass across it from time to time. For this an arch of wooden *voussoirs* with curved faces gives a dramatic demonstration (Fig. 49).

Limitations of the exercise

Models are naturally used later in the course as a way of exploring design ideas and sometimes these may be structural models: the above exercise

148

49 Model of arch bridge: the line of thrust must pass through the points of contact of the curved faces.

is therefore a useful introduction to this technique. But there is a difference between an explanatory model and one that may be used for simple analysis.

Therefore one has to guard against giving an impression that the model may be used as an analytical tool. Certainly some models are built for just this purpose, but the design of such models is not an easy task. Antonio Gaudi used models in the design of *Barcelona Cathedral*. Loads representing the weight to be carried were hung on wires, so that the resulting network was a mirror image of the structure to be built. The result is a direct translation of structural forces into building form. Such a method of working may well suit the design of 'thin' structural forms, for example the tent-like structures that have become possible with modern materials. Such a direct connection between modelling and design, however, must always be unusual. More often the model is used as a way of proving the initial design and analysis. The timber hoods on the *Thames Barrier* were designed with the aid of normal methods of structural analysis, although a 1:5 structural model was then built as a check on this and as a way of exploring the method of construction.

In general the design of models as an aid in structural engineering is a difficult task in itself and simple models are unlikely to be good analytical tools because of the distortions caused by changes of scale or means of construction. Robert Mark has carried out a comparative study of the structure of Gothic cathedrals using photo-elastic techniques [6]. This method provides a striking visual display of the stress conditions within the model when it is loaded. It is, therefore, a very attractive method for demonstrations. However, a stone building is not elastic and so its behaviour is not exactly like that of the model. Thus, while the modelling technique may be useful, some care is needed in interpreting the results that it gives.

Construction process

Hilson's experiments, described above, concentrate on the understanding of simple building elements and the way that their design derives from their structural behaviour. While structural behaviour is an important consideration in the design of a complete building and has occupied discussion here so far, the problems of construction are equally important because there are cases where the choice of means of construction affects the choice of structural form. The simple basic structure of the *Forth Bridge* is an example. In bridge design it is clearly desirable to limit the number of footings that have to be built in water. A few large footings are much easier to build than many small ones under such circumstances and this, together with the resulting spans, may suggest the type of structure to be used.

In contrast to the domes discussed earlier, Brunelleschi's dome of *St Maria Del Fiore* is not a hemisphere – either internally or externally. Instead it comprises eight ribs between which are singly curved panels of brickwork and the overall shape is more pointed than a hemisphere. The choice of structure for this building was dependent upon the method of constructing the dome. To have provided a temporary timber centring would have been a major engineering problem in itself: instead of this, Brunelleschi devised a form and a method of construction that dispensed with the need for such a structure. The form of the dome was such that it was self-supporting at all stages during its construction [7].

The limitations of structural materials and the problems of construction may occasionally be demonstrated by a careful choice of modelling material or technique. However, like the Gothic cathedral model, such demonstrations require more sophisticated modelling than can reasonably be expected from students who are trying to understand the basics of structural behaviour. Morever, these influences on the design of the structure may not be apparent. Because they are too important an influence on design to be ignored, even at this stage, their effect needs to be brought out by the teacher during discussion of the student's work.

Secondary lessons

In looking at the structure of the chosen building, the student will be concerned with relationships between the two-dimensional drawings that are the source of information and the three-dimensional model. Plans, sections and elevations will be translated into volumes and this is an important secondary lesson that the programme provides. It is one of the skills that students must continue to develop to which this exercise forms an introduction at an early stage of the course. At the same time, the student should come to realise that structural forces within a three-dimensional form must themselves have a three-dimensional character, but one which is normally represented by two-dimensional diagrams in the structural analysis that they are taught. There is a parallel here between the limitations of conventional architectural drawing as a representation of space and the conventional structural diagram as a representation of structure. These lessons may be conveniently brought out in studio discussions with the students while they are working on their models.

This exercise, as described so far, is concerned with a qualitative understanding of structure, while the purpose of conventional structural analysis is quantitative appraisal. If an aim of the project is to demonstrate a link between analysis and structural forms, then a quantitative element is desirable. It is often not clear to the student that structural analysis is an abstraction; a simplification of the real structure. More important, the degree of abstraction is within the designer's own control and is chosen according to his or her particular needs. All too often students follow a known analytical routine when much simpler techniques would suit their purpose. Moreover, they may be unwilling to attempt a quantitative assessment of their design proposals because they are unaware of simple techniques and daunted by the task of working through the methods they have been taught.

Paradoxically, perhaps, a way of overcoming this is to ask for some quantitative assessment of the student's chosen building. A detailed analysis of the structures involved is well beyond the capacity of the simple analytical techniques which the student will have been taught. However, some simple quantitative analyses can be accomplished using the most elementary analytical tools for even quite complex structures. By setting simple questions, like asking for the force in the buttress of a cathedral building, the student will be attempting to apply common sense in order to use the techniques at his or her disposal. Howard, in a useful book on structural design, shows the value of this approach [8]. He tackles the structural design of a number of buildings; the simplest of which is a single-storey school building with a timber structure, for which he works out the sizes of all the members. His most complex example is the structure of Saarinen's *Foster Dulles Airport*, for which he only works out the major forces in the frame. Howard's essentially simple technique enables architects to prove the overall design form of buildings, whatever their structural scale and complexity.

Discussion

Of all the discussions with the students, the most important takes place during the presentation of the models at the end of the exercise. The most useful way of conducting this is as a whole class event, rather than dividing into smaller groups. This may be more difficult to handle and certainly requires careful preparation by the teacher. Its value is that students, by seeing each other's work, will be introduced to a range of structural techniques and become aware of their architectural possibilities.

The advantage of this exercise over a 'design' exercise is that the teacher will be aware of the relationships that exist and will be able to explore these in questioning the students. One can also see the way that structural ideas are formed by each student. Sometimes these are similar to one's own, sometimes they are wrong and may be corrected, and sometimes they show an imaginative approach that may be illuminating for the teacher. This diversity is also valuable because the student may be shown that there is no single way of approaching an understanding of something. There are many, and it is important to seek the one that is most useful to oneself.

In its presentation this is an analytical exercise, but it analyses a set of relationships that might otherwise be seen separately and whose contribution to design should not be underestimated. Any design actively involves an attempt to predict the performance of the object being designed. At its simplest level, this can be done by trial and error, and research has shown that a good deal of this occurs, even in the work of experienced designers [9]. However, the process is more efficiently carried out if the relationships being manipulated are understood at a more abstract level. The relationships between structural form and stress – and between plan, section and perceived space, which are involved at a secondary level in this exercise – will be developed further elsewhere in the course.

The primary aim for the student, to explore the relationship between architectural form and structure, is a much more complex task. However, its neglect results in a student (and, perhaps, eventually a practising architect) who is unable to foresee the structural implications of design decisions. At a later stage in his or her career, a designer or design student who has not developed this understanding will adapt to the lack, just as one adapts to any other handicap. A common form of adaptation is to rely upon the trial and error technique. In practice this results in an extended dialogue between the architect and his structural engineer, sometimes with considerable distress to both parties. Another form of adaptation is to assume fixed relationships between structure and architectural form. If the relationships were fixed, one might adopt a pedagogic approach to this subject. Sometimes this is done, presumably in the belief that there are fixed relationships that can be taught. My own view, however, is that the vast majority of relationships are not fixed, and must be explored by the designer for each problem. They may best be taught by encouraging the design student to begin this exploration as early as possible.

Notes and References

1 Described at a conference on the teaching of structures in schools of architecture, held at the Institute of Advanced Architectural Studies, York, 1967.
2 Examples of this kind of exercise may be found in: GREEN, P. 1974. *Design Education: Problem Solving and Visual Experience*, London, Batsford, pp. 17–24.
3 HILSON, B. 1972. *Basic Structural Behaviour via Models*. London, Crosby Lockwood.
4 The model described here is a demonstration model designed by the author, and it would be unreasonable to expect a student to devise one with such a

degree of complexity. It is sufficient for the student to be able to appreciate differences between the structure he or she is modelling, and other buildings that depend upon a similar structural principle.

5   For a description and illustration of this building see PIANO, R. and R. ROGERS. 1977. *Centre Beaubourg*. Global Architecture No. 44, Tokyo, ADA Edita.

6   MARK, R. 1972. 'The Structural Analysis of Gothic Cathedrals: a Comparison of Chartres and Bourges', in: *Scientific American* 227, pp. 90–99.

7   MAINSTONE, R. 1969–70 'Brunelleschi's Dome of St. Maria del Fiore and some Related Structures', in: *Transactions of the Newcomen Society* 42, pp. 107–26.

8   HOWARD, H. SEYMOUR. 1966. *Structure: an Architect's Approach*. London, McGraw Hill.

9   WILLEY, D. and D. YEOMANS. 1974. *Monitoring Graphic Techniques in Design*. International Conference on Computers in Engineering and Building Design, Imperial College, London.

Chapter Fourteen

CHRISTOPHER FRAYLING Some Perspectives on the Crafts Revival in the Twentieth Century

In recent years the phrases 'crafted' and 'hand-built' have become absorbed into the language of advertising and packaging, and into popular culture in general, in a particular way. We see these words and the rural imagery usually associated with them all over the place – promoting everything from cars, processed foods, new housing developments and building societies to wristwatches, cigarettes, beers and clothes. The phenomenon has become so widespread that a recent survey of the state of the language devoted a whole section to the word 'crafted' as one of those words in everyday vocabulary which 'beguile as well as inform'. 'When advertising people use "crafted" as a substitute for "manufactured"', the survey went on, 'they are attempting to delude the public into believing that something has been made by hand in a carefully old fashioned way.' The hoardings do not actually say this – they simply smuggle it in. Hence the slogan 'hand-built by robots' and its rival 'more space, more craft', in which the reassuring connotations of 'hand-built' and 'craft' are calculated to offset the less-reassuring connotations of robots and space-age technology.

Craft is trustworthy; microchips are not – at least, not yet. It is as if the advertisers are deliberately creating a confusion between William Morris the artist-craftsman and William Morris the automobile magnate, and in the process selling our own nostalgia back to us at a profit. Perhaps the campaign that has made the fullest use of this strategy is the series of 45-second films promoting Hovis on television. By means of this campaign some mass-produced goods are associated in consumers' minds with brass bands in rural Yorkshire during the early part of this century, bakeries run by early craftsmen and their even more elderly apprentices, technicolour villages of the mind to beguile the supermarket shopper into believing that it is as good today as it has always been. If the strategy works – and it seems to, even if it does create problems when you are trying to launch a new product – it says a lot about the continuing potency of 'craft' as an idea. Assembly lines may be manned by robots. The corner grocery shop may long since have been demolished. Convenience foods may seem too processed for comfort, at least for some of us. But the advertisers can rely on the simple word 'crafted' to relieve for a moment the complex anxieties which these social and economic processes have created.

Of course, the word 'crafted' is not confined to the billboards, and the ad men did not conjure this imagery out of thin air. As a result of the craft revival (so-called) since the mid-1960s, the word can be seen above just about every souvenir shop. At least they *used* to be called souvenir shops, but now they are called craft shops – along the main roads to tourist resorts, or wherever pine is stripped. In other words, it has become a fashion; and all this has been going on at a time when commercial publishing has come to depend on illustrated reprints of nostalgic reminiscences about the rural world we have lost. It is perhaps significant that many of these books, such as Flora Thompson's *Lark Rise to Candleford* and the books of folk songs selected by Vaughan Williams, originally date from the agricultural depression of the 1920s, another period of dislocation. A glance at the best-seller lists shows that this fashion for retrospective regret has been commercially stable over at least the past decade. In books ranging from *The Diary of an Edwardian Lady* to the *AA Book of British Villages* we have been offered the countryside of the pre-First World War as static object to be viewed through a car window – disconnected and gift-wrapped bits of a previous culture. When they were written, the books by Flora Thompson and the Edwardian Lady represented a continuity of experience from the 1880s through to the 1920s. Today they do not. Nostalgia, it seems, is not what it used to be – even if it *looks* just as authentic as the BBC 2 classic serials.

Perhaps the best example of the way in which the fashion for what the French call *Le Mode Retro* can distort the history it is exploiting is the pervasive use of the Saxony spinning wheel as a key symbol of the domestic crafts. This symbol can be seen in the windows of most 'craft' shops. Victorian photographs and watercolours of spinning wheels in drawing rooms, or of young ladies engaging in a spot of home spinning, appear to reinforce the association. No-one seems to have noticed, or no-one wants to notice, that it is rather odd for a late fifteenth-century piece of technology to be in general domestic use in the mid-nineteenth century at a time when spinning machines – starting with Hargreaves's jenny, Arkwright's wheel and Crompton's mule – had been around for about seventy years, and when the skilled handicraft end of the trade used the great wheel rather than the Saxony wheel. It is odd but quite explicable when we think of the Saxony wheel as a piece of furniture rather than as a piece of technology: a great wheel would have looked distinctly odd in a Victorian drawing room. It is further explained by recalling that the fashion for home spinning in Victorian times had much more to do with the desire of second-generation industrialists to pretend their wealth had nothing to do with industry, than (except in a few isolated cases) with the genuine survival of a craft. So the Victorian spinning wheel, about which we are encouraged to be so nostalgic, was to a large extent nostalgic in the first place, a symbol of status rather than of craft survival.

Now such popular images of craft and workmanship – from 'hand-built by robots' to the spinning wheel – may seem very remote from the world of the craft teacher or indeed from the world of the practising artist craftsman. However, I believe that sensible arguments in support of the crafts in education and society – arguments for the benefit of

educators, civil servants, grant givers of all description, and society at
large – are in danger of being confused with less sensible arguments,
based as they are on a mixture of sentiment, bad history, and a
misunderstanding of the Arts and Crafts movement. And it is of crucial
importance to separate the two. There *are* hard-edged arguments at our
disposal, but it is not always easy to dismiss the popular connotations of
the crafts. We have to live with them: the crafts as folksy, alternative,
rural occupations associated with a homecoming vision of the future via
Schumacher and Illich, and associated with a nostalgia masquerading as
history. For these connotations represent the most powerful perspective
on craft in the late twentieth century that there is, backed as it is by
advertising, commercial publishing, the record industry, and even some
colleges of art and design where, regrettably, the look of the Arts and
Crafts movement has been made orthodox while its social philosophy has
been abandoned.

   I shall not presume to look at the craft revival in terms of educational
theory because I think Robert Witkin, in his *Intelligence of Feeling*, has
already developed a persuasive defence of the role of craft, as opposed
to art, education in the development of what he calls 'the inner world of
sensations and feelings', and in particular the crucial role of *action* in an
individual child's balanced development. Witkin's conclusion is that
since most of the children covered by his pioneering survey wanted to
be free to express themselves *and* to work within reassuring guidelines
at the same time, and since they were lukewarm in their response to art
classes as being too free of rules to meet these objectives, the craft subjects represent the best available means of developing the intelligence of
feeling [1]. His conclusion does not need restating here, but one of
Witkin's philosophical distinctions does lead directly to my first perspective on craft: it is a distinction between types of knowing. Perhaps the
best way of introducing this distinction is to re-tell a famous story and
to add a gloss on it provided by a distinguished American psychologist.
It is entitled 'Never know when it might come in useful', and I think it
is from the ancient Persian:

> Nasrudin sometimes took people for trips in his boat. One day a
> pedagogue hired him to ferry him across a wide river. As soon as
> they were afloat the scholar asked whether it was going to be
> rough. "Don't ask me nothing about it" said Nasrudin. "Have
> you never studied grammar?" "No". "In that case, half your
> life has been wasted". Nasrudin said nothing. Soon a terrible
> storm blew up. Nasrudin's crazy cockleshell was filling with
> water. He leaned over towards his companion. "Have you ever
> learned to swim?" "No" said the pedant. "In that case,
> schoolmaster, *all* your life has been wasted for we are sinking".

As Ornstein notes in *The Psychology of Consciousness*:

> The two characters in this story represent two major modes of
> consciousness. The verbal rational mode is portrayed by the
> pedagogue who's involved in and insists on neat and tidy
> perfection. The other mode is represented by the skill of
> swimming, which involves movement of the body in space, a

156

mode often devalued by the neat rational mind of the pedagogue. On one level these two characters represent different types of people. The verbal logical grammarian can also be the scientist, the logician, the mathematician who is committed to reason and correct proof. The boatman, ungraceful and untutored in formal terms, represents the craftsman, the dancer, the dreamer whose output is often unsatisfactory to the purely rational mind [2].

Now this distinction between the pedagogue and the boatman has been formulated in many different ways. Sometimes it has been a hard and fast distinction between knowing how and knowing what, between knowing how to do something and knowing some information. Sometimes it has been presented as part of a continuing process which encompasses a whole spectrum – knowing what, knowing who, knowing when, knowing where, knowing why and knowing how. Sociologists distinguish between formal knowledge and tacit knowledge, the kind that can be found in books and is easily articulable, and the kind that cannot since it can never be articulated in verbal terms. The best example of this, which sociologists always use, is from Wittgenstein's description of people learning algebra, where he says that a person coming out of an algebra class can say 'I learnt how to do equations . . . you cancel one side and then you cancel the other'. But what the person cannot say is that the equation was written on the blackboard, that it was written with chalk, that it means the same thing whether it was written with chalk or biro, and so on. In other words, *all* things that he takes for granted about the lesson in algebra he cannot really articulate because he cannot ever recall in words everything about what happened when he learnt something. The distinction is, of course, between the formal knowledge that is the algebraic equation and the tacit knowledge that is all the things that a person has experienced in the classroom by being socialised into the idea of being taught. It is a distinction which runs right through modern sociology and anthropology.

Design theorists distinguish between recipe knowledge, where an individual can never be sure of the outcome each time he or she acts upon it, and knowledge of principles, where it is assumed that individuals and even groups *can* be sure of outcomes. Philosophers distinguish between knowledge and know-how, and this distinction has led to a battle royal in the world of design theory, between those who reckon that you can and should reduce the contents of George Sturt's classic book *The Wheelwright's Shop* [3] to a set of abstract and logical design principles, those who reckon you cannot and should not, and those who reckon there is nothing to be gained by trying. But the distinction between knowledge and know-how was perhaps most forcefully expressed by the philosopher Michael Oakeshott. Oakeshott expressed the fear that the educational system was becoming too geared to the transmission of what he called 'formal knowledge'. It was downgrading know-how at its peril – not because this could be directly linked to vocational training, which is the standard argument, but because it represented a way of knowing which was the most important for getting around in the world. He did not present his argument in terms of education *versus* training, but rather as education *through* training. Here is a characteristic example quoted from Oakeshott's *Rational Conduct*:

> Doing anything both depends upon and exhibits knowing how to do it and though part but never the whole of knowing how to do it can subsequently be reduced to knowledge in the form of rules and principles, these propositions are neither the spring of the activity nor are they in any direct sense regulators of the activity. The characteristic of the carpenter in the ordinary conduct of life and his relations with other people and with the world is a knowledge not of certain propositions about himself, his tools and the materials in which he works, but the knowledge of how to decide certain questions and this knowledge is a condition of the exercise of the power to construct propositions after the event. Consequently if rationality is to represent a desirable quality in an activity it cannot be the quality of having independently premeditated propositions about the activity before it actually begins. There is in fact no way of determining an end for activity in advance of the activity itself and if there were, the spring of activity would still remain in knowing how to act in pursuit of that end and not in the mere fact of having formulated an end to pursue. A cook, for example, is not a man who first has a vision of a pie and then tries to make it. He's a man skilled in cookery and both his projects and his achievements spring from that skill. Nevertheless we may be agreed that it is preposterous to suppose an activity can spring from the premeditation of propositions about the activity but we are still apt to believe that in order to teach an activity, it is necessary to have converted our knowledge of it into a set of propositions: the grammar of a language; the rules of research; the principles of experiment; the canons of good workmanship – and that in order to learn an activity we should begin with such propositions. It would be foolish, of course, to deny that this device has an educational value but it must be observed that not only are these rules an abridgement of the teacher's concrete knowledge of the activity and therefore after the activity itself, but learning them is never more than the meanest part of education in an activity. *They can be taught but they are not the only things that can be learnt from the teacher.* To work alongside a practised craftsman is an opportunity not only to learn the rules but to acquire also a direct knowledge of how he sets about his business and among other things a knowledge of how and when to apply the rules; and until this is acquired nothing of great value has been learned at all. But it is only when we think of this as of no account in comparison with the learning of the rules themselves or when we reject it as not teaching in the proper sense or not properly knowledge, that the character of learning an activity seems to support the view that activity itself can spring from independently premeditated propositions about it [4].

The point seems to be a crucial one in terms of marshalling arguments about the crafts because this quotation neatly – some would say too neatly – states the knowledge/know-how distinction and it flies in the face of much modern educational theory, to say nothing of some contemporary practice in the art and craft world. The argument, part of a sustained explanation of what the concept of rationality means in everyday life, progresses along the following lines. I have adapted Oakeshott's examples to suit the case of a craftsman working in wood.

A: The activity of doing something (for example, making a piece of furniture) clearly supposes a certain know-how and this know-how may be organised as a set of formal rules after the event, but the formal rules should never be confused with the activity itself. Craftsmen may impose a certain order on the design, on the various stages through which a piece of work went, as they later reminisce about the making process: to put this another way, they may postrationalise the process. But the know-how which went into the making process at the time can never be successfully transmitted in this verbal way. It is a little like Wittgenstein and algebra.

B: The craft activity and the relationship between the craftsman and his world do not in any sense depend primarily on knowledge of these formal rules (of the kind that *Do-It-Yourself* manuals represent) or even on formal knowledge about the craftsmen's tools and materials (of the kind that dictionaries of tools and guides to technologies represent) but rather on what Oakeshott calls 'knowledge of how to decide certain questions'. Until the problems arise (they may, for example, be new to the craftsman) the skilled person cannot necessarily articulate how he would go about resolving them. Again formal rules, which can be applied to all eventualities, should not be confused with the know-how which can only express itself in the process of resolving those problems that arise during the actual making.

C: The rationality of an activity has very little to do with thoughts about that activity conceived before it commences. This is where Oakeshott gets onto tricky ground. He is saying that theorising about an activity before or after the event is not the same as finding a rationale for it (although it may be the same as persuading someone to give you a grant for it, but that is not the same thing). Such a rationale arises from the activity itself; for example, the end of the activity, or the goal in view, may change during the process. The real spring of activity remains knowing how to handle problems as they arise.

D: To adapt the example cited, a furniture maker is not a man who first has a complete vision of a chair or table in a vacuum – some designer-craftsmen may disagree with this – and then tries to make it. He is a man skilled in furniture making and both his projects and his achievements spring from that skill.

E: Even if we accept the argument so far (and it has to be admitted that Oakeshott expresses it in an extreme way) we may still hold to the view that the only way to teach carpentry, assuming we have experience ourselves, is to convert our experience into formal knowledge which is transmittable. It is easier, accessible, knowable. Oakeshott includes as an example of this knowledge the canons of good workmanship or the principles and grammar of craftsmanship, things that could be found in a craft manual or even in a specialised commentary such as David Pye's *Nature and Art of Workmanship* [5]. This formal knowledge may have some educational use if it provides a context for the activity, he says, but — and this is crucial – it also represents a post-rationalisation on the part of the teacher, an abridgement of his or her concrete knowledge, and it can contribute no more than the most basic, meanest part of an education in carpentry. It has the advantage of being teachable but, as Oakeshott neatly puts it, other things can also be learned from the teacher even if they cannot be formally taught.

F: And finally, how can aspects of the activity itself be transmitted? Oakeshott's answer is very clear: through observing, working side by side with, and participating in the life of, a skilled craftsman who is also a sensitive teacher. In this way the apprentice or pupil has the opportunity not only to grasp the formal rules but also to acquire a knowledge of how the craftsman works, of his know-how. Only then can things of value be learned about. Yet such a mode of teaching by example plus practice is often downgraded, says Oakeshott (and he first wrote this in the 1940s), while the learning of formal rules by heart is promoted as the proper way.

Now Oakeshott's argument is radical in its implications even today, and perhaps because of this it has a slight 'either/or' feel to it which some philosophers and educationalists would wish to reject. After all, the brain controls the hand, so it is dangerous to move even a small way towards restating the age-old 'mental/manual' distinction in a clear-cut way. But Oakeshott does not actually fall into this trap since his argument centres on the implication that the craft activity *is a form of knowledge* and it stands as the most clearly stated challenge to those who would wish to turn craft education towards more formal types of knowledge. The pressure was there when Oakeshott was writing, and many would agree that it is there today. So the argument is still valid as a source of stimulus to thought and debate, particularly among craft teachers and practising craftsmen, and as an important contribution to a contemporary philosophy of knowledge. This, then is my first major perspective on craft.

My second one arises out of the first, and relates to the thorny question: What is a skill? Most writings on craftsmanship, Oakeshott's included, make huge assumptions about the importance of skill, but there seems to be no general agreement about what the word actually means. Does it refer to manual dexterity, craft experience, conceptual activity, general know-how, or a shifting combination of these four? If the word means something different in each different kind of work, as some people have said, are any generalisations about skill possible? This is not just an academic question, for in the end most arguments about the crafts, in social terms at any rate, boil down to the value we attach to the exercise of what are known as 'certain skills'. Since practising artist-craftsmen are by no means agreed about this, some of them rejecting or downgrading manual skill or technique as a component in their creative work as artists, it is important that we try to find some common

160

ground. Otherwise, it is possible that the art and craft world will increasingly cut loose from the assumptions which lie at the root of the crafts in education – assumptions about the coordination of perceptual and motor activity, or, to put this another way, of intellectual and manual work. I mean if an artist-craftsman who believes that his art has little or nothing to do with technical skill visits a school workshop, what exactly will be the benefit of his teaching by example? He may encourage children in their ambitions to be artist superstars, but that is surely not the point. As David Pye has said, in recent years 'skill' has become a word to start an argument with.

It may be necessary to re-examine the analysis by John Ruskin, William Morris and others of the degradation of work *in general* in the late nineteenth century, a tendency that has become known as 'de-skilling', in order to find a more hard-edged use for the concept of skill in today's complex art and craft world. After all, the invention of the artist-craftsman or the fine art workman was indirectly based on Ruskin's and Morris's analysis of skill. Indeed it was intended to be a response to it, so if there is any common ground perhaps it will emerge from the same sources. On the face of it, the Arts and Crafts line on de-skilling in society at large remains persuasive. If we place a plate from Diderot's famous *Encyclopédie* published in the mid-eighteenth century (a picture of a small-scale manufactory) side by side with a late nineteenth century print (of a large machine-factory) the main difference is striking and obvious. In the former the worker's relationship to the equipment is that of a musician to a musical instrument: in the latter the worker's relationship to the machine is that of a cog or lever.

Our eighteenth-century example is of a pin factory (Fig. 50), and it is of some interest because Adam Smith used the example of a pin factory nearly twenty years later, in *The Wealth of Nations*, to illustrate his point about the division of labour required to produce an object as simple as a pin. If we look at the relationship of the figures to the equipment they are using, in the pin factory, they are involved and participating in the equipment – *even in the classic example of the division of labour*. And if we then look at the print of a hundred years later – of a vertical planing machine from the Soho Foundry in the 1860s (Fig. 51) – we can see that the relationship of the man to his machine is that of a working part. He

50   *The Pin Factory*: from the 'Manufacturing Processes' section of DIDEROT and ALEMBERT (eds) (1751–1780) *Encyclopédie, ou Dictionnaire Raisonné des Sciences, des Arts et des Métiers.*

51   *A Machine Minder*: late nineteenth-century print of an operative at the Soho Iron Works (artist unknown).

stands alone, attending to it. The division of labour has developed since the days of the pin factory, and a new component has been added in the form of *automation*. Whereas the pin makers exercised some control over the stage of the pin-making process for which they were responsible, the machine-minder has no control at all. And it is not just a question of 'machines' versus 'people', as some intellectual Luddites have suggested: it is more a question of *the ways in which the machines are used*, and of *the context for their use*.

The point is that if we read accounts of the traditional crafts at the time of the Industrial Revolution and compare them with accounts of similar activities written a hundred years later, the contrast seems to tell us a lot about the degradation of work which happened in the interim. The eighteenth-century craftsmen, as one commentator has said, were not on the whole the unlettered tinkers of historical mythology.

> Even the ordinary millwright was usually a fair arithmetician, knew something of geometry, levelling and measuring and in some cases possessed a very competent knowledge of practical mathematics. He could calculate the velocities, strength and power of machines and could draw in plan and section [6].

By the end of the nineteenth century, however, or so the analysis of Ruskin and Morris goes, the separation of this kind of craft knowledge from craft skill was complete in most areas contributing significantly to the economy. Some contemporary, articulate critics of this separation thought they were clear as to the reasons why.

Here is one critic of the 1890s, writing about the de-skilling tendency in the *International Moulders' Journal*:

> We think of craftsmanship ordinarily as the ability to manipulate skilfully the tools and materials of a craft or trade but true craftsmanship is much more than this. The really essential

162

element in it is not manual skill and dexterity but something stored up in the mind of the worker. This something is partly the intimate knowledge of the character and uses of the tools, materials and processes of the craft which tradition has given the worker but beyond this and above this, it is the knowledge which enables him to understand and overcome the constantly arising difficulties that grow out of variations, not only in tools and materials but in the conditions under which the work must be done.

Instead of this combination of knowledge and dexterity, the craftsman in industry is faced with the gathering up of all this scattered craft knowledge, systematising it and concentrating it in the hands of the employer and then doling it out again only in the form of minute instructions on how to be a machine minder, giving to each worker only the knowledge needed for the performance of a particular, relatively minute task. This process, it is evident, separates skill and knowledge even in their narrow relationship and when it is completed the worker is no longer a craftsman in any sense, but is an animated tool [7].

This is a very powerful thesis and, it seems to me, the foundation of much that Ruskin and Morris wrote about – in particular the role of the crafts in society as an antidote to this tendency. However, there are, I think, problems with this 'de-skilling' thesis as an explanation of what had happened since the days of our ordinary millwright. But they are problems that can get us closer to agreeing what a skill really is. First of all, the thesis is based on a somewhat static notion of skill. According to Ruskin and Morris and many other subsequent writers about the degradation of work, skills are always lost forever rather than redistributed or reformed. I return to this point shortly. Second, the thesis depends on the rather sentimental assumption that a whole range of pre-industrial activities like plain hand-loom weaving, the most famous example, were once highly skilled, when in fact some of them appear to have been almost as mechanical as the semi-automated activities which succeeded them. This assumption can all too easily lead on to what I call the 'myth of the happy artisan', and to the image of good honest work as something done by 'tidied up, pre-Raphaelite varieties of craftsmen', in Gordon Russell's words.

Third, the thesis boldly contrasts something called 'craft' with something called 'industry' and tends to assume that more activities were highly automated in England than was in fact the case. Just after William Morris's death, the only areas which fitted this description – of machine-minders who had been utterly 'de–skilled' – were large corporations producing soap, chemicals, foodstuffs, and textiles (Karl Marx's favourite example). Most current research into this history seems to be proving that hand-work and mass-production industries existed side by side into the late nineteenth century, and that the specifically English experience of industrialisation involved a close interaction of the two. So it was not simply a matter of industry taking over from craft, but of craft *within* industry – steam technology; hand work – throughout the nineteenth century. When Ruskin and Morris evolved their famous images of automated factory work in Victorian England they may have been responding to what political economists of the day *thought* was going on, rather than to a widespread development in the real world.

Finally, and above all, the thesis does not sufficiently emphasise what may well have been the most important consideration for pre-industrial craftsmen – like the millwright or the hand-loom weaver – fighting for the status of a way of life: that is, *retaining control at the point of production.* If we add a 'high discretion content' to the usual definition of skill as a combination of knowledge and dexterity, then we may have found one of the reasons why so many people were so keen, at the turn of the century, to defend what were in today's terms unskilled occupations at the time of the Industrial Revolution. It was not necessarily a matter of protecting skills, as Morris thought, but rather of protecting the measure of control the craftsman exercised over his work – in his own time, to his own pace, perhaps with his own machinery. No-one can ever agree about what the components of skill are because clearly all skills are different. If we extend the concept to *the circumstances which make possible any skilled activity*, we can find much use for the de-skilling thesis in the present. For although today's various types of craftsmen may argue for ever about the process itself (does skill involve mental or manual dexterity, or both?) they all seem to have a common, strong belief in the importance of controlling every aspect of the work they do. And there is no need to bring nostalgia into the picture at all.

If we go further and relate this issue of *control* to the role of tomorrow's craftsmen in society, we can see why it is so crucial to abandon the rather static notion of skill held by the Arts and Crafts people. For it will be possible in the near future for whole industries to be made up of small interconnected workshops, each in specialised areas, each allowing for a large measure of control at the point of production within each unit, together catering for a market which wants well-made and customised products rather than badly made identical ones. The centre for such production in the mid-1980s has been in 'the middle Italy'. Emilia, Romana, Tuscany, Umbria and the three Venetian provinces, a region which is sharply contrasted with, on the one hand, the industrial north of Italy – Milan, Turin and Genoa (where cars are hand-built by robots) – and, on the other hand, the agricultural south where the traditional rural crafts still have important parts to play.

Here in 'the middle Italy', in small workshop-based activities, there are craft industries as diverse as shoes, ceramic tiles, textiles and furniture. In these a huge variety of craft goods is produced through the cooperation of networks of small firms each employing around ten craftsmen. The thing that has made this possible is the development of numerically controlled machine tools or robots – but robots harnessed to the ever-changing needs of small batch or short run production. These small interconnected firms have proved themselves relatively immune to economic crises of over-production at a time when large, inflexible, highly automated, de-skilled firms are going to the wall. By any definition this success is related to skilled craftsmanship; so it may not be a question in the near future of 'industry versus craft' but of 'craft with industry', of a product hand-built with just a little assistance from robots.

My analysis of skill and of the de-skilling thesis may not be satisfactory to all, but it certainly leads – without recourse to nostalgia or sentimentality – towards hard-edged arguments encompassing both the artist-craftsman, who makes unique artefacts and has the opportunity to make them better than ever before, and the craftsman who is involved in batch production. This analysis stresses the pragmatic questions of *control* and the ever-present need for flexible, transferable skills in a context which *allows* for controls. With the intention of stimulating debate, I have tried in this chapter to deal with the implications of just two of the key arguments which craft teachers, administrators, practising craftsmen, and researchers have at their disposal, revolving around the apparently simple concepts of 'skill' and 'know-how'.

It is important – in our battle with the stereotypes imposed by the mass media, with which I started – to set the record straight about the history of the crafts, a much neglected area. Some research is being done, for example by the *History Workshop* group in Oxford, into historical alternatives to mass-production, and this research has already provided the materials with which to challenge the textbook accounts of 'craft versus mass-production'. There is also the *Crafts Study Centre* in Bath which continues to build up an archive of written records and three-dimensional objects with an emphasis on the process or activity of craftsmanship (and which now helps to produce the journal *Craft History*). To return to my opening subject of car manufacture 'hand-built by robots': the latest researches show that the British car industry, unlike its American counterpart, continued right until the 1920s to rely on external supplies of components made by small craft workshops all over the country. Only then did large firms begin to swallow up the small workshops (such as George Sturt's wheelwright's shop in Farnham which had been transformed into a components craft workshop for the car industry). So perhaps the other William Morris (Lord Nuffield) was not quite such a destroyer of craft skills as the textbooks say. We need to re-write the history of 'the craft system' and 'the industrial system'.

Notes and References

1 WITKIN, ROBERT. 1974. *The Intelligence of Feeling*. Exeter University Press.
2 ORNSTEIN, ROBERT. 1972. *The Psychology of Consciousness*. New York, San Francisco, Freeman.
3 STURT, GEORGE. 1923. *The Wheelwright's Shop*. Cambridge University Press.
4 OAKESHOTT, MICHAEL. 1967. *Rationalism in Politics and other essays*. London, Methuen.
5 PYE, DAVID. 1968. *The Nature and Art of Workmanship*. Cambridge University Press.
6 Cited in LANDERS, DAVID. 1969. *The Unbound Prometheus*. Cambridge University Press.
7 Cited in BRAVERMAN, HARRY. 1974. *Labour and Monopoly Capital*. Monthly Review Press. (This is an excellent, if extreme, statement of the 'de-skilling' thesis, as it applies to the American experience, in long-term historical perspective.)

Chapter Fifteen

MICHAEL YEOMANS The Future of Design in Further and Higher Education

Depending on one's point of view, design education can be Pandora's box or a cornucopia. Not wishing to damage my eyesight further, I will focus more on the horn of plenty. Without a sense of optimism discussion of this subject could easily lead to a rehearsal of current woe. Endless complaints of cutbacks in staffing, finance and accommodation may do no more than identify those academics who claim to be designers yet adopt a most undesignerly approach to solving their management problems.

So when I write about 'design education' what do I embrace in those two words? A great deal has been written about the definition of 'design', the difference between 'design' and 'designing', the similarities and differences between art and design, the place of craft and the role of technology. Through reference to other texts I will arrive at a position which I believe is a suitable starting point for considering the future directions design education might take.

Addressing a Coombe Lodge conference in 1976, John Blake, then Head of the Information Division at the Design Council, proposed the following relationship between Art and Design:

> Art is the physical manifestation of an individual or group desire for self expression, regardless of the desires or wishes of the market place. Design is a direct response to the desires or wishes of the market place, and any designer who ignores this fact does so at his peril – and at the peril of the company which employs him [1].

Having made this distinction, Blake was at pains to emphasise his holistic perception of Art and Design. He continued:

> although art and design are different, there is no sharp dividing line between them. Their relationship, in my view, is more akin to a continuous spectrum which can be further extended to embrace engineering, technology and science.

Examining the provision of degree courses in Design it will be noted that, in most cases, they are located alongside a Fine Art course. The General Art and Design (GAD) version of the National Diploma validated by the Business and Technician Education Council (BTEC), because it is diagnostic in nature, includes a Fine Art experience. Historically, despite tensions between Fine Art and Design and political pressures that might try to separate them on the basis of cost or utility, our present education system has largely kept them together. Of course Fine Art can exist without Design and Design without Fine Art, but that stance, I believe, avoids confronting philosophical issues of importance, narrows the

166

educational experience of students and the academic stimulation of staff, and too neatly falls into an administrative pattern that suits auditors but has little to do with creative behaviour.

The practice of both Art and Design requires the exercise of theoretical and practical skills in a demanding activity. The prevalent notion that there is a division between thinking and making is erroneous and dangerous. It is deeply distressing to have heard the Director of a very large Polytechnic state at the annual awards ceremony that artists and designers will be remembered, not for what they think, but for what they do or make. This attitude perpetuates the educational fallacy that the brain is switched off when the hands are used. The worst manifestation of this attitude sends the intellectually less able to the Art Room as a dumping ground for assorted pupil problems and timetable difficulties. It prompts the misguided headteacher to announce proudly to visitors to the school's art exhibition that 'It is wonderful to see such good work coming from less bright children.' It leads Further and Higher Education (F/HE) managers to a belief that the Art and Design use of libraries and data bases is of minor importance. Such misconceptions are the result of failing to think through the relationship of subject *study* to subject *practice*. As Robin Plummer rightly observed:

> Degree courses in art and design are almost universally concerned not with the study of the subject, but with its contemporary practice [2].

The study of contemporary practice clearly involves a marriage of cerebral and physical activity. Consideration of the range of material included under the umbrella name 'design' makes this conclusion inescapable.

In a study of policy options pertaining to the initiation of a design-led national economic recovery the Confederation of Art and Design Associations (CADA) used the following working definition:

> The field of design, and hence 'design activity', includes architecture, engineering, consumer goods design, textiles, fashion, graphics, theatre and television design, etc. . . . . Also included are systems design, software design and planning.
> Design activities may or may not contain very much in the way of invention in the technological term. 'Design activity' may or may not adequately describe craft activity.
>
> Particularly, 'to design' means, 'to seek out a manner of matching a set of known, postulated or to-be-discovered needs, desires and values with a practicable, producible, marketable, and economic means for meeting them to an acceptable degree' [3].

It is this potential utility of the designer's activity that prompts governmental interest and, in its extreme form, may lead to the erosion of those educational experiences, in design courses, that do not immediately and obviously promote profitability. This danger was alluded to by Sir Ernst Gombrich when addressing the 1985 North of England Education Conference he said:

> Broadly speaking government must try to hold the balance between two legitimate interests. Those of the citizen as taxpayer

52 A five unit *Pyramint* pack, 1988.
SIMON BATES (first year HND in Product and Packaging Design, Sheffield City Polytechnic). This project was conducted in conjunction with WILLIAM THYNE LTD., Edinburgh, for their clients TERRY'S of York. Reproduced by permission of Sheffield City Polytechnic.

and those of the citizen as parent. The spokesman of the taxpayer insists that expenditure on education be kept at a minimum and that cost should at least be recouped by the returns the economy can expect from the training of students in 'vocationally relevant subjects'. The citizens as parents . . . instruct their representatives in Parliament to make sure that at least their offspring will obtain the social privileges that they connect with education [4].

Art and Design education, because of its intellectual demands and practical emphasis, is a most appropriate vehicle for meeting both these 'legitimate interests'.

The necessary ingredients for an educational programme that will equip students to become designers will include those which promote creative behaviour. As with Design, a great deal has been written about creativity. Even more has been said by artists and designers in a manner which gives the impression that not only do they know what it is, but also that they are the sole possessors of the quality. However, Arthur Koestler, in *The Act of Creation*, has clearly demonstrated that creativity may be a characteristic of activity across all areas of human experience. A more general appreciation of this fact could lead to greater understanding and collaboration between staff of differing disciplines in F/HE. Peter Gorb has endorsed this view of creativity and the designer:

Creativity bulks large in the designer's concept of self. High creativity is certainly an aspiration of all designers. It is also true

168

that many designers are recruited from educational streams which are traditionally thought of as seedbeds of creativity. Yet these self evaluations, aspirations and breeding grounds are neither exclusive to designers, nor indeed to anyone else [5].

A consistently present fundamental of creativity, evident in the writings of researchers into creative behaviour, is the making of novel connections. Unlike the God of Genesis we do not 'make' out of 'nothing'. Our creativity is in part a product of what we have already experienced. Carl Rogers' definition of the creative process is:

> That it is the emergence in action of a novel relational product, growing out of the uniqueness of the individual on the one hand, and the materials, events, people, or circumstances of his life on the other [6].

This is, in my view, only a partial definition because it does not distinguish between the purely accidental and inconsequential random act on the one hand, and the relationship of the process to decision making, problem solving or planned exploration. Most if not all design courses in F/HE include theoretical and practical studies that complement or contrast with the main subject being studied. These are generally in addition to a historical element that sets practical work in a time context. These various studies have often been the focus of debate and contention, not only because of the time allocation which some practitioners have seen as too great, but also because they have been seen as cultural 'additions'. I believe this a quite wrong view. Of course there is a significant cultural aspect to these so-called 'additions' but their major potential lies in opening doors to knowledge and experience that add to a student's directory of possible connections. As Lucien Gerardin said:

> Invention consists of connecting things never before connected and yet one must be aware of their existence before one can connect them [7].

He was explaining the thinking behind a movement in the USA which was dubbed 'bionics' before the word became debased to mean any superhuman skill. Bionics was perceived as the application of knowledge of living systems to the solution of technical problems. If one accepts these perspectives on creativity then design cannot be an isolated discipline. At its best it will be creative.

Questions of scale, materials, technique and process do not impinge on the cerebral aspects of creativity. Theo Crosby recognised this when he wrote:

> The artist has the capacity to see a visual problem in a unique and often remarkably acute way: such expertise and intelligence is infinitely valuable. So is the experience of working with different minds and talents, in the process of which the designer's own perceptions are often sharpened and his abilities extended.
>
> The orchestration of these many skills by the designer is as legitimate an expression of creative talent as any work he may personally undertake, and is far more likely to lead to the creation of something truly memorable [8].

169

One irony of our present F/HE and Secondary systems is that cross-curricular connections have become increasingly difficult, if not impossible, to make. Whereas at primary level the idea of learning many things through art is not merely an interesting theory expounded by an educational philosopher but is *practised*, by the time students leave school the use of visual skills to learn and to solve problems has often been relegated to a position substantially below the use of words and numbers.

Although the National Curriculum continues to generate heated discussion, not least in the debate surrounding the location of Design in the curriculum, at least the possibility of many subject contributions is being explored actively. What is important to the debate is that it is not constructive to weight certain subjects, such as mathematics and science, as being 'most important contributors' to design education. In certain circumstances they may be. It depends on the design problem being addressed. The study of origami may be most appropriate for architecture students solving a folded plate structural problem.

The importance of a broad, associative approach to curriculum design was recognised in a Further Education Unit discussion paper:

> Creative thinking is often characterised by applying ideas or
> principles from one area of experience to problems in another:
> through recognising analogies between apparently different types
> of problem. This approach supports the value of going beyond
> single-subject teaching as a basis for course planning to look for
> new associations of disciplines and fields of study. It also
> underlines the need for teachers to emphasise wherever possible
> the ways in which ideas and skills in one context may be related
> to, or have implications for, those in others [9].

This leaves Higher Education as the black hole into which all previous integrative, associative educational endeavour passes with only a fair chance of being continued. Perhaps it is not so surprising to have heard a Polytechnic Director, in 1988, reflect the views of the Committee of Directors of Polytechnics as follows:

> In the enhancement of human capacity, the development of the
> imagination and of the urge to create and express needs to be
> fostered along with the development of the intellect [10].

Did the Directors really believe that being creative and expressive is possible without brain activity? Or are so-called intellectuals to be regarded as non-creative and unexpressive?

There is, however, another side to the coin. Is it that art and design academics have been less than effective in demonstrating to other colleagues that the creative practice of art and design is an inseparable mix of thinking and doing? Is it that the enhanced respectability of an Honours Degree and a lengthy Art School tradition live on in an élitism that still eschews real involvement with other disciplines? If creative behaviour is really developed in the way implied earlier, how dare we merely touch the forelock to our academic colleagues in other disciplines and then return unmoved to our practices of previous decades! The fact that some of our colleagues may not be itching to become involved in Art and Design activities should be neither surprising nor a long-term

170

53 Domestic pewterware, 1988. TREVOR BARLOW (second year BA Hons Metalwork and Jewellery, Sheffield City Polytechnic). Produced by I GIBSON & SON, Sheffield. This project was sponsored by the Worshipful Company of Pewterers in conjunction with selected colleges and manufacturers. Reproduced by permission of Sheffield City Polytechnic.

barrier. If we, who see ourselves as creative, inventive, problem-solving innovators, are slow to change our spots, why should we expect others to change more quickly? Perhaps it is that false 'craft' image that still attaches to colleges and faculties of Art and Design that causes low levels of inter-subject collaboration. If this is the case it is unfortunate. The question of the place of craft has to be addressed.

One of the most persuasive cases for the place of crafts in society was presented by Fred Brookes in his introduction to the catalogue for the *Craftsmanlike* exhibition. Through his work with craftspeople, and his efforts to interpret their concerns through exhibitions, he has identified important aspects of the crafts. At this point the emphasis is on craftspeople and craft products. Brookes states that:

> Out of the totality of human making, 'The Crafts' appear as a
> fairly closely bunched group of activities related to one another
> by several characteristics: small-scale independent and self-reliant
> enterprise; hand work; production process within the conceptual
> grasp of one man; fairly low regard for financial gain; desire to
> achieve high levels of quality in design and workmanship; desire
> to fulfil the utilitarian and aesthetic needs of the community;
> taking pains . . . . The desire to have things the way one likes
> them is an important characteristic of the crafts [11].

In a recent BBC interview Richard Williams, the animator of the film *Who Framed Roger Rabbit?* made a very similar comment reflecting his own film craftsmanship. He said, 'I am a professional amateur because I want it right for its own sake.'

This concern of the craftsperson for high quality has led, as Brookes points out, to restricted accessibility to craft products because they tend to be expensive. The high cost is not a reflection, however, of the income level of craftspeople. On the whole they are prepared to accept lower rates of pay than would be acceptable in commerce or industry. However, society needs the products of craftspeople, as society needs the work of artists, as a foil to mass production and industrialisation. Inasmuch as we are influenced by the objects of our environment, the craftsperson may influence us beneficially through the original, sensitive design and making of high quality objects. The perspective of craft activity is often central to courses in institutions of Further and Higher Education: but to leave the impression that it is the dominating perspective would be misleading. In many courses it sits happily alongside the industrial perspective. It is not unusual to find students of ceramics moving to either studio pottery or industrial ceramics via the same course; and to find fashion students aiming at limited production of boutique garments or to chain store mass production via the same course.

Considerable pressure has been placed on design courses during the last five years to develop a curriculum more appropriate to the needs of industry. This pressure has come from BTEC and the Council for National Academic Awards (CNAA) who validate the majority of design courses. Pressure has also come from Government agencies such as the Department of Trade and Industry (DTI) and the National Advisory Body (NAB) Art and Design Group. Encouragement has come via the Royal Society of Arts (RSA) and its *Education for Capability* initiative and continuing *Design Bursary Scheme* and via the Confederation of British Industry (CBI). There has also been pressure from professional bodies. The bias has been towards inclusion of improved business/management awareness, information technology, engineering and languages. DTI initiatives have resulted in upgrading technology in departments concerned with education for the printing, textiles and furniture industries. This welcome investment, giving design students experience of technology closer to that available in industry, nevertheless leaves intact the tradition that artists, designers and crafts people *use* appropriate technology; they tend not to modify and certainly not to invent technology.

I have identified four interrelated components that provide a matrix within which it is possible to locate all art and design activities. My horizontal axis runs from Fine Art to Industrial Design. The axis is an unbroken continuum with Fine Art representing activities with maximum 'internal' control and Industrial Design a maximum of 'external' control. The Fine Artist operates mainly within personally defined parameters, the Industrial Designer within parameters established by industry/commerce. My vertical axis runs from Craft to Technology and represents the extent to which the Fine Artist or Designer moves from concept to product via personal manipulation of materials and tools or, remotely, via appropriate communication resulting in manufacture using mass production technology.

Within this matrix the studio potter would be located towards the Fine Art end and probably well into the craft area. The industrial ceramicist would be towards the Industrial Design end and into the technology area. It is particularly important that the artist's and designer's thinking/making processes move freely across the matrix. Much of manufacturing industry relies on craft skills in the early stages of preparation for mass production. The craftsperson freely uses the products of technology even down to pencil and ball-point pen! A sculptor may have to consider the design requirements of a public site and designers will draw not only on art drafting skills but also on the intellectual freedom of making connections of an intuitive nature during the 'concept design' stage.

172

I hope that my preceding remarks explain my perception of 'design' in an educational context. I wish now to explore the nature of the present provision, its social, industrial, commercial and political context, and its possible future. I firmly believe that the quality of provision is more the result of people than things. An institution may be fabulously equipped but if the staff are of poor calibre the students' learning experience will not be good. Those institutions that have gained designated authority from the CNAA and are now independent of local authority control are masters of their own destiny. That destiny must be dictated by well-informed perceptions of design education and its dependence upon the commitment of high quality staff. As Razik has said:

> What finally controls an institution are the values it holds for itself and the means which are used to determine whether or not the values are being attained through the efforts of the institution [12].

A self-perception of being the best in the world has been challenged by many who are involved in, or concerned about, design education – from Prime Minister to students. I too believe it is proper to challenge such a self-indulgent attitude. Such challenges have been levelled at other countries' education systems. Victor Papanek has issued challenges to, and been critical of, the American system.

> Unfortunately, education has been made into a method of preserving the status quo, a way of teaching and prescribing the moral attitudes, smug life-styles, and other sacrosanct values held by the old, and dispensing whatever is currently accepted as 'Truth' [13].

Even artists and designers can demonstrate what Donald Schon describes as 'dynamic conservatism' in the face of change. I sometimes wonder how many design staff, wearing designer clothes, growing designer stubble or hair styles, are led along management-designer desire lines to designer water and in a most undesignerly manner refuse to drink! Papanek's complaints about American education sound so much like a NAB report, yet he was writing nearly twenty years ago.

> Part of the philosophical and moral bankruptcy of universities and design schools lies in their ever increasing trend to train students to become narrowly 'vertical' specialists, whereas the real need is for broad, 'horizontal' generalists or synthesists. Nearly everything in today's university milieu militates against educating for general synthesis . . . most of what passes for 'education' today is in reality a 'crime against humanity' as defined by the Nuremburg Laws of 1945, and . . . most educators could be imprisoned for violating at least 6 out of 10 points of this same code for experimenting upon human beings, without their consent, without the subject's right to terminate experimentation, without the subject's right to change his conditions, for engaging in torture, etc. etc. It is to the credit of the young people of today that they have smelled all of this out, and are trying to change it [14].

Maybe the reason for the repetition of Papanek's comments twenty years on is that there is still a substantial body of the same staff around as in 1970 – not that long service necessarily leads to ossification, but growing resistance to change is a common characteristic of ageing.

Despite the applause, perhaps our design education system isn't quite as good as we are fond of believing. If it is so good why are more UK products not better designed? This is a point made by Kenneth Grange:

> This country's design education is perhaps the best and biggest
> in the world. Architects, industrial and graphic designers have
> proliferated in the last 25 years, a period in which Britain has
> gained a world wide reputation for design consultancy whilst the
> design reputation of its products has sunk to an all time low [15].

Ensuring a reputation for poor product design is of concern not only to industry and commerce but also to government. Not unexpectedly, in 1983, John Butcher, Minister of State for Industry, endorsed the CADA belief:

> that the quality of the Design of British goods and services is a
> crucial factor in the health of the economic and cultural life of
> the nation [16].

If there is truth in these statements regarding the quality of our design education provision and our industrial products then it is a matter of urgency to identify the problems and propose solutions. An inevitable retort will be, 'but that has been done by so many people that you have already listed: CNAA, BTEC, NAB, DTI, etc. etc. . . . So what's new?' Many of these bodies, because of their terms of reference, have addressed only part of the problem and their statements often provide an opportunity to deflect responsibility for a solution onto some other shoulder.

I intend to assemble some pointers from a variety of sources that lead me to propose a future radically different from the present. In particular the pointers will be drawn from the design perspectives of both craft and technology. First, it is worth noting those inadequacies perceived by and in students on leaving F/HE and entering the world of work. The last major survey of this transition was undertaken in the late 1960s and published in 1972 [17]. Although twenty years have passed, some of the criticisms of the system are still heard today. For instance, students from all design areas expressed particular concern at the inadequacy of the contact and communication between course/institution and industry and commerce. This led employers to comment on the poor practical grounding students had received in the requirements of commerce and industry, although employers seemed satisfied with levels of basic design skills, originality and creativity.

Where there is this lack of sustained, first-hand experience of industry and commerce, students leave institutions with high ambitions and an unreal perception of life in the first years of practice. This applies equally to industrial designer and artist-craftsperson. For many students the initial experience of the tension between an internal desire to produce work of high aesthetic quality and the external pressures of the commercial world comes as a shock. This experience should lead educators to examine the manner in which perception of quality and value are developed during design courses.

174

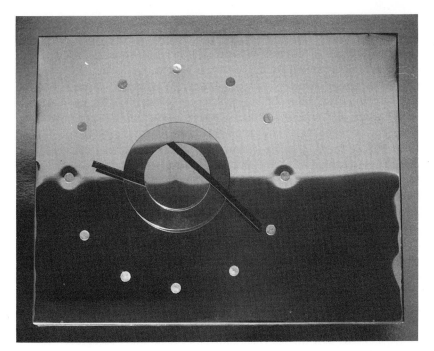

54 Prototype clock in sheet steel, 1988. SIMON TAO (second year BA Hons Industrial Design, Sheffield City Polytechnic). This project was sponsored under the Shell Technology Enterprise Programme. Reproduced by permission of Sheffield City Polytechnic.

BTEC believes that their courses better fit students for their careers than do degree courses:

> BTEC courses in design are different from degrees. No other courses in Britain are more particularly designed to help equip the new generation for careers in creative subjects. They include more 'hands-on' experience, more 'learning by doing', more day-to-day working in firms and on practical projects . . . . Relevance to the real world is a theme that crops up again and again [18].

BTEC's view of course differences is not necessarily held by the design profession. In an enquiry into the impressions of eighteen design practices, *The Designer* magazine found no outstanding evidence of real difference:

> The difference between BTEC and degree courses is meaningless; the students and their portfolios are what are finally judged and you can't tell which course is which unless you ask – and one never does [19].

The products of BTEC courses ought to be distinctive, for the Council's stated purpose is 'to advance the quality and availability of work-related education'. In order to achieve this it seeks to ensure

> that the availability, accessibility and design of BTEC courses, the quality of student learning and the standards of achievement are all relevant to occupational requirements . . . . BTEC is an important member of the national network of educational and training agencies. Each is concerned, in its own way, with improving industrial performance through the development of people . . . [20].

With such aims it would be an indictment of BTEC if the products of their courses failed to meet the requirements of the workplace or failed to contribute to an improvement of industrial performance. BTEC and design staff are aware of dangers inherent in such an overt 'feeder' relationship with industry and commerce. Apart from the possibility of a broad, creative, educational experience being replaced by a narrow training, the stance assumes that industry and commerce not only know what they want but also that what they want is what they need. 'I'll tell them what I want' does not reflect partnership but alienation.

The development of sandwich courses and the inclusion of work placement has slowly changed the nature of design education, but these forms of contact with industry, commerce and the professions are not available to all students on all design courses. Design educators have been pressured for many years to develop stronger links with the world of work and this pressure has been applied as much at the craft as at the technology end of the design spectrum. In 1951 the Royal College of Art published a collection of professors' *Inaugural Lectures*. R. W. Baker, Professor of Ceramics, spoke on 'Who Trains Designers?' Although he seemed completely to confuse training and education, he stated that:

> The production of designers must be a cooperative effort between
> the works and the schools, and the schools must recognise that
> the lesser part of a designer's training will be the education he
> receives in the works [21].

Two recommendations of the *1962 Report of the National Advisory Council on Art Education* (NACAE) continue the pressure:

> Wherever possible, arrangements should be made for students to
> obtain appropriate industrial experience, particularly during the
> later stages of their course . . . cooperation between art schools
> and industry should not be restricted to the planning and
> running of courses but should also be effective at the stage when
> students have completed their courses and are seeking
> employment, and during their early years of work [22].

In the government white paper *A Plan for Polytechnics and other Colleges*, 1966, closer and more direct links with industry, business and the professions are identified as features which would distinguish the Polytechnics from other HE Institutions. Placement in industry and the development of sandwich courses were the main vehicles envisaged for the formation of these links. Addressing the requirements of an education in Industrial Design, the Design Council stated in 1977 that:

> Education establishments should ensure that all those responsible
> for teaching design keep in close contact with industry . . . .
> Every effort should be made to place students in industry for an
> effective period during their course, to gain insight into the
> realities of the industrial situation [23].

In an effort to encourage employers to take BTEC design students into their commercial environment for a period of up to six weeks, BTEC organised a series of nine meetings in 1984. These were attended by representatives of the colleges and industry, commerce and the professions. In reporting the conclusions that had been reached BTEC stated:

One of the outstanding lessons from the nine meetings was just how incredibly successful work experience programmes can be for students, colleges, and employers when they are working well. Speaker after speaker from each side of the fence quoted examples of the transformation in students who had even a short spell in work experience [24].

After nearly forty years of pressure there are still students leaving design courses without any first-hand experience of industry. Forty years is a convenient period to review, because it is the period of teaching service which results in a full pension: there are some lecturers in design for whom, throughout their career, there has been a constant reminder that experience of industry is important for students. But I hear voices telling me that their courses have never had more than the odd day placement and all the students get jobs: why change? Papanek's reference to the Nuremburg Laws was correct. Is it not just remotely possible that students might benefit from contact with the real world of industry and design practice? The 'odd day' is an irresponsible approach. What is needed is a collaborative venture in design education on a scale never before attempted. Those institutions that have made progress with effective collaborative schemes are best placed to develop and grow. In this respect the size of institutions is immaterial: dinosaurs are extinct. What is important is the enthusiasm, determination and commitment of staff in the face of very real difficulties regarding already stressful demands on their time. It is also clear that difficulties in developing collaboration are not encountered exclusively in the academic camp. There will have to be changes in industrial attitudes to design. How many industrialists take the trouble to visit degree and diploma shows, particularly the many excellent ones outside London?

In an address to CADA in 1984 Sir Keith Joseph, then Secretary of State for Education and Science, reiterated John Butcher's message on the contribution of design to quality and the significance of design in improving profitability. He warned that:

> Those who embark on careers or professions where good design affects the success of the end product in the market place, both at home and abroad, will ignore this message at their own peril and to the certain loss of the national economy [25].

In one major Polytechnic an analysis of first destinations of Industrial Design graduates showed that over a five-year period a quarter gained employment outside the United Kingdom. The NAB Art and Design Group recognised the irony of this position and commented in their 1987 Report that there seemed little point in educating students for emigration. Worse than that concern is the fact that some of these students are now designing products for our European competitors who successfully break into the UK market. The success of our competitors is partly attributable to management attitudes to design.

The CNAA has recognised the UK deficiency and, in 1984, launched an initiative in management education under the banner *Managing Design*. Six pilot schemes have been operating at both undergraduate and postgraduate levels. The DTI has become involved with research support,

177

notably at Leicester Polytechnic in the Faculty of Art and Design. Welcome as these developments are, they are tackling the problem at student/course level and it may take many years for the effect to be felt at senior management level in industry.

Problems at management level in industry are, however, only a part of the jigsaw. Other problems have been identified. As a result of collaboration between the Department of Education and Science and the Design Council a report was published in 1983 which identified areas of mismatch between the competencies of Design graduates and the expectations of practice and industry. I don't believe that the list has changed much in five years. It includes:

> Respondents in industry were not happy about the extent to which designers were prepared to offer alternative solutions to a design problem . . . .
>
> Designers did not sufficiently appreciate the value of seeing the product in its market context . . . .
>
> Areas of weakness were found in selecting special materials, and using them cost effectively, in sensing potential safety hazards and in selecting methods of joining and assembly . . . [26].

Other shortcomings included: lack of a disciplined approach, disregard for deadlines, poor written and oral communication, an uncompromising attitude to a company's practical constraints, difficulty in operating within a multi-disciplinary team, unfamiliarity with volume production methods, inability to recognise maintenance and reliability constraints, insensitivity to engineering requirements, lack of computer aided design skill, unfamiliarity with electronic and electrical engineering, lack of commercial awareness, unpreparedness for the realities of the market and running a business. Future requirements may include a major foreign language, basic physics and statistical science. The forthcoming change in the UK's relationship with its fellow member states of the EEC may bias the choice of language towards Europe.

Whilst acknowledging, largely because of proximity, the European challenge it would be a grave mistake to ignore aspects of world competition. The Middle and Far East are not merely good hunting grounds for overseas students paying full fees and producers of cheap goods, but also short- and long-term rivals of enormous significance. In a recent address to the Royal Society of Arts, the Rt. Hon. Edward Heath drew attention to the influence of Japan and China:

> When one looks at Japan and China together, what we are going to see – indeed we are seeing more and more – is the technology of the Japanese, which is now creative, not just imitative, and the sales drive of the Japanese, applied to the raw materials of the People's Republic of China . . . all the raw materials which one could want, plus a population which is now being highly educated, thanks very largely to a number of American Chinese professors who have been going back regularly now for several years. . . . That is the combination which we in Europe are going to face: technology, sales drive, raw materials and a highly skilled labour force [27].

The Council for Industry and Higher Education is a non-governmental, independent body consisting of the polytechnic directors, vice-chancellors, heads of colleges and twenty-two heads of major companies. In 1987 the council published a paper entitled *Towards a Partnership*. It commenced with a statement subsequently endorsed by the 'Higginson Committee' in the report for the Secretaries of State for Education and Science and for Wales regarding 'A' level syllabuses and their assessment. The statement reads:

> The UK's prosperity, vitality and international standing depend
> on its becoming a more highly educated nation which recognises
> skilled brain power and applied ingenuity as its distinctive assets.

If this recipe is fulfilled then Edward Heath's eastern challenge will be met. However, the picture I have painted of the present provision of design education and the identified mismatch between the skills of new graduates and the expectations of industry must prompt the question 'Is it possible?'

Another dimension of the problem, seldom mentioned, is the massive mismatch between the technological resources available to students of design within their institutions and the resources of industry. The scale of mismatch seems to have increased exponentially in recent years. Some institutions have benefited from financial injections via the DTI in areas listed earlier. Unfortunately, too few have been helped, across a very limited range of design disciplines. The growing, already massive, application of computer power to both designing and manufacture is just one area in which institutions are unable to approach the resources of industry. This desperate position has not arisen with great suddenness. Design academics have been asking, recently not very politely, for improved laboratories, workshops, equipment, technician support and materials: instead they have seen staffing and budget reductions.

No doubt partly because both internal and external pressures for accountability, efficiency, effectiveness, personal development, research, statistical data, improved marketing and competitiveness have led to an oppressive bureaucracy which, in many institutions, has wiped out the academic credibility of most staff above the rank of Principal Lecturer, those who should be proposing and implementing radical solutions to major problems are incarcerated in remote offices pushing large volumes of academically irrelevant paper from one side of their desks to the other. They haven't noticed that since Leonardo da Vinci there has been a major shift in the educational resources required to support design activities. That may be an unnecessarily extreme statement but the principle I am making stands. From the earliest days of Art Schools, the foundation of the Royal College of Art and Schools of Art at such places as Manchester, Birmingham and Glasgow, there has been a continuing fine art and craft presence. These disciplines have traditionally relied mainly on small pieces of equipment, hand tools and readily available, often local, materials with which fine artists or craftspeople make ideas manifest.

Industrial developments often relied on the exercise, initially, of a craft skill before the emerging technology could proceed to the next stage of limited or mass production. Tool makers and pattern makers are obvious examples but so also are compositors and tracers. So it was a clear justification for the retention of such craft skill training within a range of art school educational facilities. Additionally, the designer-craftsperson tradition has not been interrupted and has always found course provision within art and design institutions. For students to experience both craft and technology aspects of their chosen design area has invariably proved beneficial for both exit routes.

To their cost, governments have found that too overt a pressure on pupils or students to apply for places on science or engineering courses has led to an opposite response to that desired. Many students seem to display a congenital distrust of authority and particularly of government, local or national. This distrust is often shared by academics who see political expediency driving the education system. Such a turning away from the wonderful world of designer-everything has recently been observed by the Association of Graduate Careers Advisory Services who note that:

> As a possible reaction to a high tech world, the last few years
> have seen a resurgence of interest in crafts, with a growth in
> craft fairs, craft parties, craft workshops with retail outlets, mail
> order, etc. [28].

This reaction and resurgence of interest in crafts is observable both in students and in those members of the public who have a sensitivity towards their personal environment and have the financial resources to pay for the unique or limited production craft item. So institutions offering courses in design find it appropriate to make an adequate provision at the craft end of the spectrum, and are often seriously deficient at the technology end. The sort of provision for serious design practice in, for instance, printing, video production and animation, furniture, automotive design, textile printing, weaving and plastics, will prove so expensive that most institutions must now follow industrial leaders. The result is often to provide students with second-hand knowledge of industrial resources.

So how are these various problems at the technological end of design to be addressed? I believe that the time is ripe for a massive opening up of collaboration with industry in a form of academic/industrial partnership which will go beyond current practice (Figs. 50–56). With greater autonomy for those institutions under the Polytechnic and Colleges Funding Council (PCFC) and with greater independence of the CNAA for those so designated, the possibility of joint academic/industrial degrees should be no more difficult than joint institutional degrees. The establishment of inhouse design and consultancy companies and design/manufacture/marketing agreements should all be viable. I do not believe that it is any longer possible for design academics to include within their courses, BTEC or degree, all the necessary subject content in the most appropriate form for their students by drawing upon institutional resources alone. Who are these dedicated academics in other departments who have such an interest in the needs of design students that they will originate suitable programmes in written and oral communications,

180

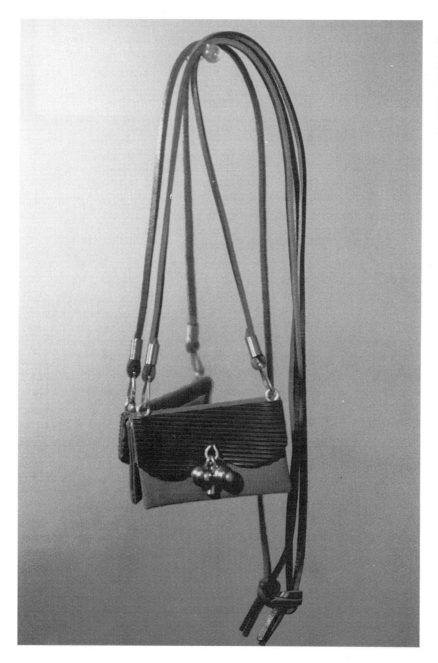

55 Bag, 1988. JONATHAN LYNCH (second year BA Hons Industrial Design, Sheffield City Polytechnic). This project was sponsored by Plain Quarters Ltd. Reproduced by permission of Sheffield City Polytechnic.

financial control of volume production, production quality control, electrical and electronic engineering, CADCAM, languages and business management?

By the time these allies in other disciplines have discovered what is needed, prepared programmes, learnt from mistakes, modified and adapted, either students will have graduated or our benefactors will have been promoted out of the area as a reward for such masochistic dedication to an alien subject. If the resources currently devoted to the failing

56 Prototype portable
cement mixer, 1988.
ALASDAIR WILLIAMSON
(third year BA Hons
Industrial Design,
Sheffield City Polytechnic)
in association with
HEIGHT DESIGN.
Reproduced by permission
of Sheffield City
Polytechnic.

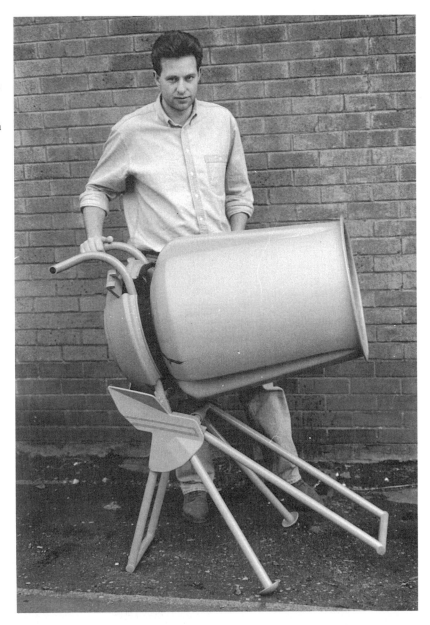

attempts at updating design provision in institutions (and these resources come both from internal budgets and external contributions) were ploughed into a more dynamic institution/industry relationship, some of the problems might be solved.

Of course there would have to be a degree/diploma plan that ensured that each student had the right mix of learning experiences. Of course there would still have to be basic, 'core' material common to groups of students. Of course industry isn't going to jump at the opportunity of deeper involvement with education: but if academics, believing this to be the only solution, approached and kept on approaching industry with a constructive package showing benefits to both sides, then change might occur. Academics would start to fulfil a very different role, as would their counterparts in industry. Many design staff do not have a specialist teaching qualification, and many designers in industry will not enter teaching because their salary and job satisfaction are higher where they are. Why, therefore, do we persist in ignoring the potential benefits of having a system of industrial-academics, who may be of more value to students in their respective specialisms than the institutional academics?

If the DTI, instead of inviting institutional bids for high tech equipment in furniture, textiles and printing, had sought bids for finance to put students into companies that had equipment, and more, it would have been better value in the long term. Unless the DTI is prepared to cover all design areas with their 'initiatives' and to repeat the upgrading every two or three years, there is no way institutions will be able to find the resource from their own budgets and the DTI investment will prove a temporary hiccup in the inexorable process of provision obsolescence. If the package offered to industry by academics were to prove so unattractive that there were no 'takers', then would it not be reasonable to assume that the academics had failed to approach the task in a 'designerly' manner and should not be in the business anyway?

Clearly, much of the low tech work can be properly provided for within the institutions. Further, the level of success in establishing collaboration with industry would probably polarise course provision further in a number of institutions, but not necessarily with the same distribution of subjects as at present. There are those who will interpret these proposals as a manifestation of free market philosophy. I prefer to see them as a pragmatic approach bearing in mind the comments, criticisms and constraints that I have identified.

If students' courses were actually based in industry with visits to the institution rather that the other way round, would students not, perhaps, have a more useful experience? If the resources are never to be provided that put institutions at the leading edge of design technology then what alternative is there but to negotiate a profitable deal with those who are at the leading edge? Amos Rapoport has some unkind but true things to say about the traditional design studios of architecture students:

> In effect the studio presupposes that apprentices learn from a master – it perpetuates the archaic master-apprentice system no matter how disguised. This has several problems. Lacking evaluative criteria, there is no way of defining who is a 'master', what constitutes mastery, or what one is master of . . . . The studio may be the major mechanism for perpetuating an invalid view of what architects are and what they should do [29].

For architects read designers and the image fits. My message is not one of 'change or die'. Education moves too slowly for that to be the case. Instead I hope that I have presented some developmental possibilities that could provide a vehicle for design education to make a real contribution, not only through the provision of a more valid learning experience for students but also to the re-establishment of the high quality design image of UK products.

Notes and References

1 BLAKE, J E. 1977. 'The Place of Art and Design in Society', in: *Coombe Lodge Report*, Vol. X, No. 1, p. 3.

2 PLUMMER, R. J. 1975. *Post-Graduate Study in Art and Design*. National Society for Art Education, p. 4.

3 Confederation of Art and Design Associations. 1983. *Design for Recovery*, p. 10.

4 GOMBRICH, E. 1985. 'The Embattled Humanities', in: *Proceedings of the North of England Education Conference*, p. 14.

5 GORB, P. 1978. *Living by Design*. London, Lund Humphries, p. 7.

6 ROGERS, C. R. 1970. 'Towards a Theory of Creativity', in: P. E. VERNON (ed.). *Creativity*. Harmondsworth, Penguin, p. 139.

7 GERARDIN, L. 1968. *Bionics*. World University Library, p. 8.

8 CROSBY, T., in: GORB. *Op. cit.*, p. 191.

9 FURTHER EDUCATION UNIT. 1987. *Creative and Arts Activities in Further Education*. DES, p. 6.

10 COMMITTEE OF DIRECTORS OF POLYTECHNICS. 1974. *Many Arts, Many Skills: the Polytechnic Policy and Requirements for its Fulfilment*, pp. 10–11.

11 BROOKES, F. 1978. *Craftsmanlike*. Coelfrith Press, Sunderland Arts Centre.

12 RAZIK, T. A. 1970. 'Psychometric Measurement of Creativity', in: VERNON. *Op. cit.*, p. 157.

13 PAPANEK, V. 1970. 'The Education of the Art Professional: the Designer', in: E. B. FELDMAN (ed.). *Art in American Higher Institutions*. National Art Education Association, USA, p. 40.

14 *Ibid.*, p. 49.

15 GRANGE, K. in: GORB. *Op. cit.*, p. 254.

16 Confederation of Art and Design Associations. *Op. cit.*, p. 3.

17 RITCHIE, J. 1972. *The Employment of Art College Leavers*. HMSO.

18 MCLACHLAN, S. 1985. *Design by Experience: Putting Industry and Design Education on the Same Path*. BTEC, pp. 15–19.

19 MCCULLAGH, L. 1987. 'Raw Recruits', in: *Designer*, Journal of the Chartered Society of Designers, May/June 1987, p. 21.

20 BTEC. 1984. *Discussion Document on Educational Policy*. p. 3.

21 BAKER, R. W. 1951. 'Who Trains Designers?' in: R. DARWIN (ed.). *The Anatomy of Design*. London, Royal College of Art, p. 61.

22 NATIONAL ADVISORY COUNCIL ON ART EDUCATION 1962. *Vocational Courses in Colleges and Schools of Art*. Ministry of Education, HMSO, p. 9.

23 DESIGN COUNCIL. 1977. *Industrial Design Education in the UK*. pp. 7–8.

24 MCLACHLAN. *Op. cit.*, pp. 71–2.

25 JOSEPH, K. 1984. Address to CADA Conference (unpublished).

26 HAYES, C., V. KELLER and B. DORSEY. 1983. *The Industrial Design Requirements of Industry*. London, Design Council, p. 10.

27 HEATH, E. 1988. 'One World: the Challenge Ahead', in: *Journal of the Royal Society of Arts*, Vol. CXXXVI, No. 5387, October 1988, p. 786.

28 FARRINGTON, B., L. JOHNSTON and A. WEBB. 1988. *Artworkers: a Report on the Employment and Further Study Patterns of UK Art and Design Graduates Shortly after Graduation*. Association of Graduate Careers Advisory Services, p. 3.

29 RAPOPORT, A. 1983. 'Serious Questions', in: *Architects' Journal*, October 1983, pp. 56–7.

Index